9TH DEC 2C

JACK NODWELL

ENJOY THE "READ"

REGARDS

Perry WOOD

DRIVEN TO SUCCEED

To Margaret Hasenfratz,
my daughters Linda and Nancy,
and all those who made Linamar the successful company it is today.

DRIVEN TO SUCCEED

HOW FRANK HASENFRATZ GREW
LINAMAR FROM GUELPH TO GLOBAL

ROD MCQUEEN AND SUSAN M. PAPP

DUNDURN
TORONTO

Project Editor: Michael Carroll
Editor: Nigel Heseltine
Design: Jesse Hooper
Printer: Friesens

Library and Archives Canada Cataloguing in Publication

McQueen, Rod, 1944-
          Driven to succeed : How Frank Hasenfratz grew Linamar from Guelph to global / by Rod McQueen and Susan M. Papp.

Includes index.
Issued also in electronic formats.
ISBN 978-1-4597-0795-5

          1. Hasenfratz, Frank. 2. Linamar Corporation--Biography. 3. Businessmen--Canada--Biography. 4. Industrialists--Canada--Biography. I. Papp, Susan M. II. Title.

HC112.5.H37M38 2012   338.092   C2012-904639-6

1 2 3 4 5   16 15 14 13 12

We acknowledge the support of the **Canada Council for the Arts** and the **Ontario Arts Council** for our publishing program. We also acknowledge the financial support of the **Government of Canada** through the **Canada Book Fund** and **Livres Canada Books**, and the **Government of Ontario** through the **Ontario Book Publishing Tax Credit** and the **Ontario Media Development Corporation**.

Care has been taken to trace the ownership of copyright material used in this book. The authors and the publisher welcome any information enabling them to rectify any references or credits in subsequent editions.

J. Kirk Howard, President

Printed and bound in Canada.

VISIT US AT
Dundurn.com | *Definingcanada.ca* | *@dundurnpress* | *Facebook.com/dundurnpress*

Dundurn	Gazelle Book Services Limited	Dundurn
3 Church Street, Suite 500	White Cross Mills	2250 Military Road
Toronto, Ontario, Canada	High Town, Lancaster, England	Tonawanda, NY
M5E 1M2	LA1 4XS	U.S.A. 14150

CONTENTS

1

Learning to Survive

Frank Hasenfratz was born in Hungary on a bitterly cold day, January 18, 1935, the second child of Anna Schaffer and Marton Hasenfratz. The midwife and other women in attendance at the birth immediately saw what a robust, healthy baby boy he was, as they bathed the newborn for the first time and wrapped him in warm cotton and wool blankets. Shortly after, Marton entered the darkened room where his wife had given birth and proudly held his new son. The baby yawned sleepily as if he, too, had been worn out by the arduous process of coming into this world. As Marton spoke to him gently, he saw that his son barely wanted to open his eyes.

According to local custom, if the baby had been born sickly or frail, if there was any chance the newborn wouldn't survive, the midwife herself would have immediately performed the rite of baptism. There would be no need for this in the case of his son, thought Marton. This baby was perfectly healthy and would be baptized in a week or so at the local Catholic Church. The young couple had previously chosen the name: if it was a boy, they would call him Franz Josef, after the much-loved emperor of the Austro-Hungarian monarchy, who died almost twenty years earlier. In Hungarian, he would be known as Ferenc.

～

Although the Austro-Hungarian Empire was dissolved after the end of the First World War, the German-speaking minority within Hungary, known as Swabians, still spoke of that era with great reverence and nostalgia. The Hasenfratz family was a proud part of this community. After all, it was due to that era that so many Germans, primarily Catholics, were enticed to settle in Hungary shortly after the Turkish occupation, which had devastated and depopulated large areas of the kingdom. Ferenc was born on Felsőkereszt utca, in the town of Szár, just on the western outskirts of Budapest, a neat, picturesque little place nestled in the plains between the surrounding Vértes and Gerecse mountain ranges. His ancestors had come to this region around 1712 from a Swiss-German border town called Stuhlingen. They were industrious people lured by the promise of tax exemption for three to five years and freedom from serfdom. They and many other hard-working families re-built the agriculture of the region, as part of a substantial wave of settlers into Hungary who numbered close to a million by the latter half of the 1700s.

As Ferenc grew, German was his mother tongue, the language of home, of his siblings and playmates. Ferenc also learned Hungarian, the language his father used in business and the language his older brother wrote and read out loud while he was doing homework. On Sundays, the priest led prayers and said Mass in German at the village's only church, St. John the Baptist Roman Catholic church. Attendance was obligatory each Sunday when all the villagers dressed in their finest outfits and attended Mass.

Szár was a self-sufficient, insular town. Young women were courted by eligible young men within the community and they were expected to be married by the time they were twenty. Outsiders were viewed with suspicion, even if they were from other nearby Swabian communities. Anna Schaffer was twenty-one when she married the handsome Marton Hasenfratz. Their first-born, Marton, arrived a year later. As the years passed and the family grew, Ferenc could barely remembered a time when there wasn't a baby in the family. He was two years old when his younger sister Maria was born at home, followed soon after by two more brothers, Jóska and János. Ferenc's paternal grandmother and grandfather lived with them and helped the family with the raising of the children and managing the farm.

The census in 1749 showed only three families with the surname of Hasenfratz, but by the time Ferenc was born, there were numerous families with the same surname. As he grew, Ferenc realized that many children in the village, cousins and distant relatives on the streets where they played, all had the same last name as his. As was customary in agricultural communities on the death of a father, land was divided among the male children of the family. Female siblings were provided a cash dowry for marriage by their brothers. But after a while, land plots became so small that they could no longer be divided and sustain a living for a family. As a result, customs changed: the oldest male heir would inherit the farm and he in turn had to "pay out" the rest of the siblings, male and female. In Szár, many men would instead go to work in the coal mines, some five kilometres away, near Tatabánya. As first-born, Marton Hasenfratz Sr. inherited the farm from his father. Even if the head of household worked in the mines, the rest of the townsfolk also grew crops and had their own cows, pigs, and chickens. Although the cows and pigs were led out to pasture every morning by the shepherds, everybody knew which animals belonged to which family, just as each animal knew which gate to stop in front of as they ambled their way home late in the afternoon. Most households grew their own crops and vegetables on small farms (under 10 hectares), always planting a few rows of grapes in their backyards to produce their own wine. The soil was rich and fertile, and with diligent work, the yield was plentiful.

After the relentless work of planting in spring and nurturing the crops all spring and summer, came the harvest in the fall. Ferenc would watch in awe as his mother and the other women in the village tackled

Ferenc Hasenfratz as a two-year-old, 1937.

the enormous task of cooking and canning the family's own fruits, creating plum jam as well as pear and apple sauce. The children helped as much as they could. Root vegetables, carrots, beets, turnips, and potatoes were placed into barrels filled with sandy soil in the cellar so that the family would have fresh vegetables throughout the winter.

To celebrate the bounty, friends and relatives filled the house to capacity as they gathered and brought baskets full of fresh baked breads, platters of stews, and sweet cakes (*kalács*). Lively harvest dances were held in the church yards or social club where the local accordion, fiddle, and harmonica players provided music. The dances were held where Father János Wenc, the local priest, could supervise, to ensure that everyone behaved. The younger men — still courting — stayed to dance with the young women, while most of the mothers sat along the edges of the dance floor, carefully watching the hands, the body movement of the young men as they swung their daughters around the dance floor. They speculated among themselves and talked about the prospects of this and that young man, and which one of their modest but sweet young daughters would make a fine wife for which young man.

The older men sat in small groups outside the hall, gossiping about what farm equipment they might buy, and how they could augment the crops next year. As they chatted among themselves and smoked hand-rolled cigarettes, they passed around bottles of home-made *palinka* (house brandy) and wine, all the while measuring, commenting on whose was stronger, whose tasted smoother. The children shrieked with joy as they played tag or other games — preferring the outdoors to the dancing inside.

In the winter, the women of the town would gather to spin their own linen cloth, embroider, knit, and share stories of the history of past generations and catch up on gossip. These spinning room sessions made the interminable, dark, and cold winter evenings pass more quickly, more pleasantly.

Ferenc grew up in a secure, loving family — but because there were so many siblings, he learned from a young age to compete for attention. "I think it taught you survival. We were tough already, growing up in a household with five kids. You had to survive," he said.

The family home had three bedrooms: one for grandmother and grandfather, one guest room, and one room for mother, father, and all the children. Even when grandmother passed away in 1941, grandfather stayed in his room, alone.

One of the advantages of having so many brothers and one sister around was that there were always playmates. The children didn't have many play things but created toys and games with everyday objects, such as pieces of wood, stone chips, and marbles.

Ferenc Hasenfratz first heard the word *war* as a young boy. He really didn't understand the term but knew it caused a lot of excitement. "By 1940, people were leaving, going into the army, and there was always talk about it and each time someone left for the army it was a celebration. Everybody was drinking and someone started waving the Hungarian flag. Some signed up for the Hungarian army, some left to join the German army."

Brass bands played and men in dress uniform with real guns marched by each time someone from the town volunteered to go off to war — to fight they said: "For our community and our country." The children marched alongside the real soldiers, laughing and imitating the stiff steps of the men in uniform, picking up pieces of wood and throwing these over their shoulders as pretend guns. The dogs barked and ran alongside the children. It was great entertainment. Each day, the town crier strode along the length of the town, pounding his snare drum, bringing news of the war from the outside world.

But as Ferenc grew older, the parades diminished, and the messages of the town crier were listened to with increased trepidation by the residents. "By 1944, they were taking sixteen-year-old boys and they were just children. One of them in particular was my classmate's older brother. And it only took about four months until they brought him back dead. He was shot by a sniper. So that's very vivid in my mind."

The sobbing of widows and extended family walking in funeral processions replaced the brave sound of the marching bands and joyful parades. The drastic change left an indelible impression on nine-year-old Ferenc. The women of the town spoke in hushed tones about tragic events as Ferenc sensed that the source of their great consternation was that something was going terribly wrong with the war.

～○

Toward the end of 1944, mere months before the end of the war, Ferenc's father received a draft notice from the military. Until then, Marton was exempt from military service due to a factory fire, from which he barely escaped with his life as a young man. He suffered smoke inhalation and extensive burns that permanently disfigured his hands. By then, he was among only a few men remaining in the town, along with the very young and very old, the priest, and a few business owners whose products were deemed essential for the war effort. Because Marton dreaded being far from his family and because he knew the end of the war was very close, he went into hiding to a nearby village on the outskirts of Szár called Szálláskut. There, on a farm owned by a distant cousin, he hid in the haymow of their barn. Each day, Ferenc and his older brother, Marton, filled their bulky pants and jacket pockets with bread, cheese, and bits of smoked meat, then walked several kilometres to take their father sustenance.

Ferenc was nine when he saw a Russian soldier for the very first time on Christmas Eve, 1944. Instead of celebrating Christmas with friends in church and then at home with family, mother, all the children, and grandfather, he hid in the wine cellar to await the inevitable arrival of the Soviet troops.

Some neighbours, including one with five young daughters, joined them. Ferenc understood from their conversations that the war had been lost, and that the arrival of Russian troops was something that filled the community with tremendous fear and anxiety. "A few days before the Russians arrived, each family opened the tap on their wine barrels and let all the wine out because they had been told that when the Russians come in, they start drinking, rape all the women, and steal everything," he said.

So, grandfather spent days taking all the barrels of wine from the wine cellar and emptying their contents onto the hard frozen ground. The children couldn't believe their grandfather was doing something so wasteful. It seemed incomprehensible after all the painstaking work that had gone into growing and harvesting the grapes, then fermenting and aging the wine. Better that, the children were told, than leave alcohol for the Russians who would become drunk and commit atrocities. Mother gathered their few valuables, such as wedding rings and watches, placed them in a small cloth bag, and then hid the bag at the bottom of a wood pile. Ferenc watched with foreboding as his first watch was hidden with the rest. It was a keepsake he had received for his Confirmation, which took place just one year earlier.

On Christmas Eve, as they waited in the dark wine cellar, they heard sporadic shooting outside. The noise of gunfire eventually stopped, and Ferenc could hear yelling in a strange language he did not understand. As the Russian voices grew closer, Ferenc could hear his mother whispering the rosary next to him. Even in the dark, he could see her close her eyes as she said the words. "Holy Mary, mother of God, pray for us sinners, now and at the hour of our death. Amen." She was pregnant with another child and holding three-year-old Jóska in her lap as she murmured the Hail Mary over and over again. She gently rocked Jóska back and forth — he was asleep and she hoped and prayed he would not be startled awake by the noise outside.

The little group of women, children, and one grandfather sat silently in the dark, each immersed in their own thoughts, as they were startled when the cellar doors were yanked open from the outside with a tremendous banging noise. Three Russian soldiers, pistols drawn, descended into the wine cellar. They shone flashlights into the faces of the frightened women and children.

Ferenc's first impression of Russian soldiers was that they looked bedraggled, unkempt, and dirty and seemed very upset to find all the wine barrels devoid of their contents. In response, they dragged grandfather out into the yard and beat him. It was dreadful to listen to the cries caused by the dull thud of fists pummelling their dearly loved grandfather. After what seemed an interminable length of time, the Russians yanked off his boots and left him. He lay on the ground for a long time afterward, bloodied and bruised. Then more and more Russian soldiers came down and picked out the women and young girls, and took turns making them scream and cry. Ferenc wasn't sure what they were doing to them at the time; he hid his face in his mother's skirt and tried to muffle the sound of the ear-piercing screams. The rampage went on for what seemed like an eternity. The mother of the five girls kept screaming and crying, pleading with the soldiers, pointing to herself, "Take me, leave our daughters please, please, take me instead." They were begging in Hungarian; no one knew any Russian words. The soldiers seemed to be revelling in the chaos, as if it was a game to them.

Unmoved by the pleading mothers, the Russians laughed and urged each other on. For some reason, they didn't touch Anna Hasenfratz probably because of her extended stomach, the toddler crying in her lap and two other children clinging desperately to her skirt. No one could escape from the wine cellar, no one knew when it would end. When the Russian soldiers grew tired, they went out of the cellar, leaving the whimpering women, crying and comforting each other, to collect themselves and their torn clothes. At dawn, the terrorized families finally crept back to their own houses. Ferenc, his mother, and the children climbed into bed together to seek solace from each other's warmth. They had survived that first terrible night.

～

During the next few days, the Russian army made camp in Szár and conducted daily house-to-house searches, and confiscated everything, anything of value. Radios were particularly targeted, as if the Russian soldiers really didn't want anyone to hear what was going on outside of Szár, nor did they want the residents to be able to contact anyone in the outside world through short wave radios. Houses, barns, chicken coops, pigsties, outhouses, anything with walls and a roof were searched for cash and valuables — especially watches and jewellery. At the Hasenfratz household, a soldier readily found the little bag of gold rings and watches their mother had hidden so meticulously in the wood pile. Ferenc stood, heart-broken but silent, as his treasured watch was pocketed by the gruff Russian. They dug up gardens in search of treasures if they noticed any recent mounds of disturbed earth. Once the valuables had been seized, they confiscated clothes, shoes, and boots of all sizes and types.

The townsfolk learned not to resist these searches and seizures, as difficult as it was not to protest even though they were forced to watch their livestock, horses, cows, pigs, and chickens gathered up and carted away. Occasionally, they outsmarted the soldiers. "Grandfather heard that the Russians wouldn't take sick or limping horses and he knew just how to precisely insert a nail into the horses' hooves to make them lame and did so with a few of our horses. It worked. They left the 'lame' horse. They killed all the pigs, but most people knew it was coming. They left us some meat when they saw how many children were in the family," said Ferenc.

The Russian army command picked one of the largest, most centrally located houses in town, the Krall family residence at 33 Fő utca (Main Street) and made it their headquarters. The occupiers set up a separate camp kitchen to feed their troops and billeted a Russian captain in the Hasenfratz home and other officers in other homes. Few reprisals in the form of killings took place because the invasion had occurred without a single shot being fired against the advancing Soviet army. Only five locals died during the occupation, among them the blacksmith who was shot when he pounded a soldier on the head with a hammer as well as the baker who was killed when he yelled at the soldiers as they carted off his baking equipment.

For the next three months, because the town was in such close proximity to Budapest, Szár became part of the front line of battle between the retreating forces of the Third Reich allied with the Hungarian army and Soviet forces invading from the east. Despite pleas from the Hungarian army military command that Budapest be spared the destruction of house-to-house battles between the warring sides, Adolf Hitler ordered exactly that.

Ferenc and his friends realized their town had become a dangerous, albeit exciting place. They learned to move around surreptitiously and avoid being seen by soldiers. When mother allowed them to go out, they played war games. Whenever a dead Russian soldier was left by the side of the road, they went through his pockets looking for anything of value they could "reclaim." They never found much, but the adventure and excitement was worth the risk. Everyone was constantly hungry following the confiscations, since hardly any food was left for the family to survive. The spring planting was out of the question with fighting flaring up in pockets all around them and troops laying mines in the fields surrounding the town.

Ferenc and his older brother made a game of sneaking into the temporary kitchen set up by Russian troops to steal food. "We didn't consider it stealing — after all, weren't the meals of the soldiers made with the flour, vegetables, cows, chickens, and pigs the Russians had taken from our families? We were simply re-possessing what was rightfully ours." Ferenc and Marton were usually successful at sneaking under the fence and into the kitchen unnoticed — where they would stuff their pockets as full of bread, potatoes, and even bits of meat as they could carry. Whatever they could lay their hands on. "If they caught us, we were usually slapped on our behinds and literally kicked out of the kitchen." Yet the game of breaking in and trying to steal food became the foremost challenge for all of them. For the most part they succeeded, because the gnawing hunger was the greatest motivator for growing boys. It kept them occupied with trying to figure out new ways of breaking in.

~⌒

The Russian soldiers loved to drink and their penchant for alcohol became well known in the community. One soldier's sole task was to seek out and find wine for dinner each evening and, despite the fact that most of the townsfolk had poured out their wines before the Soviets' arrival, this soldier somehow always succeeded in finding a hidden cache of wine. Each evening the "wine steward" — as he was known — would arrive with at least ten litres of wine, sometimes in only one pail, sometimes more than one. During the evening meal, the pails of wine were put under the table where each of the soldiers would reach down to fill their tin cups and keep drinking until the pails were empty.

Whenever the wine steward found alcohol, the beatings and violence against the townsfolk worsened. The residents could hear the drunken soldiers even from a great distance, as the shouting and singing in Russian seemingly got closer and closer. It was a terrifying sound for the frightened, distressed women, who hid themselves and their daughters whenever they heard marauding, drunken soldiers. One young girl was held captive by the Russians for days and no one could do anything to free her from the repeated sexual abuse she suffered. Her screams eventually abated with time and she was taken away by the Russians. No one was ever be able to find out where she went or what happened to her.

For a terrifying three months, Szár and the surrounding villages and towns became part of the front line of battle between German and Hungarian troops fighting the Soviet troops who were pushing westward. The civilian residents, mainly women and children, were evacuated to nearby towns that were not part of the front lines, to Bodmér, Vértesboglár, and from there later to the villages of Alcsutdoboz, Etyék, Tabajd, and Vaj.

The residents of Szár finally returned to their homes when the front moved westward at the end of March 1945. One of the disadvantages of having the front stationary there for so long was that whatever the German and Hungarian troops didn't blow up in retreat, the Russian troops confiscated or burned.

In April 1945, when the Hasenfratz family returned to their home at the centre of the village, they found all the windows broken. Mother stepped off the cart on which they had travelled, put her hand to her mouth, and gasped at the picture of devastation. In this case, the children were all stunned at the pained response of their usually calm mother. As they walked through the front door, they saw that nothing had been left intact. The beds, tables, chairs had been smashed or used for firewood. Shards of dishes were scattered all over the kitchen floor, and the cupboards and doors were ripped off their hinges. All they had left were the clothes on their backs and what little mother had packed and taken with them when they were evacuated.

In one corner of their bedroom, mother leaned down and picked up a photograph of her and Marton on their wedding day. The frame had been smashed, but the picture itself was still intact and had a calming effect on her. She stared at it for some time, then looked up at her children and said, "It's all right, we survived, we are all alive. The war is over and we will rebuild." Her optimism might have been uplifting but the family had little idea of the hardships that lay ahead.

2

Narrow Escapes

THE HASENFRATZ FAMILY MEMBERS were not alone in their loss. When they returned to Szár in April 1945, their home had been ransacked, the barn and kitchen devoid of even a single grain of wheat or kernel of corn. But every house, each family, was in the same situation: bereft of the basic necessities of life, with most of the farm animals and equipment gone.

Yet the desire to rebuild their lives was on everyone's mind: to plant something in their abandoned and fallow fields, to nourish livestock, and to restore their homes and shattered lives. People made do with what they had. The men of the village hitched themselves to cultivators to break up the soil. Not having any planting seeds, some farmers found potatoes left over from the previous year's harvest in their fields. They cut out each "eye" of the potato, then sliced up the skin into small bits, then planted these in lieu of seeds in hopes of growing a crop.

Marton Hasenfratz still had one horse and a wagon that he could use to haul wood from the country to customers in the city. His father had made the horse "artificially" lame so that the marauding armies on all sides would pass over it when they seized all the others in the village. Now they pulled out the nail and, luckily, still had an animal to help the family earn a living.

Anna Hasenfratz, along with the other women of the village, made soup from caraway seeds and wild mushrooms found in the woods. She gave thanks to God that they still had a cow so each morning the children had some milk. The meals were simple and always the same every day: a glass of milk with some bread and, if they were lucky, boiled potatoes. The children grew taller but more gaunt, each one as thin as ever. Although they were incessantly hungry, they didn't complain. Anna was heartsick at all the death, cruelty, and destruction they had already witnessed in their young lives, yet they seemed very stoic about the family's fate, accepting it as if it had been the most natural thing in the world. She worried terribly about her two eldest boys, in particular Marton and Ferenc. It seemed to her that they had turned into hardened street urchins in just a half a year, occupied with such things as searching the bodies of dead Russian soldiers for small treasures and learning about the many kinds of killing instruments: bullets, guns, abandoned field mines, and bombs that failed to detonate.

The war was over, but there were piles of ammunition everywhere. The soldiers on both sides had left so hurriedly, they hadn't even made an effort to take the ammunition with them or camouflage these stockpiles. They were simply left on the side of the road, wherever the fighting ended. One group of boys in the village found an undetonated bomb. They poked at it with sticks, rolled it down a hill, and threw rocks at it, in the hope that they could cause it to explode, but nothing happened. Finally, the boys lit a fire under the live bomb. It exploded, killing two of them, and blinding and injuring five others. Anna Hasenfratz gave thanks that her sons were not among them.

But how could she prevent her sons from playing such dangerous games? Other than keep them tethered to the table, there was nothing she could do but pray to God to keep them safe. The structured world they had known and brought children into had collapsed; she realized only a higher being could make sense of it all and guide her children on the right path.

But the parish priest, Father János Wenc, was of little help in teaching her children the right path and the ways of God. He beat the children who misbehaved in school and Anna knew that her son Ferenc had little respect for the spiritual leader of the community. On one occasion, Father Wenc asked Ferenc to deliver the parish newspaper to one of the parishioners, a Mrs. Bohm. Ferenc, not wanting to have anything to do with the priest, shook his head and stepped away just in time to avoid being swatted hard with the newspaper. The priest became incensed. That evening, he called on

Anna and Marton to complain about the behaviour of Ferenc. Sharing his son's dislike for the religious leader, Marton took his son out in the backyard and told him to pretend he had been reprimanded, to come back into the house wiping away tears as if he had been crying.

Anna tried to discuss all this with Marton, when the children would get back into a normal routine, but simply surviving and settling in with life occupied their days. She was happy if they were at least able to exchange a few private words after they said evening prayers with the children and fell asleep, exhausted.

Anna considered herself fortunate that she still had a husband. Of the 300 or so men who had enlisted in the army from the village, many had died, disappeared, or had been taken prisoner of war and hadn't yet returned home. Who knew if they ever would? Once the war was over, the Soviet army stayed and became an army of occupation. The Soviet occupying force announced that all men between the ages of eighteen to fifty must volunteer for "Malenkij Robot," or three days work. No one in Szár trusted the Russians. The villagers were convinced that once you were taken, you would never come back. Marton was grabbed by Russian soldiers on three separate occasions, but he was able to escape each time. The older children, Marton and Ferenc, believed their father was superhuman to have escaped the Russians so many times. Although they had heard the stories before, they never grew tired of them and repeatedly begged their father to tell them how he had managed to extricate himself from the hands of the Russians. It was usually in the evening, before going to bed, that these adventures were recounted.

"Father, tell us the first time," Ferenc pleaded.

After all the children chimed in with a bit more coaxing, Marton began: "The first time, I was ordered to march in a long line of men, I noticed there were few guards and many men. I worked my way to the centre of the group, as the guards were always stationed at the beginning of the line and at the end. It had been raining for three days and I saw that the ditch beside the road was full of water, there was lots of mud everywhere. I made a plan and waited until dusk. Daylight was fading fast and when it was nearly dark, I quietly took a sudden step off the side the road and rolled into the water at the bottom of the ditch. The mud was so thick, I just sank into it. I stuck my nose out above the water so I could breathe. When I thought that the long line had passed, I crawled out of the ditch, and using the forested pathways, returned home."

Then teasingly, he said, "Your mother hardly recognized me when I came in the door as I was completely covered in mud."

They all laughed. Marton, the oldest, piped up, "And the second time, please tell us the second time." ·

"The second time again I slipped away from the hostages, but that time I hid in a corn field, in a pile of drying corn stalks. This time they came after me, someone must have informed them that I ran off. The Russian soldiers drove their bayonets through the piles of drying corn stalks, but didn't get to the one I was hiding in. Plus, all the other men were waiting on the road, and surely they were worried that they would lose even more men if they spent too much time looking for me. Again, I came home after dark."

The children were again thrilled to hear of the safe return of their father. Each time they heard these stories, they sat in rapt attention, as if they were hearing them for the very first time. Marton's daughter Maria sat at her father's side, grabbed his arm, and excitedly begged him to continue. "Please, Father, tell us about the third time."

"The third time the Russians marched us during the day and there were no muddy ditches or corn fields to escape to. We marched all the way to the railway station in Bicske, where we were loaded onto cattle cars that had no windows, just a narrow opening on top covered in barbed wire. As you know your father never leaves the house without a few tools in his pockets, such as my trusted knife." While he said these words, Marton reached into his back pocket with a mischievous smile and pulled out his knife, the kind that collapsed into the handle. He extricated the four-inch blade as the children sat watching in awe.

"As luck would have it, the train didn't leave until after dark, but by then I had cut the barbed wire as quietly as possible, and without anyone noticing, slipped out and snuck home again."

The children barely moved, frozen with excitement, their eyes like saucers in awe and admiration.

With that, Anna Hasenfratz sent them scurrying to bed. She was the strict disciplinarian in the family and really didn't like her husband filling their heads with tales of glory when in fact, the reality was that life was brutally hard, especially now, after the war. But her husband believed that the children needed to hear tales of overcoming adversity, stories that injected a bit of happiness into their lives. They had witnessed too much death and destruction throughout this past year. Anna had two brothers, the children's uncles, who had been taken away and no one in Szár had seen them since. After a while, the children stopped asking about their missing uncles.

~

By June, barely two months after they returned home, ominous new rumours were swirling around the community. Marton came home from the fields one day and barely glanced at his wife as he took her arm, led her into their bedroom, and closed the door.

Anna sensed a nervousness about him she had never seen before.

"They are compiling lists," her husband began tentatively.

By the look on his wife's face, Marton could sense she had no idea what he was saying. Anna sat down on the edge of their bed and continued to stare at her husband.

"Lists of those who will be sent back to Germany." He waited for the news to sink in, then took a breath and spoke in barely a whisper. "The men stopped tilling the soil this afternoon, asking each other, 'What is the use of doing all this work if we won't be here to harvest it?' We stood and discussed the issue among ourselves." Marton again waited a minute. "Then, within a half hour, an official from the local agricultural workers party came out into the fields and told us to get back to work. He said all the talk of deportations were rumours based on lies. He told us Szár is officially categorized as a mining community, we are essential workers in mining, important to the state, and as such, no one from Szár will be deported anywhere." Marton sat down next to his wife on the edge of the bed and looked straight ahead. Anna could tell he was still sorting through this news.

Many minutes passed before he spoke again. "Our families have built their lives in this country for over 250 years and now they want to send us back. Back to where?" They looked at each other in silence.

As the months passed, the rumours of deportation spread once again. The county councils were preparing lists. More ominously, local officials walked the main street of their village, making notes, pointing to houses, and discussing details among themselves. They often stopped in front of the Hasenfratz home on Felsőkereszt utca (Upper Cross street). Anna Hasenfratz knew she had to be strong when she noticed the officials in front of her house, making notes. She couldn't let her children know that she had an unspeakable fear of things to come.

∽

Even before the war was over, the idea of "collective guilt" was promoted at the Potsdam Conference by Edvard Beneš of Czechoslovakia, who wanted to rid the state of its sizable German and Hungarian populations. By April 1945, the Kosice program provided for the confiscation of property of Germans and Hungarians and deprived them of their citizenship. The Czechoslovak government openly called for the "total liquidation" of the Hungarian and German minority. In the summer of 1945, the Czechoslovak state began to summarily expel Hungarians to Hungary and Germans to Germany.

The deportations were often executed in a brutal manner. Large communities of the expelled Hungarians were settled in the region of Tatabánya and neighbouring villages, including Szár, putting pressure on the Hungarian government to find homes for these newly displaced Hungarians. News of the cruel deportations even trickled into the village from relatives, friends, and families.

∽

All over Europe, from East Prussia to Poland to Czechoslovakia, some twelve million Germans who lived outside of Germany were being cast out of their homes and forced to flee. An estimated two million perished in the journey. The ousted families were by that time made up of mostly women, children, and elderly men. That didn't matter, however, as all ethnic Germans were marked with the all-encompassing stamp of "collective guilt" following the end of the war.

Unlike other countries, Hungary had never demanded a total expulsion of her German citizens, but the Hungarian government was forced to take action on this issue by the occupying Soviet forces. Laws were passed forming the framework of such a population movement and finally enacted on January 4, 1946. The expulsion order affected anyone "who claimed German nationality or 'German mother tongue' in the 1941

Hungarian census, those who were part of the SS, anyone who changed their Magyarized surnames back to their German equivalents, and those who were part of the Volksbund." The Volksbund, officially the *Volksbund der Deutschen in Ungarn*, was a Nationalist German Socialist organization which became the official representative of Germans living in Hungary in 1940, and was directly controlled from Germany.

The villagers knew that in Szár, the few residents who had been members of the *Volksbund* had left with the German army as it withdrew. As a result, they concluded, the lists must have been compiled based on the census statistics, but many villagers doubted that there was any reason for the list except for the fact that a resident had a nice home, a substantial piece of land, and hadn't bothered to "Magyarize" their German names.

By early April, the lists were finalized. To the Hasenfratz family members, the news that they were not on the list brought a tremendous sense of relief. Yet, they watched the departure of these unfortunate souls, their neighbours and friends, with heart-wrenching sadness, knowing full well that they could have also been included among them. Those on the list had a few weeks to pack their meagre belongings, limited to twenty kilograms per person. The children really couldn't understand, no matter how many times the parents explained, why their dearly loved playmates were being sent away. May 11, 1946, was the date set for the first deportation, with 162 families from Szár packed up and shipped by train to Dingolfing in southern Germany. The pastor, Father János Wenc, wrote in his diary: "Last night we said goodbye to many of my parishioners and my heart nearly broke as I felt like a father saying goodbye to his children. They were sobbing, not knowing where they were going and what would be waiting for them when they got there. The local police were amazed at the self-restraint and good conduct of those being deported. They wove a cross wreath onto one of the railway cars and wrote below it: 'God sends trials to those he loves.'"

Ethnic Hungarians expelled from Czechoslovakia were brought in and given the houses left vacant by the deported families. They came from places like Átány and Iszkaszentgyörgy. They were called "new settlers" and were viewed with suspicion by the original, or native settlers. Resentments and misunderstandings developed. The peace and well-being of the village had been upset.

Newspapers were full of reports of the miserable living conditions of those ethnic Hungarians who had been deported from Czechoslovakia. According to historians they lived in cramped quarters, abandoned warehouses, anywhere where temporary housing could be found. The close to 105,000 ethnic Hungarians evicted from Czechoslovakia between 1945 and 1947 put further pressure on the Hungarian government to find housing for them.

Talk of further deportations ceased for a while, but within a year, officials were again seen walking the main roads of the village, scouting out houses and making notes. Despite this, everyone tried to carry on as usual.

The Hasenfratz family was well known and respected in the village. Because the Communist Party was amalgamating power in the entire country, new officials were regularly sent to the village. Many of them heard that to find out what the locals were doing and thinking, they should speak to, among others, the Hasenfratz family. Marton Hasenfratz was suspicious of the communists in general. Marton and many other villagers believed it was a political system imposed on the country by the Soviet army of occupation, and once it left, the power of the Hungarian Communist Party would collapse. Everyone made a game of quietly speculating when the Russians would leave.

While most of these officials assessed the village for their own purposes and left, Mr. Szigethy was different from the rest. Szigethy visited with the locals and befriended Marton Hasenfratz and his family. He was sympathetic and seemed to understand the "fear of expulsion" felt by those who remained. Marton Hasenfratz later found out that Szigethy had been one of the many ethnic Hungarians expelled from Czechoslovakia.

Szigethy dropped in unexpectedly one day in the spring of 1948. He seemed disturbed and wanted urgently to talk to Marton, Anna, and Marton's father. The four of them sat around the kitchen table. Ferenc, then twelve years old, stayed in the kitchen and listened.

Szigethy began, "In two days the list of those who will be evicted next will be posted on the wall of the building of the county council. You will be on the list and your property will be confiscated."

Anna put both her hands to her mouth in silence. She was shocked. Marton's father stared at Szigethy in disbelief, as did his son.

"But ... why?" Marton stammered.

Szigethy continued: "The only reason is because you are a German-speaking family and you have an attractive, well-maintained home and sizable property. There is no other reason. I tried to prevent this for as long as I could but I can't do anything further to stop it." He stopped, giving them a moment to collect themselves, then continued.

"But I can help you in one specific way. You will lose all of your animals, the cows, pigs, and horses, if you don't follow my advice."

Without taking note of the stunned look on their faces, Szigethy went on: "We will go to the town hall tomorrow and you will register the sale of your animals to me."

In Hungary at that time each cow, horse, and pig had to be registered by their owners with the county clerk so they all had numbers. Nothing could be sold or slaughtered without government permission. The adults sat in stunned silence, allowing the information to slowly sink in.

Szigethy resumed: "Mind you, I won't pay you a *forint* for them, but I promise wherever you end up, I will give them back to you when you get there."

Now Anna Hasenfratz had had enough. What she was hearing from this man was overwhelming.

"No, you can't do that — we won't do that!" she cried in anger, standing up from her chair.

"If you don't sell them to me, then you will lose them all," Szigethy insisted. Realizing that this information was too much all at once, he left, but on his way out, he reassured Marton that he was looking out for their interests and that he wanted to help the family in this difficult time.

Anna Hasenfratz went into the bedroom by herself. When she returned to prepare dinner, her eyes and cheeks were red from crying. Realizing they had little choice, Marton and his father went to the town clerk's office the next day to transfer ownership of the animals to Szigethy. According to law, even if deported, the family could keep one horse.

In two days, a family with twelve children arrived at the house escorted by a local police officer. The Hasenfratz children, sensing that these newcomers were not here for a visit, simply stared at the new arrivals. They seemed poorly clothed, and Ferenc noticed the runny nose of the youngest. They were walking around, examining all the dishes in the cupboards, the pots and pans on the stove, touching the embroidered tablecloth on the table. Anna Hasenfratz, still in emotional turmoil from all the devastating news she had to absorb, held

her youngest — two-year-old Jánoska — in her lap. No one spoke; no introductions were made. The police instructed Anna, Marton, Marton's father,
and the children to move into a bedroom. They were told to knock from
the inside if they needed to come out and the door was closed behind them.
Shock and disbelief descended upon them, that the horrible, cruel process of
eviction and deportation was taking place, that now it was their turn.

Depressed and dejected, tears flowing down her face, Anna turned to
her husband and asked, "Are we to become prisoners in our own home?"

Ferenc and his older brother were much too curious about what was
going on outside the bedroom to stay still. First, Ferenc knocked, said he
had to go to the washroom, then Marton knocked and both were escorted to
the washroom by the police who stayed close by as they urinated. Both boys
came back to report that the strangers were taking inventory of the house
and their belongings, with the help of the police. Ferenc realized his parents
didn't want to hear the news of their scouting expeditions as they became
more and more distraught. Mercifully, night came and the entire family fell
asleep as the noise from outside the locked bedroom subsided.

～

The next morning at 6:00 a.m. the Hasenfratz family was rousted awake.
They were told they had a few hours to gather their belongings and pack.
They would be going to Vérteskozma, an isolated hamlet eight kilometres
away in the densely wooded foothills of the Vértes Mountains. They could
take whatever fit on one horse-drawn wagon.

After hurriedly dressing and giving the children breakfast, Anna Hasenfratz
tried to remain calm as she set about packing up their lives and thinking about
what they would need. She tried not to fret about the condition of the place
they would be sent to, but surely, they would need bedding, pots and pans,
tablecloths, dishes. The strangers were still in the house, studying their every
move. When Anna started to take one of her favourite cast iron pots off the
stove, the other mother protested: "You can't take that — we need that pot!"
The woman spoke in a loud voice so that the police officer standing outside
could hear. Anna decided they could live without the pot. She would substi-
tute it for another, but wouldn't lower herself to getting into a shouting match
with this stranger.

There were a few things Anna insisted upon, however, things that weren't essential, but represented something dear to her heart or a link to the past. There were objects she couldn't part with, such as the new chandelier in the front room. The fixture represented one of the few items they possessed simply for its beauty. They had only recently purchased it. Even if it was heavy and awkward to pack, she wasn't leaving the chandelier behind for people who would certainly not appreciate it. The entire morning was spent in a terrible tug of war of packing and unpacking. If someone in the new family wanted the particular item, he or she usually won out and had it taken off the cart. On some items, Anna was adamant and the interlopers backed down. Among her victories she kept the full-length linen tablecloth, hand-embroidered by her grandmother, that was part of her trousseau when she married Marton.

Ferenc was told to pack his clothes, for both summer and winter, including heavy coats and boots that weighed a lot. Mother told him to wear his coat, but it was warm outside. He also brought his slingshot and the other "weapons" he would need in the many battles ahead.

～

April 11, 1948, was a stunning spring morning with the sun shining and birds chirping. By the time the Hasenfratz family was finished packing, the sun was high in the sky. Their one remaining horse was hitched to the wagon as they set out on their journey. Anna, two-year-old János, and six-year-old Jóska rode, while Marton, his father, and the other three children, including Ferenc, walked alongside the wagon, piled high with all their earthly possessions.

That same day, twenty-eight other families were evicted from their homes and the village of Szár. The caravan of carts with men, women, babies, children, some grandmothers and grandfathers, and a few stray dogs seemed unending as the outcast families slowly wound their way out of the village and up the hilly paths toward the wooded foothills.

"As we went through the town, it was very interesting, nobody looked at us. Everyone was afraid of associating with us because they might be next if they were seen to be sympathizing with you. So as we went through, we didn't see a soul, we didn't see anybody. And we are all walking beside the wagon. It was horrible."

Ferenc looked straight ahead, steely-eyed, ignoring them all. He kept walking and walking and walking as if nothing mattered but putting one foot in front of the other, head held high. At one point, when he knew they were well out of the village, he looked back and realized how small Szár seemed to be from where he stood. He would not look back anymore, only forward from that point onward.

3

THE PRANKSTER

For Ferenc, the eight-kilometre walk to Vérteskozma seemed interminable. The sun beat down on the line of carts, making their journey unbearably hot. Father told the children to drink water sparingly as they didn't know how long it would have to last. Once they reached the path leading up into the tiny hamlet, the heat of the sun diminished. The road changed suddenly, from a gravel-surfaced road that was relatively easy to navigate, to an unpaved, muddy path full of potholes with large stones that had to be avoided. The woods thickened all around them and the way became a narrow path as they progressed deeper and deeper into the forest.

It was a steady, sometimes steep climb up into the mountain ridge to Vérteskozma into an ominous forest full of strange bird and forest noises. When they finally reached the hamlet, Ferenc couldn't believe what a god-forsaken place it was. A forlorn row of little houses stood empty on one side of a dirt road, and a dried-up creek bed lay on the other side with a small church and steeple and undulating hills beyond. Dusk had fallen by the time the Hasenfratz family arrived at the house assigned to them, a hovel compared to the home they had left behind. There was no running water or electricity connected to the house, so mother lit candles.

There was no furniture, no table, not a single chair to sit on. It looked as if no one had lived here for several years. Rubble, dust, and dirt were everywhere. All kinds of crawling creatures — spiders, field mice, insects — had taken up residence. Ferenc and his siblings had, until now, never lived in a house with a dirt floor. Mother swept one room while father collected barn boards, then hammered them together to make one bed for all of them. Exhausted, they fell into bed to sleep.

No sooner had the candles been blown out when Maria cried out in anguish: "Mama, there are bugs all over me, biting me!"

The other siblings felt them too. Father relit the candles and it looked as if a million bedbugs and fleas had descended on them.

"*Mein Gott*, Marton!" mother cried out when she saw the onslaught of creepy crawlies retreating from the light. Not wanting the two-year-old, János, to be covered in bites, she shielded him with her nightgown. The two youngest children began to cry.

Marton tried to stay calm under the increasingly discouraging circumstances. Ever the practical man, he once heard that fleas and bedbugs could be stopped if they had to cross a threshold of water. Marton searched the house and the yard for anything — a container to fill with water and put under the legs of the bed. He picked through a pile of debris in a corner of their garden and found a few abandoned military mess kits. He filled them with water and placed one at each leg of the bed. Then they blew out the candles and tried to sleep again. But the lice were persistent and began dropping from the ceiling. Maria cried out again, "Mama, they are biting me again!"

Father got up, lit one candle again, but returned to bed. "Try to sleep my dear daughter, tomorrow we will solve the problem, I'm just too exhausted to do anything about it now," he replied.

Ferenc could see that the little blood-sucking bugs liked his sister, his mother, and his older brother much more than they liked him. He secured a spot between them, thereby making sure that he was bitten less than they were. It was a dreadful night for all of them. Although they tried every possible solution, the battle with the fleas and the bedbugs went on for months.

~

Three days after they arrived in Vérteskozma, a horse-drawn cart pulled up in front of the Hasenfratz house. Szigethy arrived with two cows, a calf, and a horse in tow. On the cart, chickens and pigs huddled in cages.

Szigethy bowed and smiled when he saw Anna, Marton, and all the children. "Marton," he said, "your animals as promised."

Anna couldn't believe her eyes. Ferenc stood by her side and heard her say, "In this cruel world, he kept his word! It's unbelievable!"

The return of the animals meant that they could begin to rebuild their lives. Marton could start delivering wood from the forest to customers, who still relied on him for wood, in the towns and cities nearby. He could also work the land with his father and the older children.

As compensation for expropriating their land and house in Szár, the family received ten hectares of land in Vérteskozma. All the adults in the household worked on plowing and planting their acreage to make it productive. The main difference was that the land they left in Szár had already been planted with the spring crop, whereas here they had to start all over again. The land was hard and hadn't been tilled since before the war, so it was backbreaking work.

Old friends who cared about the family's fate tracked them down. A teacher from the middle school in Tatabánya, Professor Francsisi, came to visit the family often during the war. There wasn't much to eat in cities and towns, so he visited the village of Szár to try to barter, trade, or simply find food. The Hasenfratz

The Hasenfratz family in 1952 in the village of Vérteskozma, where they were deported after the war. Front from left: father, János, mother, Jóska, grandfather, cousin Gyuri Vékony. Back from left: Marton, Maria, Ferenc, uncle Gyuri Vékony.

family befriended the youthful professor and shared food with him. In return, Francsisi ensured that the two older boys were admitted to the Felsőgallai Polgári in Tatabánya, where the schooling was much better than locally in Szár, even though they had to travel sixteen kilometres by bicycle each day.

When, after the war, Francsisi heard that the family had been deported, he found out where they had been taken and rode his bicycle to Vérteskozma. When he saw the humble circumstances in which they were living, he made a promise to himself to lend a helping hand. Happy to see their friend, Anna and Marton invited him into the house, which by then they had managed to clean up and repair.

After a bit of small talk, Francsisi asked how they were doing and where the children were going to school. "There is a one-room schoolhouse across the road," replied Anna. "I'm sure you passed it on your way to our house. There are many classes and one teacher." She continued tentatively, "I don't know what if anything our children are learning there."

Francsisi took a sip of tea and breathed in deep of the fresh hillside air. He knew he would have to approach the following subject delicately. "I came here today because I want to encourage your oldest boys to apply to a technical school in Budapest. I've heard it has one of the best apprenticeship programs for all kinds of trades. It would be an excellent opportunity for them."

Anna Hasenfratz felt flush from a mixture of joy and embarrassment. She thought, "What a kind man, looking out for her sons." She kept a handkerchief in her long sleeve, pulled it out, and quietly wiped her tears of joy. She was grateful that her husband Marton spoke for them both, because she was unable to. He said simply, "We can't thank you enough."

⌁

Ferenc Hasenfratz was fourteen when he took the train by himself to Budapest to enrol in the technical school. Professor Francsisi had told both him and his brother: "Whatever you do, first you have to learn a trade." Francsisi gave Ferenc the address and directions: get off the train at Kelenfold station, take the number 49 streetcar, and walk to Calvin Square. There he found a long line-up of youngsters, all accompanied by grown-ups. Ferenc waited patiently and when he reached the front of the line, a tall man with chestnut brown eyes registering students asked him, "Who is your sponsor?"

Ferenc, honestly not having any idea of what he was talking about, blurted, "What is a sponsor?"

The man replied, "Well, you can only get into this school if a company sponsors you so that you can work there to learn a trade. The school is three days a week with three days working at an actual company as an apprentice."

Ferenc looked perplexed and unprepared, but without blinking, said, "Well, I don't have a sponsor."

The man seemed sympathetic to the young boy's plight and asked him if he could look at his papers. Ferenc complied.

"So you came from the Tatabányai Polgári?" Ferenc replied yes and told how he had been sent here from his school.

The man called over a supervisor, Mr. Szabo, who, after a bit of consultation, told Ferenc, "Young man, you look like a promising student. We will give you an exam and if you pass, we will sponsor you ourselves."

After taking the exam, Ferenc returned home, elated that he had been given another chance, despite the fact that he didn't have the required sponsor. He planted tree seedlings all summer, anxiously awaiting news of the test results. He also passed the time honing his skills as the practical joker in the family. During their early years, Ferenc was always pondering ways to challenge his siblings, especially his brother Marton, who was always eager for the challenge. "My older brother always thought he was smarter than me, but I knew I was smarter than him. So, there was a big competition in our family." He loved to devise pranks, simple pranks, to play on Marton. After the hamlet was re-connected to the electricity grid, Ferenc's foremost occupation was studying the way the electrical sockets worked. He once caught a fly and pushed it into the electric socket. He got a shock. Undeterred, Ferenc caught another fly and, after some trial and error, realized that if he pushed it into the negative side, he would not get a shock. He perfected his technique a bit before calling Marton over. "Marton, I can do something you cannot: catch a fly and electrocute the fly." With that, Ferenc put the dead fly in the negative socket and pushed it in.

"Come on, I can do that," Marton replied, up for the challenge.

Still taunting him, Ferenc watched him catch a fly and push it into the regular live socket. He got shocked, but so had Ferenc initially. "We were constantly learning things through these practical jokes. They sharpened our skills."

On another occasion, when Ferenc tried to jump over a chair in the kitchen, he hit his head hard on a thick, low supporting beam that extended across their kitchen ceiling. He hadn't even noticed the beam because he had been completely focused on clearing the chair. After placing the chair even closer to the low-lying beam, he called Marton.

"Marton — I bet you can't jump over this chair," Ferenc challenged his brother.

Marton focused intently on the chair and his brother's dare. He didn't even notice the beam above him. He prepared to jump, and as had happened with Ferenc, hit his head — but even harder. Marton lay on the floor, unconscious, knocked out by the impact. Ferenc shook his brother worriedly, finally waking him. The only thought running through his head was, "Mother is going to kill me!"

～

In mid-August, the news he'd been waiting for arrived. His sister was waiting at the front of the house with the news. "I have a letter for you!" she exclaimed, waving the letter around excitedly.

Ferenc tore open the envelope and eagerly read its contents. "I am accepted," he shouted proudly to everyone within hearing distance. "What great news!" Although he wanted to pack and travel to the school immediately, he had to wait until September 3 to leave and could hardly contain his excitement.

What Ferenc didn't know at the time was that Csonka János Gépgyár was one of the best machine tool and manufacturing companies in the country. The firm had a sterling reputation in all of Europe and was known in many parts of the world. The company was founded in 1929 by János Csonka, who kept developing designs for reliable machinery that eventually needed a factory floor to fill the orders. The factory was built in 1939 and began operation in 1941. Csonka designed the early gasoline engines and beat Mercedes to develop the first efficient carburetor. He engineered small cars that were so reliable that the Csonka cars were still on the road twenty years later. He came up with the first version of the rototiller as well as high-speed bench drill presses, gasoline-powered portable generators, portable pumps, engine parts, pistons, and piston rings. Ferenc joined this amazing new world of production, design, and creativity in

1949. The apprenticeship program was unmatched in excellence: students worked while studying and earning full high school credits. Classes began at six in the morning and went until two in the afternoon, three days a week. The other three days the apprentices worked at companies and were exposed to many different trades. Ferenc soon realized that becoming a machinist was what he wanted to do for the rest of his life.

"You could make things, things that were scarce at the time, like motorcycle parts. A guy had a motorcycle and couldn't get the parts to fix it, and he said to me, would you fix it? Would you make me a shaft? It was a great feeling."

Among many topics, Ferenc and the other new apprentices studied metallurgy, specific gravities, which ones could be heat-treated and welded and to what degree. He immersed himself in the physics and math, but chemistry he enjoyed less so. All the apprentices lived in the company's dormitory on the mezzanine level of the complex. They wore school uniforms consisting of black coveralls, part of a strict atmosphere of work and learning that Ferenc enjoyed. There was just one truly annoying aspect of his education: a non-stop flow of communist speeches, slogans, and propaganda music piped in through the school's public address system. What Ferenc didn't realize, however, was that while his family and community were going through upheaval and dramatic change, the entire country was undergoing a communist takeover.

By 1948, with the backing of Soviet troops still in Hungary and through an elaborate system of state counter-intelligence (secret police), intimidation, imprisonment, and show trials, the Hungarian Communist Party completely took power. The Stalinist regime was built on the personality cult of the general secretary of the Communist Party, Mátyás Rákosi. The seemingly omnipresent "Great All-Knowing Father" of all Hungarians appeared on street banners, billboards, posters, and had to be prominently displayed in schools, offices, factories, public halls, and cultural centres.

"From the moment we woke up in the morning in the dormitory, the propaganda was on, always on, all day in the factory. The party line and the speeches of our founding fathers, Rákosi and Stalin, were piped in. It was always on but after a while you don't hear it anymore. As teenagers, as a joke, sometimes we sang these songs. As a teenager, you do what others around you are doing. I learned, however, very early to be careful what you said and whom you said it to. Quite often, I was asked about my family and my background. I learned to circumvent the questions. Mr. Szabo asked me once if I was a Swabian. I avoided the question, replying, 'Why do you want to know?' Well, it turned out he was Swabian as well and came to visit my parents. They got along very well. I think that is why he sponsored me. But I came from a family that was very anti-communist. My father said, 'Make sure they don't influence you.' Whatever happened, they could not influence me."

By all accounts, Mátyás Rákosi was an ugly man. The playwright Gyula Háy, who met him in Soviet exile, wrote about Rákosi: "A short, squat body, as if the creator had been unable to finish his work for abhorrence: the head disproportionately large, topped by an enormous bald dome and fronted by a pallid, bloated face with a sweet-and-sour smile frozen to it."

Ferenc couldn't stand seeing the face of Mátyás Rákosi, yet each day this round, ugly face bore its way into the lives of each and every citizen on the front page of every single daily newspaper that was still being printed. Ferenc was appalled by this constant barrage. By this time, he had become friends with the company nurse. She was a stunning woman, only two years older than Ferenc, and he flirted and chatted with her often. She was also one of the few individuals inside the plant he felt he could trust. One of her tasks was to distribute the newspapers sent to the factory. Ferenc happened to be with her one day when the papers arrived, bearing the face of the "Wise Leader and Teacher of Our People and Our Party," as usual on the front page. Suddenly, he thought of a brilliant prank. He asked her if he could have some twenty papers. She agreed and without even asking what he needed the newspapers for, she gave them to him. Ferenc hid the newspapers in his overalls and went down the hall to an area where he knew no one would be around that time of day. Without giving it a second thought, he cut the picture of communist chief Rákosi out of each newspaper, creating a little pile of some twenty pictures. "There was no toilet paper in those days. Everybody always carried a piece of newspaper with them when they had to go to the washroom. So I took the cut-out pictures and placed them into the newspaper holder in the WC. Within an hour, all the administrators were scurrying to their offices and all the doors along the hallway were shutting one after another."

Ferenc expected that his prank would cause everyone to have a good chuckle, but the reaction, when it came, was anything but humorous.

The police were called in, including the secret police, or AVH, to conduct an investigation of the incident because it fell into the category of a "political crime." About twenty teenaged apprentices were taken to the nearby police station for interrogation, including suspect number one, Ferenc Hasenfratz.

"It is the worst thing in the world to be forced to stand against a wall, with the interrogator standing beside me and hitting me, asking, 'Are you ready to confess?'" By the third day, many had confessed. "The interrogators showed me the letter signed by some of the others saying that they all knew I had done it. It was bull. Only one guy, a friend, knew I had done it, and the nurse knew. No one else knew. Slowly, slowly, most of the other guys went back to work. I was left there with about four or five guys."

As the daily questioning continued, Ferenc got to know his interrogator. He was the husband of one of the women who worked in the plant, Judit, who punched time cards in the front office. Ferenc learned later that Judit pleaded with her husband not to beat him because she felt sorry for the teenager.

Ferenc was detained at the police station for the entire month of July 1951. "They took us out of our cells for interrogation whenever they felt like it. You stand against a wall, you cannot stand for longer than five minutes. You can walk for hours, but standing is torture. The questions were always the same, asked over and over and over again: 'Will you admit what you did? Nothing will happen to you, we just want to know who did it. How many of you were involved?'

"It was so hot it was unbelievable. I was completely undressed; I couldn't stand the heat. I even developed claustrophobia sitting on the bench in the tiny cell. There was a little hole in the wall, if I wanted to go out to go to the washroom, I had to knock from the inside. So I learned quickly that was a way to get some freedom from the enclosed space. It worked the first time. The second time they stood beside me and when they realized I didn't really have to go, they hit me again."

After thirty days, Ferenc was at last released, along with the few others still being held. As he walked into the company the next day, everyone came up to him, patted him on the back, congratulating him, asking him how he held out. But by then Ferenc realized that the place was full of informers, and he knew he couldn't trust anyone. "Anyway, even after thirty days of beatings, I never ever admitted to anything."

When he returned, Judit, the wife of the interrogator, told him she hated her husband for what he had done to Ferenc. "You were very brave," she said. "Everyone knows you did it."

The incident with the secret police made Ferenc realize how lucky he was to have escaped relatively unscathed. By that time, between 1950 and 1953 alone, the secret police (AVH) had recruited over 40,000 informants and had arrested and convicted more than 850,000 people on all kinds of trumped-up charges. They held records on over a million individuals, or 10 percent of the population. The country had become a police state; everyone knew what was going on.

Ferenc was eyewitness to one such incident when men were rounded up at the Csonka factory. A group of Russian officers walked through the company with a plant supervisor. The supervisor, obviously under duress, was pointing out the men who were the best technically in their fields: the most proficient welders, toolmakers, metalworkers, and motor and engine designers. As they were selected, the men were gathered together and taken away, never to be seen again. As Ferenc left the plant during the next few days, he saw the wives of these men crying. They would approach him and anyone else coming out of the plant, pleading: "Have you seen my husband? He didn't come home last night. Please tell me, have you seen him? Do you know where he is?" Neither Ferenc nor any of his co-workers could bring themselves to tell these unfortunate women that their husbands had been taken away to work to an unknown destination in Russia.

Despite the existence of spies and informants everywhere in the plant, Ferenc continued his studies diligently. He rarely visited his family and even used weekends to study. Ferenc relied on Mr. Szabo, his mentor and the plant manager, who had sponsored him on his first day of admission, to give him advice on everything. Szabo was probably the only individual who never once asked him whether he was the one who put the cut-out pictures of Rákosi into the WC. Ferenc's main worry, however, was a fear of speaking in German in his sleep. For that, he could have been dismissed from the apprenticeship program.

When Joseph Stalin, the Supreme Soviet Leader, died in March 1953, Ferenc was in night school. It was mandatory for the entire class to march as a collective symbol of mourning of the loss of our "Great Leader." Ferenc noticed classmates, even some of his professors, shedding tears while speeches were held praising the wondrous accomplishments of Comrade

Leader Stalin. Ferenc couldn't fake the tears. There was just one thought that kept running through his head: "Good. I'm glad he's dead." Less than three months later, in June, Mátyás Rákosi was called to Moscow and dismissed as head of the Hungarian Communist Party, replaced by Imre Nagy. At this news, a collective sigh of relief and a small flicker of hope were felt throughout Hungary.

Ferenc's first driver's licence, 1954.

Ferenc continued to work and study at Csonka János, but in his spare time, he developed a passion for rowing. There was something about the discipline, about the total concentration of the team focusing on one task, one goal, that drew him to the sport. He excelled at it and became friends with some of the finest rowers in Budapest. Many regattas were held in the spring and summer months, and the competition was fierce among the companies that sponsored their own rowing teams. These regattas gave everyone a chance to see who the best rowers were in the country. The skills of Ferenc Hasenfratz as an exceptionally talented rower became evident to anyone who witnessed the young man at the regattas. The best team in the country was run by the Gamma Gépgyár (Machinery) Company. Two of the team's star rowers were Mihály Bakos and József Flakner, who befriended Ferenc at the competitions. They liked what they saw and wanted Hasenfratz to join their team, but the system of employment under communism dictated that there was no freedom to change one's place of work. The place of employment and position of all adults of working age was stamped into a personal identification card that everyone was required by law to carry with them at all times.

Flakner and Bakos told their supervisor they would have an advantage by adding Hasenfratz to the team. They arranged an interview for Ferenc with the company where he was told there would be a position for him, but that "unfortunately no one can resign and transfer to another company."

By this time, rowing meant everything to Ferenc. His days were an endless routine of study and work, while rowing was the only part of his life that was challenging and exciting. Ferenc studied and worked from six in the morning until one in the afternoon, when he and the best rowers could leave for training. Daily, they had two-to-three hours of gruelling physical exercise and training, after which they showered and returned to night school. By ten at night, Ferenc fell into bed, only to begin the entire routine at six the next morning.

Ferenc Hasenfratz went to his mentor, Mr. Szabo, and told him he intended to leave.

"You can't. Don't do that, you'll get into trouble."

"I was told by Gamma they have a position for me," Ferenc explained to Szabo, who continued to warn the young man.

"If you do this, you will get into trouble. I just want to look out for you."

But Ferenc was adamant; the lure of being a member of the best rowing team in Budapest was overwhelming. Stubbornly, he insisted that he had to make the move to Gamma.

The police arrived at the Gamma Gépgyár machinery plant within a day of his arrival to arrest the newest employee, Ferenc Hasenfratz. The police officers said little, they simply handcuffed him and took him to the 8th District Police station. Two days later, Ferenc was hauled before a magistrate, who seemed completely oblivious to the young man in front of him. The magistrate presided from a podium, looking down on the unfortunate man. He buried his bald head in the papers in front of him as the charges were read out. The magistrate wore wire-rimmed glasses and one could tell from his general demeanour that this was going to be a very serious proceeding. The only bit of information Ferenc was allowed to give was his name, his address, and how long he had been working at Csonka János Gépgyár.

Then the magistrate began: "Ferenc Hasenfratz, for your crime, you are hereby banned for life from continuing your education." Then he waited a few seconds and continued: "Your wages will be cut by 10 percent, and you will immediately return to Csonka János Gépgyár as their employee." Then, as if the magistrate knew that what he was going to say next was of particular importance, he looked down at Ferenc briefly and said in a very serious, admonishing tone, "Through your criminal behaviour, you have jeopardized the five-year plan of the Csonka János Gépgyár." With that, the magistrate briefly looked up from his papers and with a look of disgust, motioned for the prisoner to be taken away out of his sight.

Ferenc realized his dreams of being on the best rowing team in the country had been crushed, but more importantly, he recognized that a system that disallowed people from changing their places of employment simply went against human nature. It was wrong. He also knew, deep in his heart, that a system that punished young people by revoking their right to further education was deeply flawed. The entire punishment meted out to him for this "supposed" crime was, in his words, "bull****." And the fact that he, a lowly journeyman student, could somehow jeopardize the company's five-year plan was laughable at best.

Ferenc returned to Csonka János and continued the journeyman program as a lathe operator, a specialist on the machine for shaping and boring metal. Within less than a year, however, in the spring of 1955, he was drafted into the Hungarian army for the mandatory two-year National Military Service. His life was about to change in ways he could never have predicted.

4

In the Army

FERENC WELCOMED THE CHANGE that the army brought to his humdrum life as a journeyman apprentice. He was eagerly looking forward to learning something new. The surroundings were anything but welcoming. The barracks, just south of Budapest, was a massive, hastily constructed hangar-style building with tin roof and walls, with no insulation, heating, or plumbing. In the winter, the hangar was drafty and cold, in the summer it was stifling hot. The recruits were issued equipment and clothing, right down to their T-shirts and underwear; they slept on mattresses stuffed with hay. The issued items were carefully inventoried and had to be turned in at the end of their time in the service or were paid for.

During the three months basic training in the spring, the group of approximately eighty recruits was woken at 5:00 a.m. and ordered to run laps around the barracks, clad only in their underwear. It didn't matter what the weather conditions were outside — rain, freezing sleet, or sunshine — the exercise routine was always the same. Sometimes the entire day was spent crawling in the mud, or clambering up and down the hillsides in the pouring rain. Yet Ferenc couldn't remember anyone in his unit ever catching a cold or becoming ill, despite the punishing training in inclement conditions.

Because the barracks had no shower facilities, once a week the entire unit marched to a nearby steel manufacturing company to shower. "Our smell preceded us. You can only imagine the smell inside the barracks on a hot afternoon with this level of hygiene." Ferenc looked upon basic training as yet another challenge in life, something he could excel at, or at least endure.

Ferenc had been drafted as a private, but his superiors quickly recognized his outstanding technical skills. After completing basic training, he received further training as a technical officer and was assigned to a reconnaissance and radio anti-aircraft unit in Soroksár, on the southern outskirts of Budapest.

Although Ferenc was being taught certain necessary technical skills, the ban on any further academic education imposed by the magistrate when he tried to leave the Csonka factory still weighed heavily on him. Rumours were circulating that a "high ranking officer" was coming to inspect the unit, and that there would be a chance for a few individuals to ask questions during this visit. His commanding officer encouraged Ferenc to speak up about completing his formal education. The visiting colonel was meticulous in his appearance and carried himself as a professional soldier. Ferenc was impressed with his bearing and demeanour.

He spoke to the group about rebuilding the country's armed forces "from the ground up" and how the army leadership was looking to train the best men for the job. The straightforward, no-nonsense speech impressed Ferenc. When the talk ended, the colonel asked if there were any questions. Ferenc, realizing he had nothing to lose, raised his hand and was recognized. "The Colonel-Comrade mentioned in his speech that it is in the best interest of the army to have well-trained and technically educated enlisted men. My education was discontinued when I was drafted and I am requesting that I be able to continue my education and graduate, even if it would be through night school. I agree with the assessment of the Colonel in that it would be in the best interest of the armed forces of the Hungarian People's Republic to have enlisted men who are well-trained, skilled, and educated."

The colonel asked Ferenc his name, rank, and the location of his unit. He scribbled a few notes, nodded, and then went on to the next question. Ferenc sat down, rather pleased with himself for raising the question.

Within a few weeks, Ferenc was notified that he had been granted permission to continue his education while enrolled in the army.

As a result, Ferenc settled into a new routine. During the week, he attended classes and studied to finish his technical education. Each night, he had to report to the base, but was only assigned duties in the barracks on weekends.

Between the army and school, he organized his own free time, which was usually spent asking stunning young women out on dates. Ferenc had a rare talent for seeking out new opportunities for fun while making some money at the same time. Dances that attracted a new generation of young, bright, and handsome people were regularly held at one of the most elegant hotels in Budapest, the Hotel Gellért. Opened in 1918, the hotel was and still is, to this day, a grand landmark in Budapest, a symbol of an era when the Kingdom of Hungary was in all its glory. The biggest problem was the limited number of tickets printed meant the dances were consistently sold out. Only the well connected and clever could buy one of the coveted tickets.

Ferenc as a soldier in the Hungarian army, May 1956.

Ferenc not only arranged admission for himself and all his friends, but he never paid a *forint* for the tickets. The ticket taker, Sándor, was a friend. For a small payment, Sándor agreed that, unlike the rest of the ticket-takers, he would not tear the tickets as Ferenc and his friends entered. That way, the two tickets used could be passed back to Ferenc, enabling him to bring in more friends several times during the evening. Only the two initial tickets were purchased. For his part, Ferenc collected a small amount from each of his friends, which was much lower than the cost of full admission. This covered the cost of Sándor's fee and left enough for Ferenc to take his date out for a drink afterward. Because Ferenc danced well and always seemed able to arrange tickets for this most sought-after event, he was seen as a man of some influence and a most desirable partner in the eyes of the ladies.

Once a year, all Hungarian anti-aircraft units were sent to a forest in northern Hungary, near Nagyorosz, for training and joint exercises, which included target practice as well as breaking down, transporting, re-assembling, and setting up camp and all the equipment. The units pitched their tents in a densely wooded area. Planes flew through the practice target area, dragging their drones — large aerial balloons — about a kilometre behind them. The assignment of the units was to identify the exact location of the plane, target the balloon, and try to shoot it down. There were eight anti-aircraft cannons, one for each unit. Each 90 mm or 110 mm flak gun had a crew of seven, the most important of them being the vertical aimer and the horizontal aimer. Each unit was required to shoot eight rounds of ammunition before the training session was complete and then everyone could go back to Budapest. The problem was twofold. First, it had been a particularly wet spring, which in turn brought out a profusion of caterpillars, making everyone's life miserable. Second, that week, it was overcast and rainy, making it impossible to identify aircraft overhead either with the naked eye or with the rudimentary Russian-made manufactured radar equipment they were using.

As one of three men at the main command post, Ferenc sat at a round table with two others, a sergeant and a captain, with their eyes glued to the radar-tracking device. Their task was to identify the plane, pinpoint the location of the balloon, and pass the information on to the units, who in turn fired their anti-aircraft guns based on the orders received.

The conditions couldn't have been worse. Ferenc remembers: "There were so many caterpillars on the ground, you couldn't walk without stepping on them. The crunching sound made by our boots was dreadful. The smell of dead caterpillars was unbelievable. Everyone wanted me to find the plane, so they could fire off the required number of rounds and go back to Budapest. But you can only shoot if there are no clouds in the sky and it had rained for days. Finally, they were begging me, 'If there are no clouds, make sure you find the damn plane. We don't want to stay here any longer than we have to.'"

Ferenc reassured them that they would locate the plane; being out in the wet woods with all the caterpillars exasperated him just as much as it did everyone else. When the anti-aircraft guns located the drone, they locked onto the target and followed it. The anti-aircraft units never actually saw the target drone, they only followed orders of where to shoot. It was entirely left to the command post manned by Ferenc, the captain, and the sergeant to verify that they had seen and identified the plane.

Finally, there was a clear day and Ferenc was able to give the command: "Enemy aircraft approaching at eleven o'clock. Eleven o'clock. Got it. The directions are then confirmed by all eight units, and eight shots are fired."

Within seconds, there was a commotion as several jeeps were driving wildly, directly toward them, carrying the joint Hungarian and Russian army command. Ferenc and the other two spotters realized something had gone very, very wrong. They glanced at each other and knew instantly that none of them had actually seen the plane. "Before the jeeps arrived, I quickly opened the compass, loosened two screws, and gave it a good kick." When the jeeps got there, the commanding officers shouted at them, ordering the three of them to step away from the measuring equipment.

They were each asked, in turn, "Did you see the plane?"

Ferenc confirmed he had.

The sergeant confirmed that he had seen the plane.

Finally, the captain was asked and he also confirmed that he had seen the plane.

"I didn't really see a plane. The sergeant said he saw a plane, so did the captain. They were all liars. As it turned out, we were shooting at the front of the plane, not the back. We could have easily shot down the plane. But we all swore we saw the plane. I had to lie. Anyway, everyone cheered because we could go back to Budapest. The three of us were taken to a military jail and were interrogated for three long days. Meanwhile, they checked the instruments and determined that the compass was off and that it did indeed need to be re-calibrated."

~

Ferenc regularly ran afoul of authority for other minor infractions and had occasion to become acquainted with the inside of a military prison. He learned to cope with these short-term incarcerations without taking them seriously, realizing the system was fundamentally flawed and that there was nothing he could do about it. He tried to find humour in the incidents. On one occasion, when Ferenc called an officer an "idiot," he was sentenced to prison for insubordination. The timing was very inopportune, however, because he realized he wouldn't be let out in time for his sister's wedding. Again, luck intervened, as Ferenc happened to know one of the guards from his rowing days. Ferenc cajoled and pleaded with the guard, a sergeant, to let him out for an afternoon so he could attend his sister's wedding. But there was another problem. Even if he could somehow convince the sergeant to let him sneak out on compassionate grounds, Ferenc didn't have anything to wear to the nuptials but his prison uniform. Fortunately, the sergeant, feeling some compassion for the talented former oarsman, both let him out and loaned Ferenc his own uniform.

On the way to the wedding, however, his luck ran out. Unbelievably, Ferenc saw his commanding officer, Captain Roman, sitting in the same train compartment, his eyes fixed on Hasenfratz. Ferenc nonchalantly tried to look out the window, but he knew that he'd been spotted. Captain Roman walked straight toward Ferenc, stopped right in front of him and said in a serious tone: "Hasenfratz, where have you been? Well, why don't you say it, where have you been? I know you're supposed to be in jail and now you've been promoted in jail? How did this happen? We'll talk about this later." Without giving Ferenc a chance to respond, Roman turned and left.

Captain Roman never brought up the incident again. Each time he saw Ferenc, however, Roman gave him a look as if saying, "I know about you."

～

Ever the schemer and practical joker, Ferenc figured out ways of earning a bit of extra cash while playing pranks, this time on his fellow soldiers. The walls of the barracks were very thin, to the point that a small opening could be made with a simple hammer and the point of a hunting knife. Ferenc organized a few of his friends to set up a rudimentary "peep show" in one of the few private rooms. Ferenc described the event as "top-secret" and told a few mates that by chance, a woman was undressing on the other side of the wall. They could take a peek, if they remained completely silent, but they would have to pay to look through the small opening while she was disrobing. In fact, the opening was so tiny that if the person undressing remained very close to the opening, the viewer would only see skin, and the sex of the individual would not be evident at all. What Ferenc had done was convince one of his army buddies, whose arms and legs weren't too hairy, to stand on the other side of the aperture and undress.

Ferenc believed no one would guess because viewing would be brief. "The problem was we had a tough time keeping a straight face through it all."

The peep show didn't last long. When his army buddies found out it was a hoax, they were initially upset as to how they could have fallen for such an obvious ruse, but with time, everyone admitted it was a clever one. They all had a great laugh at their own gullibility, but they also learned to be cautious of anything Ferenc Hasenfratz said, even with a straight face.

By the summer of 1956, twenty-one-year-old Ferenc Hasenfratz was in his prime. He was tall, handsome man, increasingly confident and optimistic about his future, respected by his supervisors and peers, and dating several good-looking young women. Despite all the hardships life offered, he maintained and refined his sense of self and humour. No one could have predicted that historic events unfolding later that same year would dramatically alter the future course of his life.

5

THE FREEDOM FIGHTER

OCTOBER 23, 1956, WAS a sunny and warm Tuesday afternoon in Budapest, and the gentle lingering rays of the October sun fell softly. Ferenc Hasenfratz was riding on the number 49 streetcar, his thoughts still immersed in the events of last night — a quiet dinner with Mitzi, followed by dancing at the Gellért Hotel. He thought about how perfectly she fit into his arms as they swung around the dance floor. He knew that the foremost obstacle to asking for her hand in marriage was the fact that her father was an influential leader in the Communist Party. As for his parents, they would never understand.

Then, as the streetcar pulled into Calvin Square, Ferenc was yanked out of his daydreams. He couldn't believe what he was seeing from the window. He had just left the military barracks and was still in army uniform. There were large crowds of university students and other young people, walking together with hopeful, joyful smiles on their faces. They were carrying placards that alone should have landed them in prison, but much worse were the incredible things they were chanting: "Down with Gerő," "Nagy into the Government, Rákosi into the Danube," and "Russians go home."

Ferenc sensed that this was far from the usual forced march orchestrated by the Communist Party apparatus; this was a real demonstration. Lately there had been a thaw as the winds of change blew in from Poland where people had dared to raise their voices in protest and demonstrate against the excesses of communism. News of their defiance leaked through to the other Warsaw Pact nations and this demonstration appeared to show solidarity with the Poles. The crowd was headed for Bem square, named after the Polish-born Hungarian hero General Jozef Bem. Moreover, just last year, Soviet troops withdrew from Austria and, incredibly, just this last summer, many of the landmines at the Austria-Hungarian border were being dismantled. For the first time in many years, a glimmer of hope was kindled in the hearts and minds of Hungarians. If the Russian troops could leave Austria, could Hungary be next?

The streetcar couldn't proceed anyway, so Ferenc got off the streetcar and was quickly caught up in the melee.

The crowds were becoming more emboldened as tens of thousands of additional students and workers streamed into the heart of the city to join them, the mass of moving people protesting peacefully, but insistent in their demands. Some of the protestors had grabbed a Hungarian flag and were ripping the hated communist symbol — the hammer and sickle — out of the middle with a pocket knife. Soon more and more student demonstrators were holding high the Hungarian tricolour with the glaring empty hole in the centre. Late afternoon, the crowd had swelled to over 200,000 and Ferenc was convinced of the crowd's immense strength. Something powerful was happening and he boarded the streetcar going back to his barracks to tell his fellow soldiers and commanding officers all he had witnessed.

After he left, events moved quickly. A large group of demonstrators went to the parliament building, demanding to hear from Imre Nagy. It was several hours before he appeared. Another crowd tore down an enormous statue of Joseph Stalin on Dózsa György Road using blowtorches and ropes, toppling and defacing an important symbol of the system. All that remained standing were Uncle Stalin's boots: massive, black, empty shells.

A third group of university students and demonstrators made their way to the radio building, demanding that their fourteen points, the rallying cry of the university students, summarizing their demands for change, be read into broadcast.

It was here that secret police shot into the unarmed crowds, attempting to disperse them. Rather than quell the uprising, the shootings of dozens of unarmed civilians made the demonstrators more determined, defiant, and angry. The turning point here came when soldiers from the Hungarian army's 8th Tank Regiment, arriving to reinforce the defenders of the radio building, joined the demonstrators. The soldiers distributed weapons among the demonstrators.

~

When Ferenc returned to the barracks, his fellow soldiers were full of questions: "We heard there is trouble? What did you see?" After one of his commanding officers warned him that he shouldn't say much, Ferenc downplayed the drama. Forty-six officers were present in the barracks at the time; no one knew who might be an informant for the secret police. As the hours passed, more and more news filtered in about the spread of fighting on the streets of Budapest. Late that evening, when word spread that the secret police had fired upon and killed unarmed civilians, the residents of the city exploded in anger. Streetcars were set on fire, cars overturned. Small arms were obtained from police stations and army barracks. By the next morning, the army military command of Ferenc's anti-aircraft unit decided to defect to the side of the revolutionaries, as did many other Hungarian army units.

"We joined the revolutionaries, and by doing so, we were fighting on the Hungarian side, not the Russian side. Some of the communist officers, the political officers, they simply disappeared."

~

Party Secretary Ernő Gerő, head of the state security police, was one of the two most hated men in Hungary along with Prime Minister Mátyás Rákosi. Gerő asked for assistance from the Soviets on the first day, when fighting broke out all across the city and events spiralled out of the regime's control. Soviet garrisons around the city were notified that evening, and columns of tanks entered the city the next morning, the twenty-fourth, at dawn. The Russian commanders hoped that the show of force would quell the uprising, but they badly misjudged the Hungarian resistance. Roadblocks and ordinary plates, painted green and placed in a line across roads to mimic landmines, greeted the columns of tanks at crucial traffic chokepoints. Heavy gunfire and Molotov cocktails thrown from the apartments above made the tanks ineffective for the fierce urban warfare that ensued. On October 24 alone, more than twenty Soviet soldiers were killed in the fighting.

Ferenc saw that the army was recruiting civilians for fighting and he knew that was not wise. He was taught that in the army only about one-third of the personnel are actual combatants, most are support staff who are charged with getting the supplies, moving equipment, and many more mundane tasks.

"We needed volunteers, to help in supporting the army. I got into a jeep along with two other soldiers from my unit, and we went up the Castle District to the dormitory of the Technical University. When we arrived, we went into the courtyard where a crowd of university students gathered. I gave a speech and told them that the country was changing, we in the army had joined the revolutionaries, and we needed volunteers to help as support staff. There were lots of guys who volunteered immediately." Ferenc sought out his brother Marton who lived in the dormitory and found him playing cards with some friends. "My own brother Marton wouldn't come. He warned me about getting involved, telling me that the uprising was doomed to fail, and he wasn't going to help," he said.

"Was I surprised by the uprising? Of course, I was surprised. I got caught up in it. I was glad to see it and thought, let's move with it. Did I think they were going to win? Not really, but I was willing to sacrifice for it. I had seen injustices for so long. I liked it. I enjoyed it. I don't know, maybe I'm a masochist. I realized whatever was going to happen, we were probably going to die."

~

Ferenc, a reconnaissance and radio operator, and his unit set up near Soroksár, on the main road leading south toward Kecskemét.

"Anti-aircraft units were set up all around Budapest because for years we were told that the Yankees were going to come and bomb our capital. It was stupid propaganda, but you needed propaganda to scare people. That's the direction one column of Russian tanks came from."

Because there were several anti-aircraft units stationed all around Budapest, they all took credit, for instance, whenever a Russian plane was shot down. "One plane flies through, everyone shoots at it, they saw it smoking and spiralling down, and they all believed they had shot down the plane. So each unit reported a plane shot down, a total of eight planes, when in actual fact there was one plane shot down by eight units. When you are a soldier, you want, you need success. It gave the unit such a feeling of euphoria."

Ferenc, back row, third from left, with army buddies and a sniffer dog during a lull in the fighting, October 1956, Jutadomb, near Budapest.

The unit used anti-aircraft cannons against tanks as well, but the ammunition was inappropriate and unable to penetrate the outer steel shell of the tank.

"Ideally, you should shoot the first tank and the last tank in a column, so they can't go back and forth, and then demolish the entire line. According to the book, this works fine, but in reality it didn't work so well."

Ferenc was elected to represent his unit as a member of the Revolutionary Council, a body that coordinated the role of the army, university student organizations, and factory councils. From the point where he was elected a member of the Revolutionary Council, Ferenc Hasenfratz was no longer involved in the day-to-day fighting. "While I was there, I personally remember our unit destroying two tanks and an ammunition truck. After that I was no longer involved, I worked behind the scenes. I don't think I ever pulled a trigger after that."

⟨⟩

Fighting spread to other cities and towns outside of Budapest. On October 26, a general strike was called, making it clear that the uprising was supported by a large percentage of the population across the country. There were also demands for the withdrawal of Soviet troops from Hungary, dissolution of the secret police, and multi-party democracy. Soviet tanks and troops simply couldn't gain control of several parts of city, such as the Corvin Passage and Kilian Barracks. With much less firepower and inferior weaponry, the revolutionaries seemed to have gained an incredible victory over the overwhelming force of the Soviet army. It was unbelievable. A general ceasefire was declared by the end of October. The residents of the capital walked around the rubble filled streets in a dazed, but euphoric state. People hugged strangers and cried openly in their joy. Imre Nagy, the well-liked populist politician, took over once again as prime minister and announced that his government would recognize the revolutionary organizations, disband the secret police, and begin negotiations for the permanent withdrawal of Soviet troops from Hungary. Prisons were opened up, setting free political prisoners as well as common criminals. Cardinal Josef Mindszenty, Primate of the Catholic Church, was among those liberated.

As a member of the Revolutionary Council, Ferenc occasionally attended ad hoc hearings of accused communists. He was uncomfortable at these hearings as he thought about the many times he was interrogated.

"They brought in a man one day, a tall man, and they're giving him a hard time. They say he's a communist and this and that. I looked in the room and asked, 'Why are you beating him?' The revolutionaries were using some of the communist tactics to interrogate as well. They don't like to hear that, but that was the way it was. It turned out that someone accused the man of having an affair with his girlfriend, so he called him a big communist. As a result, some injustices were done as well. Eventually they let him go."

The Hungarians began to publish free newspapers, organize political parties, and clean up storefronts, but their newfound freedom was short-lived.

~

The final decision to intervene by force took place in Moscow on October 31, and preparations began. As a ruse, the top Hungarian military leaders were summoned to meetings with Soviet leaders on November 3, purportedly to discuss the details of the Soviet troop withdrawal. In attendance was Colonel Pal Maleter, the highest-ranking officer in command of the revolutionary forces in Budapest, along with other leaders. A former communist partisan, Maleter deliberately wore his Soviet military medals of distinction to the meeting. The Soviets placed Colonel Maleter and the others under arrest at the meeting, depriving the revolutionaries of their military leaders just prior to the second, more brutal invasion by Soviet forces.

Operation "Whirlwind," as it was called, began in the early morning hours of November 4, when strategic airfields, highways, and bridges were secured. Because the Soviets feared resistance by the Hungarian army, the barracks were the first targets. At five in the morning, Imre Nagy informed the world of the invasion through a dramatic radio broadcast, pleading for help for Hungary. The prime minister then took refuge in the Yugoslav embassy.

Ferenc remembers that day clearly. "At four in the morning, they started bombarding our barracks, but we had been tipped off about a day before that the Russians were moving closer by our reconnaissance people who saw the advance. So, under cover of darkness, we moved closer to the Danube, about one kilometre away. We moved all night. At four in the morning, when they bombarded and flattened our barracks, no one was there. So the entire barracks was flattened, we were the first to be attacked. Our unit was part of the command centre, the *harcállás parancsnokság* (HÁPOS), and we were the only ones who had an underground command post."

Ferenc and his small unit eluded the Russians underground for several more days, moving to the Jutadomb barracks, where the fighting was incredibly fierce.

Eleven Soviet soldiers and four secret police officers lost their lives in the fighting there. The unit defending Jutadomb didn't know it at the time, but the Hungarian military delegation, including Colonel Maleter, who had been arrested and detained by the Soviets just before Operation Whirlwind began, were being transported in a Russian armoured personnel carrier from Budapest toward Soroksár, when they came under direct fire by the Hungarian defenders of Jutadomb. While the Hungarian prisoners were not injured, one of their accompanying Soviet guards was killed.

Ferenc and his unit fought there and tracked the seemingly endless column of incoming Russian troops and tanks, reporting the numbers to the other units. The radios operated by the revolutionaries eventually fell silent one after the other.

"I knew we lost, well, we didn't want to admit it, but we did, at least I did. There is no way without a command that you can continue that. Our commander in chief, Maleter, was already arrested. So there were no orders coming. It's like with a company, when there is no management. If there are no orders, what are people doing? The average person is a follower. Most, you may have 20 percent who are leaders, the rest are followers. So, when you have no command, what do you do? Where do you shoot? Who do you shoot at? You go out on your own? You need a command and that's what we didn't have. I'm convinced Russia would not let Hungary go at the time."

By November 6, there were some 30,000 Soviet troops in Budapest, inexorably crushing the resistance. Most of the fighting was over by November 11, although sporadic activities, such as blowing up railway lines and localized strikes, continued well into the winter. According to conservative figures, an estimated 3,000 Hungarian civilians died in the fighting of October and November, and over 19,000 were wounded. At least 185 Hungarian soldiers were killed, and 137 were wounded. The Soviets counted 720 dead, 1,540 wounded, and 51 missing. Over the next several months, some 200,000 Hungarians, most with only the clothes on their backs, fled their homeland rather than live under continued repression.

～

Ferenc Hasenfratz realized he was in grave danger. As he attempted to return to his barracks, as all enlisted men had been ordered to do, even before he reached the main gate, a fellow soldier warned him to flee, saying, "Don't you know that policemen have been here, looking for you?" Ferenc knew he had little choice: flee the country or stay and face the cruel punishment of the regime's wrath with, at best, years in prison, or, at worst, execution. He decided, along with five other enlisted men he had fought with, that they were going to leave. They were already condemned men for their role in the uprising; the fact that they were following the orders of their commanding officers would mean nothing in their defence.

First, Ferenc felt he had to go home to see his parents and Mitzi one last time. He knew he couldn't let them know or even hint at the fact that he was leaving, the less they knew the better in case the secret police came to interrogate them about his whereabouts. He had no idea when he would see them again, if ever, and he wanted to see them one last time.

When he arrived in Vérteskozma, Ferenc realized that his parents had been relatively isolated and knew little regarding the extent of the bloody uprising in Budapest. Still, he could sense that his mother was worried. Never one to show much emotion, she kissed him gently and caressed his face as he entered the house. She asked him if he was hungry, but he told his parents he could only stay for a little while, as he had to hurry back to his army unit. He reassured his parents everything was fine. After a short visit, he kissed his mother goodbye and walked with his father to the gate. Suddenly, his father turned to him and said, "You know, I'm so proud of all my children, that you all stayed, that none of you boys left." Ferenc leaned in to embrace his father, choking back tears, knowing he was on his way out, trying desperately not to transmit a hint of his emotional state. He knew only too well that none of his siblings participated in the revolution, none had served on revolutionary councils, and none had fought. They were relatively safe from the regime's retribution.

At Mitzi's house in Szár, the family invited him to stay for a meal. Mitzi's father, a member of the communist party, had been following the events on the radio and had heard about the mass exodus. Ferenc could sense that he was quite disturbed. At one point during the meal, he turned to Ferenc and said, "Listening to Radio Free Europe and all these stories — these people will be begging us to be able to come back." Ferenc didn't respond; he sat quietly finishing his meal.

~∽

Ferenc and his fellow escapees took the train from the outskirts of Budapest toward the town of Kőszeg, very near the Hungarian border with Austria. They were all still in Hungarian army uniform, hoping that the military garb would shield them from the many military checkpoints set up on the way to the border. When a large group disembarked in Csepreg, one stop before Kőszeg, Ferenc and his army buddies decided to follow them. They went with the group until they all ended up at a wedding, where, fortunately, although they were unknown to either the bride or the groom, they took part in the festivities and ate and drank their fill. Afterward, one of the guests they met offered them a place to stay for the night.

The next day they headed further west on foot, in the direction of Kőszeg.

When night fell, they crept into a barn, sleeping behind cows on straw. Ferenc remembered, "Some of the guys complained about the smell. I thought, 'What smell?' That's the way farm animals smell. I didn't mind, it was good."

They decided to cross the border after dark the following evening. There was a full moon in mid-November, and a dusting of snow covered the ground. Ferenc realized the light from the full moon and from the snow on the ground would make it easier to be detected, but they had come too far to turn back, they really had no other choice but to keep going.

They set out after midnight and proceeded on foot in a westerly direction, always checking their compasses, walking for hours. They crossed clearings and wooded areas and kept walking. Then, in a distance, they saw a group of Russian soldiers. With a sinking feeling in their hearts, Ferenc and his friends realized they had been spotted, so they decided to take cover behind some trees. The Russians moved closer and closer, also moving under cover. The Russians were armed and they knew the Hungarians were armed as well. They began to shout to one another, each group hidden by trees.

"*Stoj!*" (Stop!) One of the Hungarians spoke Russian, but what they were saying was so basic it was understood by all of them. Ferenc and his friends identified themselves as Hungarian soldiers. Then, unexpectedly, the Russians yelled over, "*Devaj chasy!*" (Hand over your watches!) Ferenc remembered how many times he had heard that expression as a child when the Russians first entered his village. They did as the Russians demanded, after which one of the Russians pointed to his watch and raised an index finger at them, signalling that they had one hour to get out of the area.

Ferenc and the others hurried out of the wooded area, crossed another clearing, and continued until they saw a road with lights from cars and trucks in the distance. At this point, they weren't even sure whether they were in Austria or still in Hungary. They were getting very cold and tired. Ferenc directed two of his men to crawl down to the road, hide in the ditch by the side of the road, and check the licence plates of passing cars to determine if the group had crossed the border. The two did as they were instructed. An hour later, they came back to report that they were still in Hungary.

"Can you imagine that? It was terrible. All these smart army guys with compasses going around and around and we were still in Hungary."

By this time the first light of dawn had started to spread over the horizon, their window of opportunity for escape had passed, they would have to go back to find another place to sleep until the next night.

Soon they found a farmhouse with a barn. There were a lot of dogs around and one of the group thought he spotted a Russian army vehicle nearby. They weren't sure what they were up against, so they decided to risk knocking on the farmhouse door. The owner of the house opened the door and immediately blurted out, "Is there anyone left in Budapest?"

They introduced themselves and told him they needed shelter for the evening. The owner of the farm seemed amenable to letting them stay, but he had some conditions. "I will tell you which way to go and where to cross the border. When you get there I want you to send me a message on Radio Free Europe that 'the red hawks have arrived in Austria safely.'" Ferenc agreed.

But there was more. "You can stay overnight, but there are two people in the farmhouse that I want you to take with you."

Ferenc asked if they were civilians. When he replied that they were, Ferenc shook his head, pointing out that they were soldiers and couldn't have civilians tagging along. No way could they take them along.

The farmer insisted, saying they wouldn't be able to stay in the barn if they didn't agree. Ferenc realized they didn't have a choice. They reluctantly agreed to take the two, a mother and her university-aged son.

That night, armed with better directions, the group again ended up walking for hours and hoped they had crossed into Austria. They heard small arms fire in the distance and dogs barking. The scene seemed surreal with the full moon and snow on the ground. They realized the forests and clearings were probably thick with Russian troops. "No one spoke, there was very little talking, except to ask: Ferenc, do you think we should go this or that way?"

Ferenc was lost in his own thoughts. "I knew I was leaving Hungary for good. The situation was such that you could never come back. When I said goodbye to my dad, I knew that was it. I'd never see him again. Going across that border, it was very dramatic."

They had been told that they had to cross a small creek, the Rápca, but when they reached the creek, they saw that the fall rains had turned it into something more like a swollen river. The mother was inappropriately dressed for wading through a river and she was wearing heels. Ferenc realized he and another soldier would have to carry her over the water. Her son, the university student, began to whimper and cry when he realized that he too, would have to cross the foreboding body of water. As they set out, Ferenc felt the freezing temperature of the water as it first seeped into his boots. By the time he reached the deepest point, he was up to his waist in the ice-cold waterway. He kept telling himself, "I will get through this; it's not so bad; it will be over soon." The worst part was the whimpering, crying young man. To Ferenc, it seemed incomprehensible that someone would be crying over something that had to be faced, something that was unavoidable in order to reach a goal. When they reached the other side, all the men were soaked from the waist down and they knew they had to keep moving and find warmth fast. They emptied their boots of the icy water. The woman had stayed relatively dry.

Finally, they saw a farmhouse with a light on inside. The little group conferred to decide what to do next. Ferenc said there really was no point in continuing. They might as well knock on the door to find out where they were. Because he was the only one in the group who spoke German as well as Hungarian, it was decided that Ferenc should knock on the door. Ferenc was cold, wet, tired, and hungry; it didn't take long to decide to go to the front door of the farmhouse. He tried to walk quietly to the front door, but the crunching of his boots on the icy snow was all he could hear. Through the window he saw a man reading by a light. He seemed to be alone.

Ferenc gathered his courage and felt his heart pounding as he knocked. He heard the chair as it moved back, scraping the wooden floor. The man came to the door, opened it, saw Ferenc, and, without asking any questions, immediately announced in flawless German, "Welcome to Austria. You are okay, you are in Austria."

Ferenc's knees went weak with the joy of learning that they were all safe. It seemed that this man had been greeting such strangers at his door on a regular basis in the past few weeks. The man directed them to the nearest village, named Eberau, where a school had been set up to accommodate the daily inflow of refugees from Hungary. After being registered in Eberau, Austria, on November 22, 1956, they received hot tea, bread with jam, and the offer of a place to sleep on hay mattresses on the floor of the school gymnasium. Tired to the point of total exhaustion, Ferenc slept soundly for the first time in over two weeks.

~⌒

The crushing of the revolution was followed by years of repression in Hungary. An estimated 33,000 people were imprisoned or sent to labour camps, and 230 were executed. Imre Nagy and Pal Maleter went on trial in 1958 and both were executed. Their followers received long prison sentences. The army was thoroughly cleansed, with 570 soldiers sentenced to life imprisonment for participating in the revolution, and thirty executed. Of the military trials that were held, those of the leaders and soldiers who fought at the Jutadomb, where Ferenc Hasenfratz served, were dealt with in a particularly harsh manner. The military trials took place in July 1958. They were known as the Jutadomb trials, or Mecseri trials, named after the general in charge. Fifty-two soldiers received life imprisonment, eleven of them, including General Mecseri, were sentenced to death. Ferenc Hasenfratz was one of the lucky few who managed to escape to freedom.

6

Life as a Refugee

Aﬀﬀter their harrowing journey crossing the border, it took Ferenc a while to recognize and remember where he was, safe in an Austrian village schoolhouse, his feet were warm and dry, he no longer had to deal with the freezing cold, icy river crossings, and forests infested with Russian soldiers. He couldn't remember the last time he had slept so soundly. Scores of refugees like him were sleeping on mattresses filled with hay, side by side, covering every square metre of the floor of the school classrooms. The woman, who they had carried across the river and guided across the border, had disappeared almost the minute they arrived in Eberau, along with her whining son. A car had arrived and whisked them both away. "That's gratitude," thought Ferenc.

Austrian officials requested that he surrender his sidearm, an army-issued pistol, but he stayed in his army uniform. In the little town of Eberau, with one church and one little schoolhouse directly next to the church, the local villagers were so kind and accommodating.

"I stayed at the school house, because I couldn't leave right away. I remember people coming in and enquiring: Who would like to come to dinner? We need three people, four people. Because I spoke German, I was frequently chosen. They were very good to us."

Within a few days, Ferenc and his army buddies were sent by bus to a much larger refugee camp at Eisenstadt, about 100 kilometres away. There,

Ferenc saw for the first time the enormity of the refugee crisis thrust upon Austria and the West by the events in Hungary. Eisenstadt was engulfed with refugees and hundreds more were arriving daily. Austrian bureaucrats were overwhelmed with registering and providing food and accommodation for the tens of thousands who had already arrived, most with little more than the clothes they were wearing. Various aid agencies were busy organizing the distribution of food and medical supplies, blankets, clothing, shoes, baby formula, and even toys for the many children. Emergency medical services simply couldn't keep pace. As soon as camp officials learned that Ferenc spoke impeccable German and Hungarian, they asked him to work as a translator for the aid agencies in the camp. They were desperate for translators.

The revolution happened so unexpectedly and was crushed so quickly that Western nations were slow in reacting officially. The United Nations appeared impotent during the crisis. Following the suppression of the revolt, the world's sympathy became focused on aid for the Hungarian people and for the refugees. Countries from around the world decided to open their doors to the refugees, sending delegations to Vienna to interview and approve prospective immigrants.

In response to the Soviet action, mass demonstrations condemning the brutal clampdown were held in most major Western capitals in Europe and North America. The membership of communist parties plummeted in Western Europe as card-carrying members publicly destroyed their member-ship documents in disgust. Well-known leftist writers and poets wrote articles condemning the slaughter of workers and students in Hungary.

~

In Canada the Liberal government of Prime Minister Louis St. Laurent felt enormous pressure to open its doors to the refugees. The youthful and intel-ligent minister of citizenship, Jack Pickersgill, was entrusted with advising the federal government on how to proceed. Minister Pickersgill was determined to convince the government to accept a large number of refugees. One of the major hindrances for the refugees was, until then, the cost of passage. Because Canada was so far away, travel was expensive and newcomers had to repay any government assistance once they arrived and found their first job. Pickersgill learned one of the reasons Hungarian refugees were reticent to choose Canada was that they didn't want to begin their lives in a new country burdened with a debt they might not be able to repay. By the end of November 1956, the cabinet decided to offer free passage of any Hungarian refugee who wanted to come. The decision was historic for Canada, the first non-English, non-French speaking refugees who arrived in the tens of thousands, starting with nothing but their skills, education, and diligence.

Shortly after cabinet decided to offer free passage, Pickersgill was sent to Vienna to visit the refugee camps and to advise the government on the refugee crisis. Pickersgill witnessed that a large percentage of the Hungarians were under the age of forty, well educated, highly skilled, and anxious to start a new life. Pickersgill concluded that Canada should cut the red tape, ordering that these refugees be processed "one a minute."

It was in the Eisenstadt refugee camp that Ferenc Hasenfratz met Minister Pickersgill. Ferenc was sitting with camp administrators translating for a group of new arrivals when Pickersgill arrived with a small group of Canadian and Austrian officials. Minister Pickersgill smiled and nodded to Ferenc and the other interviewers, clearly indicating that he didn't want the proceedings to be interrupted on his behalf. Pickersgill sat and observed for a short while, then left quietly with his small group. Ferenc was very impressed with the Canadian minister, but he was not considering going to Canada at that time. "I eventually wanted to go to the United States; I just thought Canada was a frozen wasteland."

Minister Pickersgill made special arrangements to accommodate the best and brightest, many of whom were university students. For example, almost the entire forestry department — faculty and students — from the University of Sopron left en masse. Pickersgill found a new home for them so that they could continue their education as a group at the University of British Columbia.

Ferenc really didn't have any idea of where he wanted to go except that he knew he wanted to get out of Eisenstadt refugee camp. The place was terribly overcrowded and each day, Ferenc heard the same stories. "They were all free-dom fighters and they killed many Russians. If as many Russians were killed as the refugees collectively said were killed, there would be no Russians left

in Hungary. They were saying what they thought the administrators wanted
to hear. The refugees quickly found out that there was great sympathy in the
United States for the freedom fighters, so they all wanted to present themselves as freedom fighters."

Ferenc noted that everything everyone said during these official interviews was hand-written by a recording secretary in a sizable ledger binder.
"One day, surprise, surprise, the big book of testimonials disappeared,
along with a few of the alleged refugees, who, as it turned out, were actually
Hungarian secret police who had infiltrated the camp. So everything the
refugees had stated about their past, real and fabricated, was now in the hands
of the Hungarian government. It was a big scandal." Everyone worried what
reprisals would come to loved ones still in Hungary.

To alleviate the overcrowding in Eisenstadt, the Italian government
announced it was opening a refugee centre for the Hungarians. When one of
the Catholic organizations asked Ferenc if he would travel with them to the
new refugee centre in Italy, to work as a translator there, Ferenc immediately
accepted. By early December, he was on his way to Italy. To him it was progress
in his bid to reach the New World.

⁓

As they crossed the Dolomites by bus and travelled south through major
urban centres in Italy, such as Padua and Bologna, Ferenc was amazed at how
much brighter and livelier the cities were in Italy. Streetlights twinkled in the
distance; everything seemed to glitter. Their destination was Calambroni,
near Pisa, where a former youth camp built under Benito Mussolini had
been designated for the Hungarians.

Conditions weren't much better or any less crowded at this refugee centre than they were in Austria. Ferenc believed there was something wrong
with a place where no one worked, where everyone simply sat around all
day, wasting time, chatting, waiting for their fate to be determined by a third
party. Arguments were the only break from the boredom and monotony. The
refugees stood in line for meals three times a day; otherwise, the routine was
interminable. It was an unnatural environment to live in, as they lived in a state
of suspended animation. Temporary classes were organized for the children,
but the adults couldn't work and were unable to continue their education.

As had been the case in Eisenstadt, three main organizations were actively recruiting single young men in the refugee camps: the U.S. Army, the South African Railway, and the French Foreign Legion. The U.S. Army promised citizenship once the recruit served the standard term of service. The South African Railway needed strong, young men to serve as guards. It didn't matter that the recruits didn't speak the language; the pay was enticingly high. The French Foreign Legion promised a life of adventure with excellent pay, but it was unable to name a precise location for service other than it would be outside of Europe. All the recruits were sent to Le Havre in northern France where they embarked by ship toward their new life as a French Legionnaire.

To the great consternation of Ferenc, rumours were rampant that the Hungarian government was demanding all army deserters be repatriated to their homeland. Whether the stories were true or not, they served to convince Ferenc even more that he had to find a way to get out of Europe and evade the real threat of the spread of communism. Moreover, the refugee camp was in close proximity to Livorno, a district rife with communist sympathizers, the place where the Italian Communist party, *Italiano Partito Comunist* (IPC) itself was founded in the early 1920s. Following the end of the Second World War, the IPC became the largest communist party in the West. The brutal suppression of the Hungarian Revolution created a split in the leadership of the IPC. Their leader, Palmiro Togliatti, insisted that the Hungarian insurgents were counter-revolutionaries and not freedom fighters. Togliatti railed against the Italian government for taking in the refugees. Ferenc was fed up with communist agitators. Within two weeks of arriving in Italy, completely discouraged with his present situation and location, Ferenc decided to take the train to Le Havre, where he intended to join the French Foreign Legion. While Ferenc was walking on a highway in the rain, wearing his army uniform, a raincoat, and a French beret, a man stopped. "A guy stops and asks me where I'm going. I tell him I'm going to the railway station in Pisa and from there to France." The stranger offered Ferenc a ride. Ferenc, who was in a particularly bitter mood, replied, "No, you Italians are all communists, go away!" But the stranger wouldn't be deterred; he persisted. The driver guessed who Ferenc was from his dress and demeanour, and was genuinely curious about the Hungarian refugee. He replied, "How can I be a communist when I'm driving an American car?" The argument went back and forth between Ferenc and the Italian.

Finally, Ferenc, by this time tired of walking in the pouring rain, agreed to get into the car.

The Italian introduced himself as Pierro Gabrielli. They conversed further, Ferenc in his rudimentary Italian, while Gabrielli patiently asked about the group of Hungarian refugees living nearby. As they neared the train station in Pisa, Gabrielli enquired about when the train was leaving. Ferenc replied that he didn't have any idea; he just wanted out of Italy and was willing to wait for any train going north. Gabrielli then invited Ferenc for dinner. Ferenc at first refused, then, realizing he was getting quite hungry, accepted the offer. They went to a restaurant in Pisa called Bar Alfea. Within fifteen minutes, a group of Italians arrived, friends of Gabrielli, who were all anxious to meet a "real Hungarian refugee." They heartily ate creamy pasta, platefuls of antipasto, fresh bread, and drank copious amounts of wine and beer. Ferenc realized it was the finest meal he had consumed since he'd left his homeland and in such joyful company. After dinner, Ferenc was invited to stay the night as a guest in the Gabrielli home. Ferenc agreed, reluctantly at first, feeling a bit sheepish as he laid his head on the clean, crisp sheets, realizing how arrogant he must have seemed with Gabrielli earlier. The following morning Ferenc asked if Gabrielli would drive him to the railway station. Instead, Pierro told him, "No, no, no, I've told my sister about you, she wants

In Italy en route to Canada in 1957 with newfound friends. Bottom row from left: Mary, Ferenc, Olga, Clara, Giovanni. Back row from left: Piero, Carlo, Carla.

you to come for lunch. She's invited all kinds of people to meet you." And so began one of the most enjoyable periods of Ferenc's life. He abandoned his travel plans and returned to the refugee camp to work as a translator almost every day, since the invitations continued.

At night Ferenc enjoyed the warm hospitality of a long list of relatives and friends of the Gabrielli family. Everyone wanted to meet and chat with the newcomer. While many topics were discussed, Ferenc also told his Italian hosts about the reality of living under communism. In turn, he realized he was mistaken in his preconceived notion about all Italians being communist sympathizers.

The weeks in Italy passed pleasantly as Ferenc, the exotic refugee from Hungary, was practically adopted by the Gabrielli family. Gino, a close friend and high-school teacher, asked if Ferenc would donate his Hungarian army uniform for the local museum. Ferenc agreed to the request and the family, in turn, provided him with civilian clothes. He would later regret his donation and would try, unsuccessfully, to find out what happened to his uniform.

Ferenc sent a message to his family through Radio Free Europe — in the form of a coded message — that he was alive and well. He recorded the message using the names of two distant relatives, Vékony and Gazdag, saying they had arrived safely. Ferenc knew that many villagers listened to the banned radio station secretly and would understand that the message was meant for his parents and family.

Despite the warmth of his reception in Italy, within a few months, Ferenc became restless. His life in Italy was not leading anywhere. He was learning Italian in the morning, translating at the refugee camp in the afternoon, and having wonderful dinners with his Italian friends, but there were no jobs and he could see no future for himself. By April, he was determined to leave Europe and decided the French Foreign Legion continued to be the best way to leave the continent. Sadly, but with a new sense of determination in his heart, he said goodbye to the Gabrielli family and all of his friends and departed for Le Havre.

～

Life in Le Havre as a recruit with the French Foreign Legion was a bit of a shock for Ferenc. Everything seemed to be frightening or surreal. He was assigned to live in a dormitory with a group of other recruits for two weeks or until a sufficient number of men had been assembled to fill a ship to Algeria. "Those guys scared me. I always thought nobody could scare me, but those guys did. Most of them were English, German, or Austrian, with quite a few Hungarian refugees signed up. We weren't doing anything; the only thing we did was make our bed and sweep the floor. There was nothing else to do. They were a bunch of crooks, a lot of gambling went on all day." They were provided simple khaki uniforms without any identification. When the registration took place, Ferenc was asked, "What name would you like to be known as and what birth date would you like to have?" That question alone was so bizarre, Ferenc realized that before the ship sailed for Algeria, he had to find another future.

Just before they were shipped out, a group was invited out for a drink by an officer. At a local bar, Ferenc met some Italians who he began to converse with. They were sailors working on a Greek-owned transport ship called the *Ascania*. They were amazed at how well Ferenc spoke Italian. When Ferenc asked them where they were going next, they replied, "To Canada." His vision of Canada as a frozen wasteland suddenly changed. This could be his destiny. Ferenc enquired if he could join them on the journey. The sailors spoke to the captain, who was elsewhere in the bar, and the word came back "You can come with us, but you have to work!" Ferenc agreed enthusiastically, grateful to escape the shady world of the French Foreign Legion.

In Italy with friends, winter 1957. From left: Olga, Ferenc, Clara.

⌒

Ferenc spent nine days on the *Ascania*, a 9,500-ton transport vessel that was formerly a troop carrier. The ship had been sunk during Second World War, then refloated and repaired as a trans-Atlantic merchandise carrier following the War. The *Ascania* steamed out of the harbour at Le Havre on May 7, 1957, with a stop in Southampton, England, before heading across the Atlantic to its destination: Quebec City. Almost as soon as the ship reached the ocean, enormous waves tossed the it back and forth, making the passengers feel as if they were on a terrifying roller coaster. Ferenc's bunk was in the bow of the ship and he was seasick for most of the journey.

As the *Ascania* finally reached the calmer waters of the Gulf of St. Lawrence with Canada visible to starboard, Ferenc was stunned to see remnants of snow, like cotton puffs in the distance, scattered here and there on the ground and hillside, even though it was May. He thought of the incredible fullness of spring he had already enjoyed in Italy in April. Here the ground still looked frozen, the trees barely in bud. Still, he was happy to be in Canada. "I wanted to settle in Canada for one reason, to get across the border to the U.S. When they said Canada, well, I didn't want to stay in that cold country, but it's close to the American border."

Ferenc landed in Canada on May 15, 1957. He said goodbye to his Italian friends and disembarked in Quebec City. He was interviewed by a Canadian immigration officer. "First of all, I told him I was a Hungarian refugee. I explained that until now, I had been in an Austrian and an Italian refugee camp, which I could prove with papers. He asked me what level of education I had reached and if I had learned a trade. I told him about my education, for which I didn't have any documentation. He asked me about my family. They were all simple, ordinary questions. He was very nice. Then he gave me a stamped paper, $5, and said 'welcome to Canada.' Can you imagine that? Five dollars and wished me good luck. He also gave me some advice, telling me there were jobs in the forest industry and in mining. I thanked him and didn't mention that I wasn't interested in either of those fields. The whole interview took five minutes."

Ferenc really didn't have any idea of where he was going to spend his first night in Canada. He had $5, but he considered that his savings — he wasn't going to touch that. Unknown to Ferenc at the time, the programs of social assistance providing shelter for the Hungarian refugees lasted only until the end of March 1957 after which they were expected to live on their own in Canada. But Ferenc had no desire to go to a refugee centre; he had enough of those places in Austria and Italy. "So where do you go when you have no place to stay? When you are newly arrived to a place and you don't know anyone and you don't speak the language? Where do you go? Someone mentioned the bus station or the railway station. It's warm there and you hear about job opportunities there."

Ferenc Hasenfratz, utterly alone in this new place called Quebec City, boarded a bus with his small shoulder bag containing all his worldly possessions: a toothbrush, shaving kit, soap, and the $5 gift from Canada. He observed people as he rode, trying to melt in as much as possible. No one asked him for the bus fare, and he didn't know what he would have done if someone had. He changed buses several times and it took him hours to locate the train station. Once he found it, he settled in on one of the wooden benches for the evening, watching people come and go until all activity gradually ceased. When the station quieted down for the evening, he put his shoulder bag under his head as a pillow, put his feet up, and fell into an uneasy sleep. All night, he felt the hardness of the wooden bench pushing on his bones, it was unrelenting, his body too thin to cushion the wooden slats of the bench. He slept fitfully at best.

The days passed slowly. During the day, he tried to look like someone just waiting for a train, but it became a challenge to keep up the appearance of someone waiting all the time. Eventually, the station guards and railroad personnel couldn't help but notice the young man who was sleeping on the bench in the railway station. Some were friendly, greeting Ferenc each morning as they arrived at work, jokingly asking, "Are you still here?" One railway employee brought him an apple every morning. His status was a lesson in humility. "When you walk down the street and see a homeless person, don't judge too early, they could have a mental problem or a physical problem, or both. That experience taught me never to judge a homeless person."

Facilities were available, but he needed a job. "I washed every day at the station's washroom, shaved every day, but I washed only from the waist up. I must have smelled like you wouldn't believe. So I asked how I could get a job somewhere. I was told, 'You want a job? Go to the car dealers, wash cars.'"

Ferenc didn't have any idea what a car dealership was or even where they were, since there was nothing like that in Hungary, but after persistent questioning and gesturing with his hands, he found out there was a car dealership nearby. "I was paid 25 cents to wash a car. Well, I could wash two, three cars in an hour, making 75 cents. A loaf of bread was 18 cents; a quart of milk was 19 cents. I could live on a loaf of bread and a quart of milk each day without a problem. I saved money and had very few expenses. I made $4 or $5 washing cars. I didn't need more than maybe a dollar, that's all I spent. Shaving cream I had, soap I had."

After a few days, Ferenc had enough money to feel confident enough to travel to Montreal where he again lived in the train station, found a car dealership, and washed more cars. He communicated in any way possible. "You can communicate if you want to — with your hands, with whatever. I spoke a few words of English by then and made myself understood."

From Montreal, he continued travelling west to Toronto. Ferenc had the address and telephone number of

Immigration card received upon setting foot on Canadian soil.

his mother's brother — Uncle Jake — who came to Canada in the 1930s and lived in Ariss, near Guelph, an hour further west again. As he had never met Uncle Jake, he felt reticent about simply showing up, penniless, on his doorstep. Ferenc felt it was important to make his own way to Guelph. In Toronto, he approached a railway employee who looked friendly and asked him if he would make a telephone call on his behalf. In broken English, he told the man, "It's long distance. If it was short distance, I would walk there." The man smiled at the little joke and obliged him. Jake answered the telephone and asked to speak to Ferenc, instructing him to come to Guelph right away, telling him the exact time the train left Toronto for Guelph. After Ferenc gave the phone back to the man, Jake asked him to make sure Ferenc was on the next train to Guelph. His nephew travelled all the way from Quebec City for free. He never bought a ticket and no one ever asked him to show a ticket.

Ferenc arrived in Guelph at one-thirty in the morning. Uncle Jake was standing on the platform, waiting. Six weeks had passed since his arrival in Canada. Although Ferenc had never met Jake, the family resemblance was undeniable. Ferenc walked directly to him and said, "You must be my uncle." They shook hands and hugged each other warmly. Then, Jake asked, "Are you hungry?" Ferenc replied that he was indeed very hungry. Jake guided him to a restaurant called the Intercontinental directly across from the train station. "Why don't we eat here?" Jake asked. "You can tell me why everyone is looking for you, nobody knows where you disappeared to." When they received the menus, Jake asked Ferenc what he would like to eat. He began by reading and translating the specials: "Chicken breast with roasted potatoes and vegetables, pork chops with mashed potatoes and carrots."

"I'll have that," replied Ferenc, feeling famished, as if he could have eaten all of the menu items at once.

"You can't have that," replied Jake as he continued to read the menu. "Roast beef with mashed potatoes and gravy."

"I'll have that," Ferenc piped up again.

"You can't have that either," replied Jake.

By this time, Ferenc was increasingly anxious. "Why can't I have any of those things? I'm not fussy. I'd love to have it."

Jake looked at Ferenc and said, "Did you forget? It's Friday, it's after midnight, and you're Catholic, you cannot eat meat."

Ferenc couldn't believe it. Since he arrived in Canada, he'd been living on bread and milk, he certainly didn't think of Friday fasting. His life thus far in Canada had been one continuous fast, but he didn't want to offend his uncle and his new aunt. He smiled and replied, "So, I guess I'm going to have eggs." His new life, a new adventure in the New World, had begun.

7

Stranger in a Strange Land

For the first time after travelling halfway across the globe, Ferenc awoke in a bed with clean sheets, in a house, with the welcome sights and sounds of farm life — so familiar from his youth — out the window on that spring day in April. He took a shower, his first since arriving in Canada six weeks earlier, and revelled in the seemingly endless supply of hot water. The shower came complete with a supply of face cloths, something Ferenc had never seen before, so he soaped himself generously several times, enjoying the all-over feeling of doing something normal, getting ready for the day, and living with family again.

When he went downstairs, his uncle, Jake Schaefer, was at the breakfast table, his morning chores completed. They ate together and then Schaefer left to take his shower. Within minutes, he was back, looking a little grim. "Learn one thing," said Schaefer. "You're on a farm. There isn't enough hot water for everybody. If you use just a little bit, there will be some left for me."

Schaefer also had another piece of advice. In order for him to fit in better, Ferenc should call himself Frank. Schaefer knew whereof he spoke; he had grown up in Canada. His family had been part of a wave of 25,000 Hungarians who emigrated in the 1920s, followed by another group of 12,000 after the Second World War. Refugees who fled at the same time as Frank, arriving in Canada after Hungary's failed revolution, numbered 37,000.

The next day was a Saturday. Schaefer, his wife Adelaide, and their sons Ed and Roy had been invited to the wedding of a neighbour's daughter. Frank was welcome too, so they outfitted him with a suit, dress shirt, and tie for the occasion. After the ceremony, everyone danced to music performed by a small band. As a new arrival in the community, Frank was a bit of a novelty. He was also handsome and happy so several of the young women asked him to dance. Buoyed by their interest, Frank enjoyed the local custom of dancing cheek-to-cheek. If this wasn't Heaven, what was? At one point, Frank sidled up to his uncle and, nodding toward one among his many pretty partners, said, "This woman is after me."

"No, no," said Schaefer, setting him straight, "she's after everybody."

Frank helped with the chores on his uncle's 150-acre farm near the village of Ariss, ten minutes northwest of Guelph. Schaefer raised pigs, chickens, horses, and cows, so the work in the fields and caring for the animals was all very familiar to Frank. Not all of his assistance, however, was helpful. Schaefer's car needed repair work in the nearby village of Maryhill, so one of his sons drove that vehicle, while Frank followed in another car that would be used to bring his cousin back home. En route, Frank lost control of his vehicle in the loose gravel, flew off the road, and tore through a wire fence into a farmer's field before finally rolling to a stop. The minor damage included a twisted front bumper. After the car was hauled back onto the road, a stoic Schaefer dispatched Frank to another shop in Maryhill where a wrought-iron maker put things right.

Life on the farm was agreeable and Frank's extended family was happy to have him in their midst. But as a trained tool-and-die maker, Frank was itching to find work in his trade. There is a saying about a German: the worst thing you can do is take away his work. As a Swabian, Frank needed to put his skills and training to use. He began looking for a job and soon had an offer from Canadian National Railways. Schaefer was adamantly opposed. He could see Frank had ambition and feared that a "cushy" job with the railway would snuff out his entrepreneurial spirit. "Don't take it. You'll never quit. It pays too well."

Frank had another cousin living nearby, Ron Kirschner, who told Frank that the factory in Guelph where he worked as a toolmaker, W.C. Wood Co. Ltd., was hiring. The company made freezers for residential use and precision parts for the aerospace industry, just the sort of place for Frank's skills.

At the time, Guelph was a mid-sized city of 30,000, an hour west of Toronto. Founded in 1827 during the settling of what was then called Upper Canada, the residents of Guelph were mostly British stock, although Europeans began arriving in the years just before the First World War, a flow that resumed in the 1950s.

Wyndham Street, the three-block-long main drag, ran from the new Simpsons-Sears department store that opened in 1954 down to the city hall, built in the Renaissance Revival style 100 years earlier. Municipal bylaws stated that all commercial buildings in the core must have limestone facades, an edict that gave the city a solid but slightly dour appearance. Within a few blocks of the downtown were half a dozen Protestant churches. Sitting high atop a hill and visible from all major approaches to the city was the magnificent Church of Our Lady Immaculate, a Roman Catholic basilica based on the cathedral at Cologne.

Guelph called itself "The Royal City" because "Guelph" is derived from the Bavarian-Germanic *Welf*, a reference to King George IV, who was Britain's monarch at the time of Guelph's founding. George IV's family was from the German House of Hanover, a younger branch of the House of Welf.

According to *Maclean's* magazine, Guelph was "an attractive small city, not pretentious, prosperous, skilfully planned, and staunchly built." Moreover, said the article published in October 1940, Guelph "had produced an extraordinary number of people who had achieved not only national but world renown in a diversity of careers." Among the notables were Colonel John McCrae, author of "In Flanders Fields"; Edward Johnson, a tenor opera singer and general manager of the Metropolitan Opera in New York; George Drew who became premier of Ontario, leader of the Opposition in Ottawa, and Canada's high commissioner to Britain; children's book author Jean Little; and Charles Kingsmill, an admiral in charge of Canada's navy.

From a population of 12,000 in 1901, Guelph had doubled in size to 23,000 by 1941. At one point, Guelph was larger than neighbouring Kitchener, and boasted more industry than the Lake Ontario port of Hamilton, but those halcyon days had faded. The largest local employers included the Guelph Stove Co., supplier to Eaton's, the national department store, and two world-renowned educational institutions, the Ontario Agricultural College and the Ontario Veterinary College.

In 1954, a new industrial revolution began with the arrival of Canadian General Electric where hundreds of employees built transformers. By 1961, the city's population was 40,000 and over the next four decades more than doubled to 100,000. It was in this newly burgeoning city that Frank, the young rebel, went looking for work. Guelph was a far cry from Budapest with its towering spires and thermal spas, but here Frank was newly free and able to build a life without fear or favour.

⁓

Accompanied by his uncle, Frank was interviewed at W.C. Wood by a fellow Swabian but that kinship offered no assistance. Nor was Frank helped by his own cocky manner; his brashness far overshadowed his skill. Frank's answer to his interviewer's every question was "Yes." Yes, he could run that machine and that one, too. Yes, he could this. Yes, he could make that. "No job for you," said the interviewer. "You're lying to me; you cannot possibly know how to do all those things."

On their way home, Schaefer told a crestfallen Frank there would be other opportunities. Next time, said Schaefer, "Don't tell him you know everything, just tell him you know how to do this one thing, but these others you'd like to learn." Two days later, Jake called to apologize and arrange another meeting.

That session picked up where the first left off. The interviewer remained as miffed as before. "If you're changing your story now, then you were a liar the first time. Or if you're still telling me you did all this and you're capable of doing all that, then I also think you're a liar."

Frank adopted a new and more forthright approach. "My uncle told me if I tell you that I know something and want to learn the rest, then you would hire me."

The interviewer turned to Schaefer and asked, "Did you tell him that?" When Schaefer nodded, the interviewer again cut the session short by saying, "No job."

A week later, a persistent Frank tried a third time with an entirely different approach. "Give me a job, but don't pay me. Give me any job you think I should know, and if I can't do it, send me away." Frank not only landed the job in July 1957 but he was also paid, $52.50 for a 40-hour week.

Once he'd found work, Frank needed a new place to live. His uncle said he could continue to live on the farm in Ariss, but Frank felt it was time to be more independent and move closer to his employment near downtown Guelph. He rented a room at 29 Elora Street, two blocks from the Guelph Collegiate Vocational Institute, in a boarding house owned by Julia and Joe Mokanski, a couple who had emigrated from Hungary in 1935.

Frank's room was on the second floor of the three-storey brick house as were the bedrooms of another boarder, retired nurse Margaret Furlong, and the Mokanskis' son, Joe, who was two years younger than Frank. A German couple lived on the third floor in two large rooms that included a kitchen. Joe Sr. worked nights at International Malleable Iron; he and his wife Julia slept on the main floor in what had been the living room. Frank paid $15 a week for his room with its single bed and striped spread, armchair, radio, collection of figurines, and floor-stand ashtray even though he did not smoke. He usually ate with the Mokanski family but when he worked late, he rustled meals for himself on a stove in the basement.

On his fifteen-minute walk to work, Frank passed through St. George's Square. "The Square," as it was universally known in Guelph, was the city's central hub. Surrounding the open plaza were various shops as well as venerable branches of the Bank of Nova Scotia, Royal Bank, and the Bank of Commerce, all of which used the solid limestone that dominated the architecture of the downtown. Once through The Square, Frank headed for Allan's Bridge with the overhead railway trestle that brought him into town and past a brass plaque marking the spot where John Galt had felled the first tree at the founding of Guelph. "Others will reap where I have sown," Galt had announced. Once across the bridge over the Speed River, Frank rounded the corner to the right, and there stood the W.C. Wood factory.

The owner, Wilbert Copeland Wood, graduated from the University of Saskatchewan in agricultural engineering and worked at Massey-Ferguson, the farm implement company, until he was laid off at the beginning of the Great Depression. The Ontario government was bringing electricity to the rural regions and Wood spotted an opportunity to supply electrical equipment to those thousands of new consumers. He started his own company in Toronto in 1930, was successfully making milk coolers within a few years, and moved

Frank in his first rented room in Guelph, Ontario, May 1958.

operations to Guelph in 1941. By 1956, W.C. Wood had grown into a busy 90,000-square-foot factory.

Most of the skilled employees, like Frank, had completed their apprenticeships in England, Germany, or elsewhere in Western Europe. There, they had learned the trigonometry necessary for figuring out angles, the tensile strength of various metals, as well as the chemistry of materials and the way they responded. A tool-and-die maker cuts a piece of metal to the right length, then puts the metal on a lathe or milling machine to create a mould known as a die. Alternatively, he can take a casting and carefully remove specific portions of the casting to create a part that can usefully play a role in an engine, transmission, or steering mechanism. Tool-and-die makers operate machines manually to create one piece at a time or set up machines to run at high speeds in order to produce precision parts automatically. Once a part has been formed, it might be heat treated then ground or shaped to have a high degree of tolerance so that it fits and functions with other machined parts.

Frank might have aroused the ire of his interviewer claiming he could do everything, but what he saw all around him confirmed his belief that he was more accomplished than most. Generally, he found Canada lagging behind what he had known in Hungary. Still, he was eager to learn. Most days, after Frank had finished his shift, he would clock out and stay at the plant. Away from the shop floor there was little to do during the week but sit alone in his room at the boarding house. Better to remain at work and pick up tips and techniques from anyone willing to share what they knew.

And so it was he came upon W.C. Wood, the owner, huddled with several employees. Frank had no previous contact with the boss, but he knew Wood by sight, so he watched the proceedings with interest. Wood was attempting to set up a dial machine to make a new part for a customer. The plan was to have an operator load a part onto a circular table, carry out a step, then move the table clockwise, thereby rotating the part to the next station for a follow-on procedure by another machine. The operator then loaded another part in front of him, and set the table moving again, so the pieces moved in harmony around the perimeter through several different stations as drilling, cutting, and other steps were all carried out. Each time the table moved, the operator removed the finished part presented in front of him, placed it in a nearby bin for shipment, and loaded another blank.

At one station, however, there was a problem. A machined groove was supposed to be added, but because the part wasn't secured properly, it moved slightly during the procedure, and the groove wasn't the same depth all the way around. As a result, the overall shape of the part was incorrect and the movement threw off the next operation. After a few minutes watching and listening, Frank believed he had figured out how to fix the problem. He plucked up his courage and spoke.

"Mr. Wood, it's not going to work, you've been at it all day, and the parts are always coming out wrong."

"Who are you?" said Wood, looking irritated at the interruption.

"I work in the tool room here."

Upset at being spoken to in such a forward manner by one of his newest employees, Wood brushed Frank off, turned his back, and continued to try setting up the operation. The next day, Frank could see that Wood was still struggling, but this time he simply walked on by and said nothing.

A few more days passed until finally Wood approached Frank and said, "Tell me why the dial machine is not working." They went together to the site and Frank pointed to one of the locations, saying, "Well, when you cut it there, you put in too much power and hydraulically you cannot hold it. That's why your part moves. To fix that, change the sequence. Leave this phase to the second-last station, and the groove to the last station. That way, it will be perfect."

When Frank next saw Wood, he was all smiles and said, "It works. Thank you." After that, Wood always said hello whenever he saw Frank and stopped for a chat. Frank's helpful insight, however, was not enough to save him when the company lost a major contract and had to lay off employees. After only six months on the job, Frank was among those who were let go. Lesson learned: You might be smarter than the next guy, but when you're working for someone else, and times get tough, your skill level doesn't matter.

~

Although his time at W.C. Wood was all too brief, Frank found Guelph a generally welcoming place. As the fall of 1957 grew brisker, and winter approached, Frank owned no warm coat. Julia, the woman who rented him his room, asked Peggy McGarry, a neighbour who lived around the corner on Clinton Street, if her husband, Jack, who was about the same size as Frank, had an overcoat he no longer needed that he could give to the young man.

Indeed McGarry did. It was a stylish grey velour model with buttons on the front and a half belt at the back that he'd bought in Detroit. The coat not only kept Frank warm that winter, it became a running motif in his relationship with the McGarrys. In 1964, Dennis Mooney, purchasing manager at Allis-Chalmers, makers of forklift trucks in Guelph, introduced the two men who were both waiting to pitch Mooney about their respective lines of business. Asked McGarry, "Don't you remember me?" Frank gave him a puzzled look. "I gave you my overcoat." Thus prompted, Frank never again forgot the favour. In later years, the McGarrys attended the weddings of Frank's two daughters; the father of the bride mentioned the coat in his speeches on both occasions. By the time the McGarrys gave a party to celebrate their twenty-fifth wedding anniversary, Frank had by then been married to his own wife, Margaret, for nearly as long, and she presented the McGarrys with a tiny grey coat, no bigger than her hand, that she had made. There was a note attached saying she had washed the original garment and it had shrunk.

The coat came to symbolize Guelph's embrace of this immigrant who'd fled communism in a foreign land. For his part, Frank worked hard to assimilate, learning English from the time of his arrival. He was good at languages. He grew up speaking both Hungarian and German, and had made significant progress in Italian while living briefly in Pisa. In Guelph, Frank wrote down new English words when he heard them as a way of remembering and always carried a dictionary to look up anything he didn't understand.

He also attended English-language classes at John F. Ross Collegiate and Vocational Institute on the other side of the city. In addition to the two-hour sessions several nights a week, he bought a set of self-help vinyl records that he continually played in his room. The back-and-forth repetition between the recorded voice and Frank's attempts to mimic the phrases was so clearly audible in Margaret Furlong's room next door that she felt as if she were an integral part of the learning process. At one point, she rolled her eyes, and told Peggy McGarry, "If that guy doesn't soon learn English, I don't know what I'm going to do. All he does all day long is play English records."

As a young man who was lively and possessed a good sense of humour, Frank had many girlfriends in Hungary and Italy. For a time, Guelph was less fertile ground. A winter coat was one thing, a woman was quite another. "You have to understand when you're an immigrant, the native Canadians who are Canadian-born wouldn't look very kindly on the new immigrant taking their daughter out," said Frank. "What was even worse, I knew a couple of Hungarian families who arrived here in the 1930s, and they didn't want their daughter going out with a newcomer like me either."

A date with one young woman named Denise got off to a rocky start. When Frank arrived at her door, her father said, "Don't get any ideas. I just want you to know that I wouldn't like it if you got serious with my daughter." Frank was just happy to go out for an evening. He had no grand plan so it was easy for him to reply, "You've got my promise."

In another case, Frank didn't even get that far. He watched a woman regularly pass his boarding house, found out where she lived, and one evening knocked on her door. Her father answered, heard Frank's request to date his daughter, then called his wife, and asked Frank to repeat what he'd said. "They were shocked out of their boots," recalled Frank. Permission to see their daughter was not granted, although in later years, the couple became friends with Frank and Margaret and often retold the story about that first encounter.

Was it discrimination toward the new arrival or just protective parents typical of that era? "I can honestly say that no one ever discriminated against me," said Frank. "When you're new in a country, new in a culture, you cannot go to your level right away. It takes time. You have to learn that."

He was well aware that not all immigrants were well received. "Two types of people immigrate, those who are intelligent and have a good trade but don't see a future where they are, and then there are the crooks and the cheaters, and you get some of those, too."

Frank made the most of every opportunity to meet women. When he visited the Bank of Nova Scotia branch in St. George's Square to open an account, the teller handed him a lengthy form to complete. He could see that the process was going to take more time than he had right then. His English was improving but he didn't want to make any mistakes on something this important.

Frank was nothing if not bold, so he told the female teller that he had another appointment and asked if he could come back later in the day to do the paperwork. "The bank will be closed," she said.

"Well," he asked, "what are you doing afterward?" Not only did she agree to help but also invited him to her apartment a few blocks away. With her guidance, they filled out the form, and he began dating the single mother who, at thirty-eight, was sixteen years older than he was and had a thirteen-year-old daughter.

Frank wasn't much of a drinker, an occasional beer was plenty, and going to a movie with the boys was a rare event. Looking to expand his social life, he asked others at the language class what they did for fun. They told him the best place to meet girls was the weekly dance at the Knights of Columbus hall on Waterloo Avenue. "How much does it cost?" he asked. "If you pray, you don't pay," came the reply. The words were music to the ears of a budget-conscious young man who sent money home to his family in Hungary and was saving to buy a car with cash. For him, taking on the debt of a car loan was not an option. "If you want to get rich," his father had often told him, "you have to spend less than you make."

But to get into the Knights of Columbus dance without paying, he needed to know the holy rosary. Frank was raised a Catholic but hadn't practiced his religion recently so wasn't familiar with the prayer. Looking to solve his problem, he asked a woman he'd met at the language class to teach him the words required. When she said yes, he invited her to his room at the boarding house. She agreed to come, because two other men from the class would be present, also eager to learn the key to free admission.

After she arrived with the prayer written on a piece of paper, the three men began memorizing the words. "My landlady got all upset that there was a woman in my room. I said, 'We're praying.'" Invocations to God did not trump house rules. Julia Mokanski told them to move downstairs to a small den with a fireplace where there could be no hanky-panky in the more public surroundings. Frank learned the words well enough to pass muster at the dance.

On another occasion, Frank and his cousin Ron Kirschner went to a club in nearby Kitchener where they met two women. After an evening of dancing, they offered the women, who were also from Guelph, a ride home. Kirschner was driving, Frank was in the back seat with his new friend, and the topic turned to where he worked. When he told her, the woman blanched and said her husband worked there, too. They agreed not to say anything but she told her husband who in turn spoke to Frank, saying, "Let's keep that quiet."

Said Frank, "We only gave her a ride."

"He was a ladies' man," said the younger Joe Mokanski, "that's for sure."

However, all of the local women he'd met paled into insignificance one night in October 1957 when the young man on the move attended a concert celebrating the first anniversary of the Hungarian Revolution. The event, held in the basement of the Church of Our Lady, was already under way when Frank arrived. As he stood in the doorway at the back of the room surveying the scene, he became captivated by the young female chorister who was singing a solo:

Blue moon,
Now I'm no longer alone
Without a dream in my heart
Without a love of my own

To Frank, her vivacious appearance and beautiful voice put her in the company of the angels in the stained-glass windows upstairs. Smitten, he asked a man standing nearby, "Who's that girl?"

"Leave her alone," the man hissed, "She's for my son."

Undeterred, Frank kept asking others who she was. Her name was Margaret Ferter. She was born in Hungary in 1941. Her father died in the Second World War when Margaret was only three. At eight, she and her mother, also called Margaret, moved to Germany. Margaret remarried and the family immigrated to Canada when her daughter was eleven. At first, they lived in what is today Mississauga and then moved to a farm near Elora, north of Guelph.

Once Frank found out where Margaret lived, he phoned. When a man answered, he introduced himself saying, "My name is Frank Hasenfratz and I heard your daughter sing."

"Your name is what?"

"Frank Hasenfratz."

"Where are you from?"

"Szár, Hungary."

"That's very interesting. I'm Margaret's stepfather and I'm also from Szár." The connection, however, provided no immediate entrée. "Leave her alone," he said. "She's a little girl, only sixteen. What do you want with her?"

"Well, she gets older every day, doesn't she?"

The joke seemed to break the ice. He invited Frank for lunch the following Sunday and that led to a date with Margaret at the Knights of Columbus dance. The evening did not go well. Most of the women Frank had dated in the past were older than he was. As a result, he really didn't know how to behave with someone who was six years younger.

For several months, Frank pursued Margaret by phone for a second date. Each time she turned him down. The conversations always ended on the same note. He'd say, "I'll give you one more chance." To which she'd reply, "And I'll give you one more 'no.'"

Worse yet, Frank had competition. Another young man, the son of family friends, had been designated as her future husband. One Sunday, when Frank went calling on Margaret without an invitation, he found the favoured suitor already sitting in the living room as if he were king of all he surveyed. "I think you're in the wrong house," said Frank. Margaret's mother chided him, saying, "Don't do that, he's a nice young man."

Frank persisted and a full year after they first met, he finally began seeing Margaret regularly. Even then, her mother and stepfather would chauffer the couple on their nights out and sometimes bring along Margaret's friend, Diane Gilson, so three chaperones were on hand during

Frank and Margaret's first bungalow where Linamar was launched in the basement and garage, 1964.

an evening of dancing at places such as the Schwaben Club, the German heritage club in Kitchener. After a time, they graduated to going out on their own, he behind the wheel of his 1957 Pontiac two-door hardtop, a big step up from his first vehicle, a 1952 Ford for which he'd paid $300. He bought the Pontiac when it was only a year old. It had a cream top, bronze body, and was stylishly laden with plenty of chrome.

Frank was best man at Joe Mokanski's wedding in July 1960 and the following month Frank and Margaret were married in the Church of Our Lady. He was twenty-five; she was nineteen. They moved into a small 1950s bungalow on 150 acres of land just north of Guelph that had been owned by her grandmother, not far from Jake Schaefer's farm. Margaret's grand-parents continued to live in the original farmhouse on the property. Most of the money to buy the land and the brick house they lived in came from Margaret who'd saved $12,000 by working summers at a local shirt factory and in the tobacco fields of southern Ontario. As dowries went, it was a huge sum, the equivalent of more than $100,000 today. Frank and Margaret would raise their family, launch a business, love each other, and live all their married life together on that same plot of land.

8

Brave Beginnings

Three days after being laid off at W.C. Wood in 1958, Frank landed a job at Sheepbridge Engineering. Based in Derbyshire, England, Sheepbridge had 200 employees in Guelph producing precision parts such as gears, bearings, and bushings for the automotive industry as well as local manufacturers like Beatty Brothers in Fergus, Ontario, makers of the first agitator washing machines.

Frank quickly discovered that Sheepbridge was not as well run as W.C. Wood. Workers would arrive at 7:00 a.m., but management didn't drift in for another two hours then left for lunch before noon. During the summer, executives seemed to spend as much time golfing as working. With such lacklustre oversight, production ran behind schedule, and quality was poor. "Every year the owners came from England, every year the local managers said, 'Next year, we're going to be profitable,' but next year never came," said Frank. During those executive visits, machines would run flat out but the work was phony. When the visitors departed, everything was scrapped.

As if that weren't enough to sour him on the place, Frank ran afoul of the union. Because Sheepbridge was what's called a closed shop where the company agrees to employ only union members, Frank had to join the United Steelworkers in order to work there. During a union meeting, just prior to the 1958 election that saw John Diefenbaker's Progressive Conservative

Party win a majority, the union leaders demanded their members donate money to the New Democratic Party.

Frank was irate. "I don't believe in the New Democrats," he told the assembled. "If you believe, you should give. If you want to be a Conservative or a Liberal, go ahead, but don't tell me what I should be." No one spoke in support of his stance. After the meeting, he was taken to a back office and threatened with a beating if he refused to donate. "I can have you deported," said one man.

Frank hung tough and there was no thrashing. He did meet, however, with Alf Hales, the local Progressive Conservative member of parliament. Hales assured him that no one, union leader or otherwise, could have him deported for refusing to make a political donation. "But they scared the hell out of me," said Frank.

Frank kept his head down, worked hard, and, after three years, received a promotion to foreman. As part of management, he was no longer required to be in the union and pay dues. Sheepbridge was still losing money, but Frank felt better about his own situation because his tool room and machining area began functioning well. He made improvements by ensuring that his thirteen employees were on the job sharp at 7:00 a.m. and then followed a work plan he devised daily. "He was very strict. If I was thirty seconds late getting back after coffee break, there would be 'the look,'" said Rance Oosterveld, an apprentice toolmaker trained by Frank. "But he was very patient, eager to show you things, and gave you the confidence that you could do a job. He would show me how to make something faster and he made it look so easy," said Oosterveld. "But he was also saying, 'Well, it took you an hour last time, it should take you five minutes less this time.' The training he gave helped me throughout my career." Oosterveld was later promoted to tool room supervisor and then technical manager before going into sales.

Among the parts made by Sheepbridge were shock absorbers. An outside firm did some of the work, a step that slowed production and added to costs. "Frank was very innovative and found a way of doing it with the tooling that we had. He was always thinking, how can we finish this product ourselves and save some money. The guy is a genius, how he could fix things, and finish the job," said Oosterveld.

Frank's personal accomplishments did not win him many accolades from his supervisor, Des Archer, and the two regularly battled. "Sometimes

I agreed with Des but other times I told him, 'This is no good. It's going to cost us money and it'll never work.'" There came a point where Frank finally had enough. The issue was an oil pump the company was making for Ford. Sheepbridge was scrapping 20 percent of the pumps because the shaft kept binding in the housing. As usual, Archer wouldn't listen to Frank's ideas for improvements, so Frank went to Archer's boss, General Manager Bert Johnson, and said, "I want you to fire Des. If you don't fire Des, I quit."

"Okay," said Johnson. "You can quit."

Frank was stunned. His wife Margaret had graduated from business college, worked for a dentist, and then was an assistant to Ralph Dent, a psychology professor at the Ontario Agricultural College, but resigned to stay home with Nancy, their first child, who was born the previous year. From two regular salaries, they would suddenly have none. On the spot, Frank devised a plan. "I'll quit, but subcontract me the Ford pump. I'll make it my way and you don't have to pay me anything except the amount it costs you in scrap right now. You supply the raw material, I'll buy my own lathe, do the work in my basement, and you look after delivery to Ford."

Johnson called in Archer, told him Frank's proposal, and Archer said, "Let him have it." And so it was that Frank, a budding entrepreneur who had just recently become a Canadian citizen, was suddenly his own boss and no longer had to put up with meagre managers or indolent workers. "The name of the game was, 'The less work we do, the better it is.' I remember one guy who said, 'I had a great day; I didn't do anything.' What kind of a great day is that? That's the reason why it was fairly easy for me to start up. You get your own machine; you get the most out of it. That was the best thing that ever happened to me because I got into business for myself."

In order to help launch the new endeavour Frank sought a partner who could invest money and bring expertise he did not have. The first candidate was Don MacDonald, a chemist. They called their company H&M Manufacturing, but within days, MacDonald decided he didn't want to be involved in a start-up where there was no likelihood of drawing a regular salary for many months. Although MacDonald departed, the name of the company remained H&M.

Frank found another possible partner, Bert Wesley, a fellow foreman at Sheepbridge. The two agreed they would each invest $500 but Wesley's cheque bounced. Frank concluded he might just as well work on his own.

He had sufficient savings to get started; he didn't need the headaches that partners caused. For years after, whenever Frank saw Wesley, Wesley would ask, "How's my half doing?" Those two false starts forever coloured Frank's views about most partnerships. "A partner can hold you back. There aren't two people alike and I like working and I push and I push. If the partner doesn't carry his weight, why have a partner?"

But Frank also concluded there was a rhythm to his life. When bad things happened, something good usually followed. "He always said that it was his good luck that he didn't get along with those people at Sheepbridge because otherwise he would not have achieved what he has achieved," said Oosterveld. "He was ambitious and he was thinking about what to do with his life and where to go. He saw that he could undercut the costs and upgrade the machinery. He seemed destined to do something about it and that's exactly what he did," said Joe Mokanski.

In fact, that optimism was Frank's very essence. "When a bad thing happens, just look out the window, there's sunshine somewhere. That's what has happened to me all the way through my life. I looked at the situation at Sheepbridge, and I thought to myself, 'I can do it better,'" said Frank. That sunny disposition as well as a belief in himself and his talents was the foundation upon which he built his fledgling firm and would earn his fortune.

～

Frank installed his first machine, a tabletop-sized lathe that he bought for $1,000 from International Machinery in Hamilton, in the basement of the family home. Hardly had work begun when he decided the lathe, which he operated manually, needed modification. He could hear the household wringer washer whirring away nearby; the two machines seemed to be humming in two-part harmony. The washer had a gearbox at the bottom driven by a one-quarter horsepower motor. A shaft ran from the gearbox to the wringers at the top. He removed the gearbox, added a counterweight and a pulley, and was able to automate the lathe. Thus freed up, Frank could set the lathe in motion and get his next casting ready or load the finished product into a box for shipping. For Margaret, there was a new washing machine.

Within a few weeks, he hired four employees, added a second machine in the garage, and began producing parts around the clock. Because Frank did not want the weight and worry of a bank loan, he sent Ford an invoice daily asking for payment within thirty days. That way, he had a constant flow of cash to pay for necessary supplies and employee salaries.

H&M's second contract, for ITT Canada, was an aircraft part made from beryllium copper. All Frank had to do was drill some holes, bend each piece, and then heat-treat it for strength. He found a jobber in Kitchener to do the heat treatment, but during the process, half the pieces were damaged and had to be scrapped. Frank's complaints didn't improve quality so he read everything he could find on beryllium copper. He discovered that heat-treating was done at a relatively low temperature, 550 degrees Fahrenheit, and did not require any special equipment.

If washing machine parts could be pressed into service, what about another home appliance, say the kitchen stove? But the dial only went to 500 degrees, so he called Al Snape, an electrician friend at Sheepbridge. "Could a stove run at 550 degrees Fahrenheit with a new control installed that would hold the temperature within a range of twenty degrees for the two hours required?"

"Sure," said Snape.

"How much?"

"Twenty dollars."

"Okay, come and fix my wife's stove."

During the first attempt at heat-treating a tray of parts in the oven, the house filled with smoke as the oil from fingerprints caused by handling burned off. Just then, Margaret arrived home. "What on earth are you doing? The house is on fire." He explained the procedure, and told her if it worked, they would move the stove to the garage and vent the smoke outside. As was becoming the custom, Frank solved his problem, and Margaret got a new appliance. There was no scrap, no time wasted on shipping, and he saved $200 a week previously paid to the jobber that went into his pocket as profit.

Margaret also aided the newly born business by looking after all the correspondence. He'd tell her what he wanted to say, give her some part numbers, and Margaret would compose and type letters. Margaret was also a great help socially when Frank took clients or prospects out to dinner. "She adjusted herself to everybody," he said. "Customers liked her."

With H&M up and running, Frank hired an accountant, Bob Young. He'd met Young at Sheepbridge where he'd been a partner in the firm that did the Sheepbridge books but had since started his own practice. The two men became not only business associates but also life-long friends. "Frank is a very hard working, very smart individual. He could walk on the floor of

Frank and Margaret in the 1970s.

the shop, pick out any job, and improve it." When Frank needed a lawyer, Young recommended two names. The first wanted a retainer. The second, Hugh Guthrie, of Hungerford, Guthrie and Berry in Guelph, made no such demand, which appealed to the cost-conscious entrepreneur. In addition to doing legal work, Guthrie joined Frank and Margaret on the company board of directors where he served until 2003.

Guthrie was thirty-three, Young, twenty-nine, the same age as Frank. His two new advisors each had their separate areas of proficiency, but both offered the same counsel about how Frank should conduct himself. Guthrie was well aware of the rampant corruption in communist regimes. "I know all about those things," he told Frank, "don't try any of them here." But while Canadian business may have hewed to higher standards, there were a few slippery practices such paying off purchasing agents to win business. "Everybody else can do that. You should just do the best job that you can," said Young. "If you do the better job, you won't be replaced."

~~

In H&M'S first year of operation, Frank successfully met the payroll, bought materials and machines with cash, took out just enough money for his family's needs, and earned a profit of $20,000, the equivalent of $150,000 today. Moreover, he'd accomplished all of that with no outside investors and no debt. "He made more than he thought he would and it just kept growing. He's always been able to make it work. That's what I classify as a good manager," said Young. "What he earned he put back in the business. He worked debt-free. His ambition was to get to $1 billion."

To many hopeful entrepreneurs, such a smooth start-up seems improbable. For them, life is all complaint and commiseration. Frank made it look easy, juggling orders, getting paid on time, and always keeping a lookout for the next piece of business. As far as Frank was concerned, there was no secret to his success. "I started small and I worked sixteen hours a day. The skill, the capacity to think and be creative, doesn't seem to be possible today. It's like how no one does math using their brain anymore. If I'm in a meeting and some numbers come up, say sixty-five times sixty-five, and I say, 'It's 4,225.' The guys say, 'How did you get that number?' because they can't even type it into their calculators that quick."

Frank chased after every possible business lead. For example, he learned that a local firm, Oregon Saw Chain, was looking for someone to make sprockets. Frank phoned, asked for a meeting, and received an invitation to the plant the next Saturday morning. He described his equipment, and then made his pitch to production manager Ken Hammill and purchasing manager Charlie Bailey.

They expressed interest but said they wanted to see his operation. Frank agreed, told Margaret about the pending visit, and said he needed to create a setting that would make him look successful. George Eston, a toolmaker at Oregon, was delegated to carry out the inspection, so when he arrived Frank led him to the dining room, where they sat chatting over blueprints of the Ford oil pump and other business documents spread out on the table. Eston looked at the machines in the basement and garage, and then told Frank he'd won the contract. Later, Eston said, "You didn't fool me. I knew exactly what you were doing. But I also knew you could do the job."

Frank also arranged barter deals. He built parts for Mimic, a company operated by a friend in nearby Cambridge, Ontario. Rather than receive money in return, Frank negotiated payment in the form of a copying machine, not for documents, but one that could help automate production.

Many of Frank's new employees were, like himself, recently arrived from Europe. "You come out here, you work hard, and nobody ever asked me, 'What did your father do?' Nobody ever said, "I'll give you a job, but do you come from a good family?' Nobody cares here. If you can do the job, it's yours. And I'm the same way. If your father was a farmer, well, he was a farmer, what's wrong with that? There were many people who came out with no education, but they worked their heart out for their own farm or their own house and were very proud of it," said Frank.

Frank always ran his business slightly above capacity so employees could work overtime. That extra pay pleased them and he was happy, too, because machines were running full tilt. And, when orders slowed, he didn't have to lay anyone off. Paying time-and-a-half for overtime really didn't reduce profits by very much, given that labour accounts for less than 20 percent of the selling price. "Most of our machines cost between $300,000 and $500,000. You want to run them day and night, seven days a week. If you run them for only one shift, you go bankrupt. You can't afford to have that machine. People like to work overtime so that's why when you drive past on the weekend, almost every one of our plants has cars in the parking lot. There's no extra depreciation on the building, no extra taxes on the building, and you don't have to pay benefits on overtime, so it's really not that expensive," said Frank.

During those early years, Joe Mokanski and his young family visited the Hasenfratz family for barbecues on several occasions. By then, Mokanski was teaching mathematics at the Ontario Agricultural College, which became part of the University of Guelph in 1967. "Frank would take me out to his garage and show me proudly what he was doing. He would say that things were beginning to pile up and how he would have to expand if he wanted to continue. He expressed joy at the fact that he was coming along in terms of getting contracts with people who knew and recognized what he was doing. And, I remember this clearly, he would always say, 'I bid on a contract and I underbid everybody. I have it in my mind how to do things cheaper and in a much more efficient way.' That's how he made his company what it is today."

By 1966, two years after start-up, the business had outgrown the basement and garage. With the help of friends, Frank erected a 1,200-square-foot machine shop on his property, fifty metres from the house. For building materials, he turned to a local legend, Joe Wolfond. Wolfond had arrived in Guelph after the First World War as a young immigrant from Russia. At first, he operated a pushcart, buying and selling just about anything. That junk business became a scrap yard, evolved into a demolition business, and then became a real estate and construction firm that owned or rebuilt much of downtown Guelph. As a result, Wolfond always had a wide selection of used building materials for sale.

Frank chose what he needed and the negotiations began. They eventually agreed on a price and Wolfond said, "Okay, go and pick it up."

"No, you've got to deliver," said Frank. Wolfond grimaced but agreed, then offered Frank a drink to seal the deal and salute his negotiating skills. That first building, called Ariss after its location, although much expanded and altered, is still in use.

With the business growing, in 1966 lawyer Hugh Guthrie suggested Frank officially incorporate his company and choose a new name since the M of H&M was long gone.

Frank, Margaret, and accountant Bob Young sat at the kitchen table with a pad and pencil, doodling ideas. After a while, the talk turned to the couple's most recent arrival, Linda. By then, Nancy was three years old. Nancy's middle name was Margaret, the fifth generation to be called Margaret. All five Margarets were alive, a familial heritage so unusual that the local paper, the *Guelph Mercury*, had published a photograph of the five generations.

Young said to Frank, "Why don't you use some combination of the names of the three ladies in your life?" After a few failed attempts, they came up with Linamar: "Li" for Linda, "Na" for Nancy, and "Mar" for Margaret. They then added the necessary legal niceties and the full name became Linamar Machine Limited. The articles of incorporation were dated August 17, 1966. To this day, whenever Frank is asked about the origins of the corporate name, he'll tell the familial story, then pause and add with an impish grin, "I was the Limited one."

~

Among Linamar's early boosters was Jack McGarry, the neighbour who gave Frank his winter coat. As a sales rep for International Malleable Iron, McGarry sought customers for his company's castings. "Anything that required custom machining we farmed out to him. Anybody that required castings for his machining, he would send to us. We had a good arrangement that started around 1966 and carried on to the late 1980s," said McGarry.

If someone called on McGarry whom he thought Frank should meet, he'd set up a lunch. On one occasion, McGarry sent a prospect with a warning, "I don't think this guy is for real." Frank came to a different conclusion and told McGarry, "That's a great piece of business." McGarry and Frank both signed $1 million orders, thereby establishing new relationships that lasted three years. "He's always striving to achieve more. He's never satisfied with the status quo. He's an unusual person. He knew machining and costing — which a lot of machinists don't — and he knew how to sell," said McGarry.

The two men also engaged in friendly competition. "Something would come up and we'd challenge each other about getting a job with a certain company," said McGarry. To keep abreast of developments they scoured trade magazines and travelled together to trade shows, including the annual

Machine Tool Exposition in Chicago. Among the new products Frank spotted was something revolutionary: machines run by numerical control or NC, as it was known.

With NC machines, the machinist was no longer solely in charge. NC machines were guided by a series of numbers punched on paper tape or cards. Initially, the instructions were created manually but once that setup was accomplished, the tape or cards could be used multiple times. As a result, milling machines, lathes, grinders, shapers, saws, and planers became more efficient, and more able to make complex products with less likelihood of human error.

Frank instinctively knew he needed NC in order to be more productive and stay ahead of the competition. In 1968 — when Linamar had sales of $200,000 a year — he bought his first piece of NC equipment, a vertical Cintimatic with two-axis Acramatic. By 1975, Linamar had eleven NC machines, all in their own enclosed and air-conditioned space. Each cost up to $300,000 but production tolerances were vastly improved: as close as 0.0007 of an inch.

Trade magazines were agog, as much with Linamar's out-of-the-way location as the fact the company had more NC machines than any other shop in Canada. "Approaching the Linamar Machine Limited building in the farmland near Guelph, Ont., you know that something big is going on. Cars are overflowing the parking lot," began an article in the August 1975 issue of *Canadian Machinery and Metalworking*. "No, it isn't a cockfight. It's an NC-intensive job shop that started with a $300 [*sic*] lathe in a basement ten years ago. Now Linamar employs nearly 100 people and is bursting at the seams in 38,000 sq. ft. of floor space."

The Ariss plant, by then much bigger than its original 1,200 square feet, was producing a wide range of parts for the military, business machines, autos, and farm equipment. "We've never had a slack period since our first NC machine came in. We've bought NC machines every year since, " Frank told the publication. "Without NC I could not have gotten into U.S. defense."

As Linamar grew, media interest spread from trade publications to the mainstream business press. "The unimposing white building in the sleepy village of Ariss, near Toronto, hardly looks as if it harbors a revolution. But it does. It's the home of Linamar Machine Ltd., a machine-tooling company that has leaped to the forefront of the Canadian machining industry by harnessing computer technology to manufacturing," wrote Giles Gherson in the September 11, 1978, issue of *The Financial Post*. "It's incredible — a contract shop located in the farmlands of Canada far from the 'hub of industry' that specializes in high-precision machining," declared an article in the September 1981 issue of *Production*. "The company credits NC machines for maintaining and improving precision capabilities in spite of the diminishing supply of skilled machinists."

By then, Linamar was exporting 80 percent of production to the U.S. and had improved NC by installing computerization. Starting in 1977, Linamar paid $1,000 a month to share time via a dedicated telephone line connected to a General Electric mainframe computer in Rockford, Illinois. The computer replaced the manual creation of the paper tapes that established the patterns. Computerization reduced set-up time, enhanced accuracy, and meant further changes were easier because software was stored in the computer's memory.

The sole drag on Linamar's capacity to grow was the ability to hire. "I could employ a minimum of 200 more people if they were skilled — we have ads in the paper all the time," Frank told *The Financial Post* in 1978. Still, since 1975, Ariss had doubled in size to 70,000 square feet and Frank had built a 25,000-square-foot second plant called Linex. Three hundred employees at the two plants made everything from frames, shafts, and rollers for Xerox photocopiers to transmission parts for U.S. Army vehicles.

Throughout this expansionary period, Frank was home for dinner every night at a quarter after five. He would often go back to work once Nancy and Linda were in bed, but he rarely missed a family dinner. "You hear lots of entrepreneurs' children talk about never seeing their father or mother, depending on who the entrepreneur was, but that was never the case with my dad," said Linda. "Dad is a fantastic entrepreneur and truly inspirational as a business person in his relentless pursuit for top line and bottom line success, but I think he balanced it perfectly with an equal commitment to his family."

By 1981, Linamar had twenty-four NC machines in the two plants. Profits ran at 20 percent of sales, big money compared with the far lower rate of 5 to 7 percent of sales more typical today. "We were very low on overhead because I did the engineering, I did the sales, and everybody had multiple jobs. There was no bureaucracy," said Frank.

Profit and people were in sync. "It's a melting-pot shop, with equipment from all over and workers likewise — Hungarians, Yugoslavs, Germans, Italians, men 'from the islands' as well as long-time Canadians. 'You name 'em, we've got 'em,'" Frank told *Canadian Machinery*. "Maybe it's such a happy, hard-working shop because the boss is more concerned with what goes out the door than how the place looks. 'We clean up at night. That's enough. Where I used to work [at Sheepbridge], when the boss arrived everybody stopped to clean up the shop. Funny thing, we always lost money.'" There would come a day when Frank would return to Sheepbridge to help that beleaguered company turn a profit and make a little money for himself at the same time.

9

THE MAN AT THE MACHINE

WHEN FRANK HASENFRATZ WALKS into a room, he exudes the confidence of someone who is comfortable in his own skin. At five foot eight and 170 pounds, the lithe result of a daily workout, Frank looks younger than his seventy-seven years. His power doesn't flow from the fact that he is a founder or because he has personal wealth, it's the combination of his easy smile, twinkling brown eyes, legendary technical knowledge, and a high-octane brain that can persuade the thinking of others. At a busy trade show filled with strangers, he'll approach anyone, talking passionately about his company, always on the hunt for new business. He is assured but not arrogant, purposeful, and poised in a manner that means there's room for other egos in the room.

To be sure, his Hungarian heritage has left its mark. While he tends to trust people initially, he remains ever wary. That's the result of growing up in a society where, other than family, he didn't know for sure if someone was sincere, a snitch, or a member of the secret police. Despite all that, his gut instinct is to believe in others. "You can't go through life and assume people are not trustworthy. I find if you are straightforward with people, most people reciprocate. There are certain people I don't want to associate with, but very few. When I used to hire people, if a guy told me how bad his former employer was, I was a little suspicious. It may be legit, but why talk about it?"

Money can cause problems in relationships. "If my brother wants money, I don't lend him money, I give him money. You've got to be careful with friends and family." Frank applies similar thinking to strangers who bring him investment ideas. "Quite often I see people make deals and they don't know what they're doing but they would like you to be part of it." If a proposal appeals, he'll turn it over to others at Linamar to scrutinize. That way, many minds pass judgment. If the idea is worthy, the company takes the risk and reaps any reward that follows.

There are always those in this world who will never be won over. "When you're successful, there are some people who prey on you. And the same people cheer when you fail," he said. Frank's rule of thumb is simple. Work hard and be compensated; take short cuts and suffer. "He had a very nice personality about him in terms of dealing with people, but don't cross him," said Joe Mokanski. "If you crossed Frank, then he wouldn't think much of you at all. He doesn't show a temper, just a disgust with individuals that he displayed at times."

Of all the political leaders Frank has observed, he most admires former Prime Minister Margaret Thatcher for single-handedly altering Britain. He agrees with the philosophy of Thatcher who famously said, "You don't tell deliberate lies, but sometimes you have to be evasive." Said Frank, "In business, if you lie and get caught, you're a liar for the rest of your life."

For Frank there are parallels between commerce and his favourite card game, bridge. Bridge requires a mathematical mind as well as a toughness and intensity that Frank enjoys. "In business and in bridge, quite often you find out that people reveal something that could be misleading, or they're testing you. You have to be cautious. Of course, they all play the same game as we do. We want to get as much for our product as possible and we want to pay as little for what we buy as possible. In bridge, you never reveal all your cards, because once you do, you're beat. Hold the cards close, bluff a little, and don't lie."

Frank plays bridge well enough to be a master but has never bothered to collect the necessary points to hold that ranking officially. He wants to win but will not cut corners to do so. If someone inadvertently shows his cards, Frank will say, "Hold your cards up. I don't want to see them. I want to legitimately beat you." He likes the recently introduced system where players no longer declare their bids orally but instead use pre-printed cards selected from a bidding box. The room is quieter, bidding history never has to be reviewed, and there can be no advantage gained between partners who might use different tones of voice to send special messages about their cards. "I cannot understand the Italian pair who got caught in the world championship sending foot signals to each other. What's the sense in cheating?"

Once, when Frank was accused of lying by a client, he lost his temper. The incident took place in the early days after Frank won a contract to make shafts then told the client the design was wrong and the product would readily break. The client told him to go ahead anyway. As he predicted, the shaft broke so Frank called and said, "Let me put a radius on the groove so it won't crack the next time." Again, the client refused to allow any changes and accused Frank of lying just to delay delivery. Frank drove to the client's office and laid the broken parts on his desk, saying, "This is Thursday's, this is Sunday's, and don't ever tell me that I lied to you," then walked out. The client spread the word about Frank's hotheaded behaviour. "It's maybe the only time I really lost my temper. It was a very bad thing to do. It cost us, in my opinion, a lot."

But Frank doesn't dwell on his miscues or mistakes any more than he'll brag about his achievement. He's more likely to poke fun at himself by diminishing his own success. Asked by a stranger at a reception what he does for a living Frank might just say he's a machinist to see how quickly the questioner flees to find someone more important.

After that first profitable year in business, growth came at such a pace — 30 percent per year — that Frank built seven additions to the Ariss plant during his first decade in business, expanding it from 1,200 square feet to 70,000 square feet. During that time, he hired only the best by personally conducting all interviews in a small office that he shared with his secretary. He didn't just seek talent, he wanted people who had the right chemistry to be part of his team as well as the perseverance to see a job through to its conclusion.

Skilled workers were hard to find, secretaries included. His first two became pregnant. Once their babies were born, they stayed home to raise a family rather than return to work. In an attempt to impose some continuity, Margaret and a friend interviewed the next batch of candidates, seeking someone more likely to remain on the job. They chose Gladys McCreary, a woman who'd already had her family. A son, Bill, was a long-time NHL referee. McCreary not only was an efficient Girl Friday, but also did the bookkeeping and stayed for years. She became such an integral part of everything that she'd move into the house and mind the girls if Frank and Margaret went away for a few days.

Frank also had the courage to hire those who had been rejected by others. One such hopeful was Peter Neck who presented himself at Frank's office after losing his job at Guelph Tool and Die. Frank called his previous employer and learned that Neck had been fired but kept coming in to work

Frank in his office at Linamar's first plant, Ariss. (Kitchener-Waterloo Record)

anyway. Frank admired his spunk and concluded that he was a valuable person who just needed a chance. "This guy was such a good worker that once he learned a job, nobody could outwork him. Not only was he very loyal, mathematically he was a genius. The engineers would ask him for help in working up formulas." Neck, a bachelor, bought shares in Linamar every payday for years. When he retired, he was a millionaire.

Early growth — measured merely by the number of additions to the Ariss plant — seems phenomenal, but Frank now wishes he'd expanded more quickly. "I never thought big enough. I always had a goal, but I waited until I almost reached that goal, then I had another goal. But we were never big enough because I don't believe in bank debt. You don't want to be caught with your pants down one day because bankers are not good businesspeople. They can't see very far out," he said. "I believe you should make enough money to pay for expansion and that held us back. We could have done a lot better."

Because Frank was observant and inventive, brainstorms were forever whirling in his head. One idea for a new product combusted when he wondered why all tow trucks used drums, cables, and winches. Why not make a hydraulic cylinder that could be installed on any truck, operate off the battery, and hydraulically hoist an incapacitated car for towing? While his idea was still in development, a local businessman offered Frank $300,000 for the concept and he accepted. Two years later, the buyer sold the business for $18 million. "Now, that was a very bad business decision, except I had $300,000 to expand," said Frank. "I could never have done that otherwise."

Frank instinctively knew that building the business meant moving forward, forever embracing change. Some leaders scrimp their way more slowly to the future by saying, "If it ain't broke, don't fix it," but he realized that the status quo was not a business plan. He saw too many firms ride a tide of rising sales then become lazy and assume their products would always appeal. According to Frank, around every corner there's a competitor waiting to challenge any front-runner. "In manufacturing, if you don't change, you die."

～♡

With Linamar well established by the 1970s, Frank began to relax a little and take regular family holidays. In summer, they'd rent a cottage at Sauble Beach, north of Guelph. In winter, they'd spend time at the Deauville on Miami

Beach. After a few times in Miami, their winter destination became the Ocean Club in Nassau, the resort built by Huntington Hartford II, heir to the A&P grocery fortune. When the girls were older, the family travelled to Hungary to visit relatives and then would go sightseeing in Paris, Rome, or Vienna. "Regardless of what was happening, he always made sure to make time for those trips so we could be together," said Linda. "I never felt like there was a hole in my life growing up, that there was somebody that wasn't there."

On their own, Frank and Margaret would ski in Colorado or stay at the Cotton House on the Caribbean island of Mustique where they'd chat with Mick Jagger at Basil's, the top local restaurant. Once, when Frank removed his bathing suit to swim nude, Margaret took off with his trunks. "There are people sitting on the beach and she's watching from the top. I'm in the water, shrinking. She didn't let me out for an hour."

They also bought a weekend place at Talisman Ski Resort in the Beaver Valley, ninety minutes north of Guelph. The chalet was modest, about 1,600 square feet, in a row of townhouses. The year-round getaway had a golf course, swimming pool, hiking trails, lifts, and ski hills with a 200-metre vertical drop. Frank and Margaret became friends with half a dozen couples who also had chalets at Talisman.

Among the long-time friends was Glen Hutchison, a Guelph ophthalmologist, and his first wife, Dorothy, who died in 1986, as well as his second wife, Marian. Hutchison watched with admiration as Frank assembled land around his property in Ariss, buying the farm next door, then another farm across the road. "He comes from a farming background so he always was interested in farming. He became friends with the farmers and retained those friendships over the years. That's Frank. He could advance to be a multi-millionaire but these people, even though they are of lowly status — and I include myself — he never abandoned them," said Hutchison. "It came to the point I remember saying to my wife, 'Here's Frank next door to us in the Beaver Valley. He could have places in Colorado or Switzerland but here is, hooting and hollering with us, having drinks and laughing it up,'" said Rudy Chiarandini, a Fergus dentist.

⌐⌐⌐

As with most successful people, Frank has enjoyed three great advantages: talent, timing, and luck. That latter benefit extends well beyond his occupation.

Bob Young introduced him to the Royal City Kiwanis Club where the weekly lunch meetings offered an opportunity for Frank to meet local businesspeople. At each meeting, there is a 50–50 draw. Members pay $1 and the holder of the winning ticket receives half the money collected with the rest going to good works sponsored by the club. "Frank never had cash. He'd always find a dollar from somebody. He won more often than anyone else," said Young.

That competitive spirit is part of his attraction to bridge and golf. The stakes might only be a penny a point, or a dollar a hole, but it's a way of keeping score. "Frank is a very competitive person. He just loves to win a dime off me," said Young, whose ten handicap is better than Frank's twenty. Once, when they were on the tee at a par three at the Cutten Club in Guelph, Young told Frank he couldn't hit the green with his first shot. Said Frank, "Yes, I can. What odds do you give me?"

"I'll give you twenty to one."

"I'll take a dollar."

Frank hit the green. "He took the $20 off me. I don't think he's hit the green since. He just needed a little incentive," said Young. But $20 was an unusual windfall, Frank would be happy with less. "He just wants to succeed. If he wins a quarter, that means he was successful. The amount has very little to do with it," said Hutchison. Frank used to play squash and tennis but had to give up both after surgery for prostate cancer in 1991. His body could no longer tolerate the stop-and-start elements of the games.

By 1979, Frank had become so highly regarded that he was named president of the Royal City Kiwanis Club. In two decades, he'd risen from an immigrant who spoke no English to an admired industrialist and local service club leader. As president, he ran the weekly meetings, arranged speakers, and designated other members to introduce or thank speakers. "It was good for me. Running a meeting was easy, but I never went to school here, and you're sort of shy speaking when it's not your native language. That brought me out a little bit," said Frank. Frank also served as a director on several boards in the region including EMJ Data Systems Ltd., of Guelph, and Com Dev International Ltd., of Cambridge.

As a friend, he was never moody, always fun, and full of stories. "Frank loves to talk about his life and his business. Pump him with questions and he'll just keep talking about what went on during the war, the things they had to do when he was young, the Russians coming in, and the way he escaped. I've heard it all at least six times. It's an interesting story, it really is," said Rudy Chiarandini.

~⁀~

Among the reasons Frank succeeded in business was that he kept an eye on costs. He prides himself on being able to visit a well-run plant and, in a few hours, find savings. To make the point to employees, he will use arresting methods. In one case, a plant was scrapping as many as fifteen transmissions a day. Frank tucked a $100 bill into a scrapped transmission and waited nearby to see the reaction. When someone found the money, Frank stepped in and said, "Does it give you a message? The housing might be scrap but the parts inside are worth money. Why wouldn't you save them?" By recovering parts for reuse, they saved $250 per unit.

This parsimonious behaviour also colours his personal life. In Rome, when Frank and Margaret were travelling with friends, Frank announced he'd pay for the taxi taking them all to dinner because he knew that the return trip, later in the evening, would be at a higher rate. Someone else could take a turn then. "He thought that was amusing because he had put one over on us. He's not mean-spirited but he would get a kick out of doing something like that where he'd get an advantage for a nickel," said Hutchison.

After Ontario instituted a refund for wine bottles, the next time Frank dined at the Cutten Club, he asked the waitress for his money back on the empty bottle. The employee, who was new to the job, thought this was normal procedure and passed along the request to the bartender. The bartender, being more familiar with Frank's foibles, just laughed.

Once when Jack and Peggy McGarry were holidaying on Paradise Island in the Bahamas, they ran into the Hasenfratz family. Everyone went out to dinner together and, when it came time to return to the hotel, Frank launched into negotiations with a taxi driver to reduce the price of the trip. He had almost convinced the driver to take a lower fare when another driver arrived on the scene and urged his colleague not to drop his price. Frank declared if he wouldn't negotiate, they'd all travel by bus, and so they did.

On the bus were two young nurses from Detroit that Frank had met on the beach earlier that day. They had asked him to take a Polaroid photo of them topless so they had proof of their risqué conduct to show friends at home. Frank took a photo and, when the finished print came out of the camera, glanced at the result, and said it hadn't turned out. He tucked the photo in his shirt pocket, saying he would throw it out later rather than litter the beach. He took a second shot, pronounced it suitable, and gave it to the women.

In fact, the first photo was just fine. He held on to the racy keepsake for years and, during his time as Kiwanis president, slipped it into the presentation by a speaker from the University of Guelph who was telling club members about his research work in the Sahara. When the topless women appeared, the speaker was aghast, declaring he had no idea where the image had come from. Frank laughed along with the rest of the audience, delighted to have enlivened the proceedings.

Frank punctuates most of his conversations with humour. He has a storehouse of jokes, one-liners, and ironic comments to lighten any situation and remind the world not to take itself too seriously. Anyone can be the butt of his humour, even his wife. One time, there was standing room only on a bus taking them to the ski lifts. Frank and Margaret had seats so he said to a standee, "Would you like a seat?" When the individual declined, Frank said, "Are you sure? Because I could ask Margaret to get up." Even his political heroine, Margaret Thatcher, is a target. "Why didn't they let Prime Minister Thatcher wear a mini-skirt?" he'll ask, then supply the answer, "They didn't want her balls to show."

Frank will go to great lengths to play a practical joke, an aspect of his mischievous personality that hasn't changed since he was a teenager and put cut-out newspapers with the picture of Mátyás Rákosi in the toilets. One such modern-day prank involved Luigi Sartori who worked at Linamar for thirty years and had four sons who were also Linamar employees. Sartori, who was retiring, was forever bragging about how he enjoyed sex "almost every day." Frank called Sartori's wife and told her if she would say what he asked her to at the event celebrating her husband's retirement, he would give the couple two tickets to Italy as a parting gift.

Once he had coached her answer, he was ready for the evening attended by hundreds of employees at Bingemans, a banquet hall in Kitchener. With Sartori onstage, Frank said, "Luigi, thank you, you worked for us for thirty years and you did a great job. You're in good shape, physically and mentally. But I still have trouble with your claim that you have sex almost every day."

Sartori maintained that what he said was all true.

"Luigi, do you mind if I call Mrs. Sartori up here?"

Luigi protested, saying her English wasn't very good.

Frank invited her to the stage anyway and asked, "Mrs. Sartori, what's the truth about 'almost every day'?"

"Yes it's true. Almost Monday, almost Tuesday, almost Wednesday...." The hall erupted with laughter.

Frank can also have fun at his own expense. A typical self-deprecating remark that also offers social commentary is, "The sad part of it is that today I would not qualify to come to this country. I couldn't speak English when I arrived." Another favourite line is, "I only work half days — from 7:00 a.m. to 7:00 p.m." Frank always has handy a thoughtful quotation, one from about two dozen that he believes in and lives by. His sources are many and varied. Among them are:

- "Find out what you like doing best and get someone to pay you for doing it," from British writer Katherine Whitehorn.

- "Knowing is not enough; we must apply. Willing is not enough; we must do," from Johann Wolfgang von Goethe, a German poet and scientist.

- "If you can give your son or daughter only one gift, let it be enthusiasm," from American businessman Bruce Barton.

But Frank's tongue can also be sharp. Glen Hutchison ran into Frank one hot, humid summer's day and told him that he had just attended a funeral. "My aunt passed away and we cremated her," said Hutchison. "In this heat?" asked Frank. Jibes can become running gags. On a trip to Greece with friends, the group hired a guide to describe sites. Some of the ruins were being restored by donations from Austria, Germany, and Britain. In other instances, there were only bits and pieces from the ancient world strewn about.

Frank ribbed the guide incessantly about how the Greek government should be more active in using foreign money to preserve the past. "You need to get Disney over here to put the whole thing together, do a lend-lease arrangement, and you'll get your money back in about ten years." The guide disliked Americans, didn't want to have anything to do with such an arrangement, and grew riled by Frank's constant kidding. "Margaret had to calm her down and get the two of them apart," said Hutchison. "That would be his philosophy: this is business, the hell with your communist attitudes, get the thing put back together again."

Frank's parents visited Canada annually, beginning in 1968. Anna, Frank's mother, spoke German to the children so, as a result, Linda speaks some German and Nancy speaks German fairly well because she also attended school in Germany. Once when the couple stayed for six months, Frank's father, Marton, said he wanted to earn enough money to be able to buy a car for each of their two youngest children still living in Hungary. The two older boys already owned vehicles, but Frank's sister and younger brother did not. The waiting time for a new car in Hungary was five years but, if you paid in hard currency, U.S. dollars, delivery was immediate.

Each car cost about $3,500 so Frank found his father a job at Linamar that would pay a total of $7,000 over the six months. So that no one got upset by what they might see as a special deal, Frank arranged for the $7,000 to be taken from his own salary. Once the money was in hand, arrangements were made for the two older brothers to pick up the cars in Hungary, drive them to their siblings, and make the presentation in the presence of their parents. It was an emotional moment that Marton and Anna talked about for years. Frank's father died in 1976 at seventy. His mother died in 1993, aged eighty-four.

Although he is a wealthy man — his Linamar shares alone are worth about $300 million — Frank spends very little on himself. The house he and Margaret lived in for most of their marriage might have been worth about $400,000. It was only in her final years before dying of cancer that Margaret built her 13,000-square-foot dream home on the original farm property. Frugality has been part of Frank's existence since his youth. Why bother buying or owning anything when the Russians or the communists or someone else might swoop in and take it all away? "I like to make money; it's a great pleasure. I don't get pleasure in spending money. It doesn't mean anything to me. I like to have a good dinner. I like comfort. But I never had any problem not having money. Or wanting more than I have."

Frank owns no expensive toys nor does he have a winter home in warmer climes. He drives a new Mercedes 500SEL, but he drove his previous Mercedes for eight years and 200,000 kilometres before he traded it in. On business trips, he'll spend less than a teenager does in an afternoon at the mall. On one recent weeklong stay in China, his total out-of-pocket expenses — after hotel and food — amounted to $12. Even personal clothing is of little interest. He likes to dress well but he's no clotheshorse. His housekeepers purchase items for him, lay them out, and say, "You need this." He agrees, adds them to his wardrobe, and thinks no more about the new apparel.

Once when he visited friends in Florida, he arrived with a rip in the seat of his pants. He hadn't brought a second pair and said the tear didn't matter because no one could see it when he wore his jacket. Margaret marched him off to buy a new pair of pants before she would permit any further appearances in public.

His ski outfit, black pants and a yellow jacket, is probably fifteen years old. "All the time I've known him, material things never concerned him," said Hutchison, the Guelph ophthalmologist. "He's never showed his wealth, he never boasts about it, he never talks about it. He never, ever makes you aware that he is much wealthier than you are."

Those who try to benefit from his wealth, however, do so at their peril. "If he thought people were taking advantage of the fact that he was wealthy, that would upset him a great deal. If you're going out with Frank, you pay your way. Now, if he wanted to be generous, that would be up to him. But he'd never tell you, 'I paid X dollars and I want you to be aware of my generosity,'" said Hutchison.

Often, when someone does him a favour, Frank will say "*Dio ti pagera*," an Italian phrase that means, "God will pay you." Says Rudy Chiarandini, with a laugh, "I've been waiting. I say, 'This God is not paying me, Frank. I'm not getting returns on this.'"

In fact, religion plays almost no part in Frank's life. While the children were growing up, Margaret took them to Knox Presbyterian Church where she sang in the choir. Frank attended a few times a year. Most Sundays, he stayed home. "I went so often to church when I was young, I didn't have to go. 'You can pray for two,'" he used to tell his wife. "She thought I was sacrilegious."

As far as he's concerned, all religion is manmade. "There is more trouble because of religion in this world than anything else. I would like to believe something beyond myself, but I've read a lot about the universe and I can't find a heaven. I can't find a hell. All I ask is that you don't use your belief to hurt others."

Portrait of Frank, December 1976. (Robert Lansdale)

Above all, family and the business both matter to the man many call Mr. H. "I remember one time coming to Guelph for a wedding and I had to drop off some prints at the corporate office, which was part of Hastech at the time," said Ken Rossman, account manager at Linamar Sales Corp. in Southfield, Michigan. "Mr. H. saw my wife and I pull up and invited us into his office. We must have sat there for forty-five minutes talking about our families. Now, when I see Mr. H., he'll ask the two or three business questions that are on his mind, but then he always asks about my family."

Other employees agree. "He cares about what I do and asks about my family all the time. When you have that, that's a differentiator in an organization," said Brian Wade, vice president of operations. "He knows the leadership team has to have family support to be in their jobs because it's not a nine-to-five role. And he gives back his dedication. How many people in business can call their chairman on how to process a problem? I'll call him and say, 'I can't figure it out. Come over, for sure you've seen it somewhere.' And he shows up an hour later because that's his priority." But no captain can control every event or easily solve every issue. The "Good Ship Linamar" also sailed in some turbulent times.

10

HITS AND MISSES

THE STORM CLOUDS FROM White Farm Equipment, based in Brantford, Ontario, blew in without warning in October 1980 when the company stopped paying its bills. After placing an initial $1 million order with Linamar, White Farm had been a major customer for half a dozen years. During all that time, the combine maker had always paid promptly. Suddenly, White Farm owed Linamar $100,000 and there seemed little likelihood those arrears would be paid anytime soon.

White Farm had recently introduced the 9700, the largest rotary combine on the market. The 9700 could do the work of two conventional combines by harvesting wheat at the rate of more than two bushels per second. In addition to the technical advancement, the operator's cab boasted tinted glass, air conditioning, and insulation to keep out noise and dust.

The agricultural sector had never before seen such a behemoth, but the world was sliding into a recession and farmers couldn't afford such power and prestige at $150,000 apiece. As sales collapsed, the industry consolidated. Case merged with International Harvester, and a German firm bought Allis-Chalmers, later renamed AGCO Corp. White Farm was the smallest, with about 20 percent of the Canadian market and less than 5 percent in the U.S. Production in Brantford exceeded demand, inventory soared, and cash flow dried up.

Frank phoned White Farm President Andrew Zaleski. The Polish-born Zaleski came to Canada from Argentina in 1958, then worked for Canadian Admiral Corp. and Beach Appliances before joining White in 1978. "You're not paying your bills," said Frank. Replied Zaleski, "In Canada we're making money, but the U.S. is in receivership." White Motor Corp., the U.S. parent, had filed for protection under Chapter 11 of the Bankruptcy Code. Once that happened, the Canadian subsidiary went into voluntary receivership to protect its assets from creditors of the parent company. Canadian production was halted and the company was placed in the hands of a receiver, Clarkson Co., of Toronto.

White Farm had an honourable heritage that began in the nineteenth century as the Brantford Plow Works. Renamed the Cockshutt Plow Co., the firm made plows that were sold around the world. During the Second World War, the plant produced wings and tails for the de Havilland Mosquito fighter-bomber, while continuing to develop combines and tractors. By the 1950s, Cockshutt tractors shone with particular lustre. The famed industrial designer Raymond Loewy, responsible for the iconic look of the Studebaker, conceived some of the Cockshutt models. In 1969, three firms — Cockshutt, Oliver, and Minneapolis-Moline — merged to form White Farm Equipment. White Farm had made as many as 2,000 combines annually in Brantford, but after the company went into receivership, 950 production workers and 350 office staff were laid off.

In addition to farm equipment, White made Western Star trucks in Kelowna, B.C. That plant was also closed so there was growing political enthusiasm for a made-in-Canada solution to save manufacturing jobs in both locations. Several tire-kickers looked at buying operations in Brantford but, in the end, the sole bidder was TIC Investment Corp., of Dallas, Texas, the company that owned the U.S. White Farm assets. Then suddenly, and without explanation, TIC withdrew its offer.

In January 1981, with no bidders on the horizon, Frank Hasenfratz began to consider buying the Brantford operations. It was an audacious plan. Linamar had only $10 million in annual sales compared to White Farm's $200 million. Rather than continue to grow organically at the rate of 15 to 20 percent per year, White offered Linamar a unique opportunity to expand exponentially through acquisition.

Frank studied the White Farm financials and concluded that if Linamar could obtain government support and convince the creditors to take less than they were owed, a reinvigorated White Farm might be able to flourish again with Linamar supplying far more parts than previously. At the time, 80 percent of all the parts White Farm used in the engines, transmission, axles, and wheels, were made in the U.S. "I knew how they did it and how long it took them. I knew we could do it a lot better. And that would have grown Linamar, big time, right away," said Frank. "I just thought we had the opportunity of a lifetime."

Terry Godsall, of Shieldings Investments of Toronto, a dealmaker with a nationalist bent, helped put together an offer. Godsall and Frank gained the backing of Zaleski and other members of White Farm management. Frank spent the next few weeks holed up at a Toronto hotel so he'd be close to the legal team helping him with the negotiations and paperwork. "I looked forward to any new business but this took too long and the negotiations involved at least twenty-five lawyers. It was a nightmare, but no M.B.A. course could teach you as much," he said.

The tedious pace troubled Frank, who would rather do than dither. He knew everything must be conducted with the appropriate legalities and precise contract wording, but for him, some of the proceedings were nothing but a waste of time and money. Once, as Frank sat at a boardroom table surrounded by a dozen lawyers and accountants, one of the participants told a joke. Frank timed how long the tale took — three minutes — and did a quick calculation of his cost to pay the all the professionals who had listened. "That joke just cost me $150," said Frank. "From now on, when we make jokes, we clock out, okay?" The lawyers kidded Frank for years about his comment, but he'd made his point.

Frank was able to line up $20 million in government financing, two-thirds from Ottawa through the Enterprise Development Board, one-third from the Ontario Development Corp. About one-quarter of the funds came in the form of a grant, the rest were loans at below-market interest rates. "The Canadian government saw an opportunity to nationalize our manufacturing plant," said Zaleski. The government money would be used as working capital to pay salaries, buy supplies, and cover other day-to-day costs. Frank had a rule of thumb: a company needed cash in hand equivalent to a month's sales. In the case of White Farm, that was about $16 million, so $20 million in working capital gave him enough leeway until production ramped up and revenue flowed again.

Linamar would be the majority owner with 55 percent, Zaleski and three members of management would hold 25 percent, and Shieldings 20 percent. The group believed its package was unbeatable: government backing, management expertise, and Canadian ownership. Then, the situation altered again on February 19 when White Motor Corp. fired Zaleski with the full approval of the Canadian receiver. Even though there was no other offer on the table, the U.S. parent didn't like the idea that Zaleski was part of a bidding group that might end up owning the Canadian assets.

Dallas-based TIC, believing it had dealt the Linamar bid a fatal blow, then renewed its own offer. Frank and TIC President Stratton Georgoulis, a Texas millionaire who owned several companies, bid each other higher, pushing up the end price. Frank concluded that because he had government support, his offer was intrinsically better. He decided to make a final offer of $1 million that included taking on all liabilities.

In March, the two bidders, buttressed by scores of lawyers, appeared at the three-day Chapter 11 proceedings in Cleveland, Ohio, home to White Motor Corp.'s head office. "The judge was under considerable pressure from the U.S. creditor committee. They were afraid of a standalone Canadian company because they could lose the control of the combine business," said Zaleski. As a result, the judge called Frank and Georgoulis to his chambers and urged them to form a partnership. Frank agreed, but only if he were the majority owner with 50.1 percent. Georgoulis consented to hold a 49.9-percent interest. The management group and Shieldings withdrew and the court approved the newly created team. As with most such partnerships, there was a "shotgun" clause. If at any time one of the partners offered to buy out the other at a specific price, the second partner had the right to buy out the first at the same price.

In order to appease creditors and convince them to accept the deal even though they stood to be paid less than they were owed, Frank and Georgoulis each increased their investment to $1.5 million. Georgoulis backstopped his bid with a corporate guarantee from TIC to give creditors comfort that the transaction was solid. However, despite the presence of numerous lawyers and accountants, none of them noticed that Linamar did not give a similar corporate pledge. "Linamar never signed anything. I always signed as Frank Hasenfratz. By the time they found out, we'd bought the company and all the negotiations were done. Nobody realized that Linamar was not on the hook," said Frank. (During the same proceedings in Cleveland, the truck division was sold to Bow Valley Resource Services Ltd. and Nova Corp., both of Calgary, and was renamed Western Star Trucks.)

Following court approval, final negotiations were conducted at a downtown Toronto law firm under the auspices of the Canadian receiver. The last agenda item was pension liabilities. Frank was willing the buy the company as it stood, but refused to take on retired workers' pensions. When he was told they had to be included, Frank said, "Then there's no deal."

With a midnight deadline just a few hours away, Frank and his team departed for dinner nearby at Hy's. At 10:30 p.m., an emissary arrived at the steakhouse pleading for their return. Frank agreed, only to hear the same demand on pensions. "You may as well go home now, you don't have to wait until midnight. I will never sign that. The company could never survive with that liability," he said. At five minutes to midnight, all sides agreed to the deal without the pensions, which were partially assumed by government. In the days that followed, the Canadian courts and the Foreign Investment Review Agency approved the creation of a new company, White Farm Equipment (Canada) Ltd.

Signing the White Farm Equipment acquisition: From left: Frank, President Andrew Zaleski, and Dallas-based partner Stratton Georgoulis, 1981. (Jack Jarvie)

For Frank, White Farm was a blockbuster deal. Linamar paid far less than the enterprise value, shared the risk with a partner, gained new business, received government money, and didn't have to provide a guarantee. On March 16, Frank rehired Andrew Zaleski as president and chief executive officer (CEO) to run the Brantford plant and be in charge of bank financing, relations with governments, marketing, and improving morale among employees as well as the 235 dealers across the country. With Frank as board chair, the two men made a strong team. "Andrew knew a lot more about how to run a big company than I did, and he was good at marketing a product to the end user, but I knew a lot more about what to do on the floor," said Frank. "He could walk through the plant, make observations about what he saw, and 90 percent of the time he was right," agreed Zaleski.

As a first step, Zaleski negotiated a new three-year contract with the union that represented employees, the United Auto Workers (UAW). In return for wage increases of 3 percent a year the union agreed to improve productivity, defer bonuses, and adjust some benefits. With labour peace achieved, the plant began producing combines at a slightly lower rate than before the shutdown. Even that cautious production level was a mistake; there was already plenty of dealer inventory to fulfill the still weak demand during a recession.

A windfall in another area offset the poor sales of new equipment. The purchase price included inventory but there had been no mention of $50 million worth of spare parts available for repair and replacement that cost the new owners nothing. "We went to all the dealers and said, 'Any spare parts you order before such-and-so a date, you get 40 percent off.' We made money like you wouldn't believe," said Frank.

Day-to-day operations, however, continued to be troublesome. After Frank and Margaret attended a concert in Hamilton one evening, he decided they'd take a circuitous route home to Guelph and visit the Brantford plant on the way. As he walked the assembly line, Frank came upon four men playing cards. "Who's your foreman?" he asked. When the foreman arrived, Frank fired all five on the spot.

The following day, Frank received a phone call from an irate union leader, who said, "Do you know who I am?" Frank said he did. The caller then launched into a diatribe laced with expletives, arguing Frank had no right to fire workers.

"If you don't work, you don't get paid. And if you break the regulations, you're out," said Frank.

"I'll teach you a lesson," said the union rep. "I'll pull everyone out on strike."

"That's fine with me," said Frank, "we've got three months' inventory to work down." In the end, they reached a compromise; two of the five men were rehired.

Meanwhile, Zaleski sought to change some of the pre-existing arrangements between the Canadian and American arms of the business. He also tried to change production schedules so that the Brantford plant could do longer runs rather than always be retooling to suit the whims of the U.S. partner. "One of the major differences between Frank and Stratton was that Stratton wanted to maintain the status quo. I felt it was my obligation to rationalize and rectify some of the inequities and treat both shareholders fairly," said Zaleski.

Stratton Georgoulis also wanted to take money out of White Farm, thereby realizing a return on his investment. Frank refused, believing that they should pay off the debt first. Such tussles created tension between the partners but an even more serious issue was finding financing for combines when they were sold. Under an arrangement called "floor planning," when a piece of farm equipment was shipped to a dealer, as the manufacturer, White Farm received 90 percent of the wholesale price through financing by Borg-Warner Acceptance. The dealer paid nothing for the combine. When a farmer bought a combine the money from that deal repaid the financing, covered the dealer's profit, and the 10 percent still owed to the manufacturer. But the transaction was not yet complete. There would often be a trade-in at a value determined by the dealer, so the dealer would have to obtain financing from Borg-Warner on that used item while trying to find a buyer for the second-hand equipment.

However, Borg-Warner's representatives in Canada didn't seem to be as proficient as their U.S. counterparts. Borg-Warner would dispute dealer trade-in valuations and slow down the payment process in an already difficult market. "They were an American company with what I would call a branch plant mentality in Canada," said Zaleski. For Borg-Warner, the much bigger

U.S. market was of far more interest. Still, Canadian dealers needed secure financing on a timely basis; any delay hurt their ability to close sales. "If a dealer can't finance the trade-ins, buyers would go to John Deere or someone else who could," said Zaleski. Frank and Zaleski tried but failed to find another finance company to replace Borg-Warner in Canada.

Such attempts to change business practices and secure new financing did not endear either Frank or Zaleski to TIC or Borg-Warner. From the Canadian side it seemed that the U.S. interests were trying to cause strife so that Frank would give up and sell to Georgoulis just to be rid of the headaches. Matters became so heated that they were the subject of debates in the Ontario Legislature. "Ever since the rejuvenation of the Canadian firm about a year ago with an American and a Canadian partner, with the Canadian partner in control, I believe the American interests had been harassing the administration and the Canadian ownership in a completely irresponsible and unconscionable way," said Robert Nixon, the Liberal member for Brant-Oxford-Haldimand, in a speech delivered at the time. "The American partner was consumed with a desire and a commitment to regain control of the Canadian industry."

~

Despite the increasing stress at work, Frank tried to keep things on even keel as far as his wife and children were concerned. He took them on their regular winter holiday to the Ocean Club in the Bahamas. Georgoulis ratcheted up his pressure tactics by visiting Frank there. As they walked the beach together, Georgoulis announced that he had the backing of Borg-Warner and demanded Frank do what he hadn't previously done and give a Linamar guarantee or Georgoulis would withdraw his own guarantee. Frank refused, knowing that the threat by Georgoulis was legally impossible. Georgoulis then warned that Borg-Warner would cease financing unless Linamar gave a guarantee. In response, Frank told Stratton to buy him out if he was so unhappy with how the company was being run.

Following the encounter, Frank phoned Zaleski to call a board meeting. "If they don't back off the demands for a guarantee, I want you to lay everybody off and shut the plant down," Frank said. "The only people I want on the job are sales and top management, nobody else." In the midst of the brouhaha, a reporter from the *Globe and Mail* phoned Frank who had set up an office on the balcony of his hotel room so his business calls wouldn't disturb the family. Asked the reporter, "Do you know what's going on in Brantford? Do you realize that your plant in Brantford is burning?"

Workers at White Farm Equipment, 1980s.

Replied Frank, "Excuse me, let me put down my fiddle." It was a classic Frank quip, an attempt to defuse a tense situation with a joke comparing himself to Nero, the Roman emperor. The reporter used the quote; Frank was not amused. The battle escalated when Borg-Warner made good on its threat and refused to provide further financing. With no other finance company willing to step in, the plant was closed. In March 1982, a year after Georgoulis and Frank had been yoked together by the court, Georgoulis invoked the shotgun clause and offered to buy out Linamar. Frank was eager to sell but decided to keep Georgoulis guessing about his intentions until nearer to the end of the offer's thirty-day life.

Two weeks after Frank returned home from holiday, he had a visit from the Ontario Provincial Police. The officers told him they'd received a tip from someone who'd overheard a conversation indicating that Frank and his family were in danger from persons unknown. While the OPP officers had no further information, and did not know what form the hostilities might take, they said they took the threat seriously. The police told Frank to stop going into the office, move out of his house, and go into hiding. While he was gone, they would maintain a twenty-four-hour watch on both his home and his office.

Frank was shocked by the news and the OPP's recommendations. Such menace and intimidation were more common in the communist regime from which he had fled. In Canada, however, these were very unusual circumstances for anyone in business. If Frank had been on his own, he might have stood his ground, but he did not want to put his wife and daughters at risk. Frank and Margaret took the girls out of school and they all lived at the Four Seasons Hotel in Toronto sixty miles away. Only his secretary knew their whereabouts. All personal messages and work-related instructions were relayed through her. After two weeks, when nothing had come of the threat, the family quietly moved back home and resumed their normal lives.

Frank let the offer from Georgoulis go right down to the wire, finally accepting on the twenty-ninth day. He made $1.5 million, doubling his money in a year. In addition, Linamar booked a profit of $2 million by machining more parts for White Farm than in the past. "He always takes pride in saying he's the only guy that made money in the farm equipment business during that era," said Zaleski. Georgoulis, the new 100 percent owner, immediately fired Zaleski, putting him in the unusual position of being one of the few people ever to be fired from the same job twice. Zaleski joined Trimac Transportation Services Ltd. in Calgary where he became president until his retirement in 2001.

For FIRA and the governments of Ontario and Canada, there was little they could do but approve the American ownership in order to preserve jobs. In 1984, White Farm brought out a new combine, the 9720, but even that wasn't enough to spur sales in the face of continuing poor demand. Linamar continued to make parts for the new owners, but soon White Farm was back to the same sad place as before, not paying Linamar in a timely manner. For a while, Linamar shipped on a COD basis, then stopped selling to White Farm altogether.

But running White Farm, even so briefly, had the effect of reinforcing Frank's long-term ambition to turn Linamar into a much larger company than it otherwise would have been. "I would never have been satisfied any more to do $10 million in sales. So, it was a big lesson to learn, a little stressful, but I like stress," said Frank. "What White Farm did for me is open my eyes. There was an entire industry out there that was not being run properly."

~

While Frank is at heart an optimist and became an opportunist always looking for growth, two other forays in the 1980s were far less successful. For the most part, Frank's business instincts are good, but they could also go glaringly wrong. "I haven't got the time to talk for hours about how we're going to do such-and-so," said Frank. "And there were occasions when I didn't take the time I should have. We got into the plastics business, a business I knew nothing about. I was arrogant. I thought if I'm good at what I'm doing, I must be good in everything. It backfired, big time. That's the big danger with an entrepreneur; he thinks he can do no wrong."

In 1988, with 1,300 employees and $113 million in annual sales, Frank believed it was time for Linamar to diversify. Research scientists at Urylon Development Inc. of Conyers, Georgia, claimed they were "close to making billions of dollars" and Frank was in their thrall. Linamar paid $1 million for the equipment, patents on a family of new resins, and the services of their developer, Stuart Smith. The equipment was moved to Guelph and installed in a new facility. The renamed Urylon Canada Ltd. appeared to be on the verge of coming up with a way to replace traditional injection moulding processes for automotive parts using lower-cost material. Still, Frank kept Urylon on a short leash and gave them two years to create something with commercial potential.

To help bring the plastic resin technology into production Frank lined up a $4.2 million grant from the Ontario government and invested a matching amount from Linamar. Urylon was able to develop a few products such as spray-applied foam for the U.S. Navy and coating materials for roofing membranes but sales were modest. When the two years were up, Urylon had made little progress, although the company remained convinced that it was "that close" to making big money. Despite their pleas to extend the deadline, Frank refused further funding. Urylon was sold in 1990 at a loss to Linamar of $6 million. "The worst business decision I ever made was going into plastics," said Frank. "That was an absolute disaster."

Years later Urylon was no further ahead but still claimed to be "that close." Once, in Pisa Airport, Frank stood near Sophia Loren. Margaret took note and said, "You were 'that close' to Sophia Loren." Replied Frank, "And it didn't do me any good, did it? 'That close' isn't good enough, except with a hand grenade."

Losing money in Urylon wasn't the only negative impact on Linamar. "How do you measure the aggravation and the time it took me and some of our other people away from doing more productive things? I had a couple of deals like that," said Frank. "You do dumb things."

～⌒

Another business proposition that failed was a partnership with Horst-Dieter Esch, a German who immigrated to the U.S. in the 1960s. Esch made a series of bold acquisitions — including the purchase of the Terex division of General Motors in 1980 — to create IBH Holding AG, the world's third-largest construction-machine business after Caterpillar and Komatsu. In the heady days when Esch was building his empire, Linamar signed a licensing agreement with IBH to build road construction rollers. The joint venture, owned 51 percent by Linamar, was called Duo-Pact Equipment Ltd. Launched in 1977, its 35 employees in Guelph made compactors for road construction.

The business did well until 1983 when IBH went bankrupt. Several executives were jailed, including Esch, who was convicted of fraud and sentenced to three and a half years. After his release in 1988, Esch bought Wilhelmina, a New York modelling agency, and later gave it as a twenty-first birthday present to his daughter, Natasha. After the bankruptcy, Linamar continued to make the rollers using its own design but eventually some of the components made in Germany became unavailable. Linamar sold Duo-Pact to BNR Equipment Ltd., of Kitchener. "Getting involved was a mistake, but on the other hand, if you don't make any mistakes, that means you're not doing anything," said Frank. "That business should have been huge for North and South America. If you add up all the losing things we did, it was always things in which we had no experience."

While mistakes teach, they should never tether. "Entrepreneurs like me are all oddballs. We see things, we want to do things, and sometimes it's hard to get us off that. The big danger is you get an idea and you think 'I'm going to get into that.' We get carried away and we think we're good at everything and that isn't the case," said Frank. "It always brings you back — stick to what you know. It's good to learn from your mistakes but it's better to learn from your competitors' mistakes. That doesn't cost you anything. I made many mistakes but I can forget about them. They're not in my mind. Don't try to manage from yesterday. Don't look back all the time, remember what happened back there, but look forward. If you look back all the time, you're going to trip going forward."

~

Another foray in that era was far more successful. In 1985 an opportunity arrived for Frank to improve operations at Sheepbridge, the firm he'd left in 1964 to start his own business. The company had changed hands. It was now owned by Bundy Corp., of Detroit. General Manager Wayne Corbett joined Sheepbridge in 1963, so he knew Frank. "I liked Frank right off the bat because he was a no-nonsense guy. He got the job done and he didn't mess around like a lot of other people tended to do," said Corbett.

When a lengthy strike reached its sixteenth week, Bundy decided to close Sheepbridge unless Corbett could find a buyer. A despondent Corbett sought out Frank. "This is a mess. I feel badly for my people."

Said Frank, without hesitation, "Why don't you buy it?"

"I don't have the wherewithal."

"We can make it work," said Frank.

Frank phoned his local Bank of Montreal branch in St. George's Square and told them to lend Corbett the $1 million purchase price that Bundy wanted. "It was almost a situation where the money was waiting when I got there." Frank was not a guarantor and did not invest any money.

"Basically, he just told them to do it," said Corbett.

For his help, Frank received a 50 percent interest in Sheepbridge. Frank's only demand was that his name was not to be involved. As far as the world was concerned, Corbett and a partner, David Schaefer, were the new owners. Both Corbett and Schaefer put mortgages on their respective houses of $35,000 so they had some of their own money in the deal.

They changed the name of the company to International Sintered Metals, settled the strike, and put the plant on a sounder footing than under the previous owners. Frank made a few phone calls to send some business their way. "Frank was a good sounding board. He would always listen to you. There were times I'd get down in the dumps. I'd go to him with what I felt was a plan to make things move forward, and Frank would either agree or disagree. His insight was so very important to me," said Corbett.

In 1988, after only three years under new management, the plant was put up for sale again. Krebsöge, a German company, was willing to pay the asking price of $3 million. Schaefer became plant manager and Corbett moved to Krebsöge's Detroit office where he remained for four years.

The return on investment was huge. Of the $3 million, Frank received $1 million for no initial outlay; Corbett and Schaefer each got $700,000 for their $35,000. The rest went toward paying down the bank loan with the new owner taking over the remaining debt. "I've seen Frank with people he's befriended," said Corbett. "He gives them all kinds of second chances." Frank was supposed to put a symbolic dollar into the original purchase but never did. For him, it was just another case of "*Dio ti pagera*."

11

GOING PUBLIC

IN THE EARLY 1980s, the world economy was mired in the worst recession since the Great Depression. Output cratered, interest rates soared to
19 percent, and millions of jobs vanished. Faddish business practices such
as re-engineering came into vogue but for the most part companies simply
laid off workers to survive what for many CEOs was the toughest time of
their careers.

Frank Hasenfratz devised a more creative approach than downsizing
his way to corporate health. He met with employees at his three plants
and offered them a choice. They could either face across-the-board lay-
offs or forego their breaks and wash-up time at the end of the day. By
doing so, each employee would work twenty-five minutes more per shift.
Frank said he would take that 5 percent gain in output and reduce prices
by an equivalent amount, a step he believed would attract new business.
The employees agreed; orders poured in. Within a few months, there was
enough new business to restore breaks and wash-up time as well as give
each employee a Christmas bonus.

By 1985, Linamar had 500 employees in five plants with a sixth under
construction. They were all clustered together in northwest Guelph like
freckles on a boy's face. In keeping with Frank's desire to keep bureaucracy
to a minimum, there were only six people in head office — including the

founder. Rather than spend money on administrative staff, he bought up-to-date numerically controlled machines.

Employees not only worked with top equipment but they also knew the precious value of their time. "We constantly preach that if a machine stands idle for five minutes that's 80¢ a minute, or $4, we've lost," Frank told *The Financial Post*. "You have to make sure a machine has paid for itself in three years. Because you know that in 10 years it's going to be worthless and that there'll be an infinitely better machine on the market at a lower price."[1]

Employees and machines were intimately linked. "Some of Linamar's precision-grinding machines today are nearly as large as Frank's spartan corner office. The men and women who mind them are as much their 'managers' as their operators. They'll be continually testing for quality while the machine grinds away," wrote Patrick Bloomfield in *The Financial Post*. "But productivity still depends on their commitment. That's why they're treated as key players and brought into the planning as soon as a new job comes in for quotation."[2]

Each plant operated as an independent profit centre headed by a general manager aided by a small management team — called a plant operating committee — that included corporate finance, cash management, material, and marketing. That independence allowed each plant to book new orders, pare costs, and run incentive programs to reward quality work and productivity gains. As part of their compensation, general managers received a salary plus a portion of the plant's annual profits so they would feel and act like entrepreneurs with a stake in Linamar's success. "If a general manager of any one plant doesn't know every employee personally, and any work-related or personal problems that employee may have, then he's not going to be with us very long," said Frank.[3]

Frank copied the plant size and management incentive plan from another immigrant in the auto parts business, Frank Stronach. Like Frank Hasenfratz, Stronach was a tool-and-die maker who came to Canada, in his case from Austria, in 1954. He started Magna in 1957 and by 1986 had 11,000 employees at ninety plants. "I've always been a big admirer of Frank Stronach. He's a genius the way he set up his plants as stand-alone profit centres. We have duplicated that all the way," said Frank. "I like his business model and he attracts a lot of good people. The best come from the bottom up."

The first Linamar plant, known as Ariss, was opened in 1966. By 1985, it employed 175 employees from twenty-one countries making auto and defence parts, highway equipment, and hydraulics components. Ariss was also home to Frank's first lathe displayed in all its glory on a wooden stand in the boardroom.

The second plant, Linex Manufacturing Inc., at 301 Massey Road, opened in 1980 and expanded to 60,000 square feet by 1983 with 175 employees making components for Xerox business machines, propulsion units for mass transit, and suspension systems for the U.S. Army's light-armoured personnel carrier. Frank moved from Ariss to Linex, but his new office remained as modest as before, an eight-by-ten room, cheek-by-jowl with plant management and the small number of head office employees including Chief Financial Officer Larry Pearson who joined Linamar in 1980.

Armoured personnel carrier with parts made by Linamar in the 1980s.

The third plant, Hastech Inc., opened in January 1985 with 125 employees in a 40,000-square-foot building making transmission components for the Bradley Fighting Vehicle. Spinic Manufacturing Co. Ltd. opened in October 1985 with sixty employees working in 42,000 square feet producing transmission parts and front wheel spindles for automobiles. Spinic was the first of what would become many Linamar plants where the entire production was under a "sole-source" contract, the emerging trend in automotive. This arrangement meant that companies like Linamar became the only maker of a specific precision-machined part for one of the Big Three automakers: General Motors, Chrysler, or Ford.

For Linamar, profits were higher with sole-sourcing because contracts could run for three years or longer compared to short-term jobs requiring constant retooling that slowed production for the 500 different products made by Linamar for eighty different customers. Sole sourcing also created new sources of capital because the customer would sometimes help pay for machinery and tooling as part of the closer bond between maker and client.

Linamar's total sales in 1985 were $36 million with 50 percent in the defence and aerospace sectors; 20 percent in transportation; 15 percent in automotive; and 15 percent in heavy equipment, office equipment, and other items. Almost 75 percent of the production was exported to the U.S.

Sales had been growing at a torrid pace of 25 percent a year since 1981. Profits almost tripled from $668,000 to $1.7 million during the same period. The future appeared boundless. Defence spending in the U.S., which had been US$157 billion in 1981, was forecast to reach $286 billion in 1986. The West was playing catch-up. The Warsaw Pact nations could marshal five to seven times as many tanks and armoured personnel carriers as NATO. As a result, Frank knew he needed more capital for expansion.

Other matters were coming to a head at the same time. In January 1985, Frank turned fifty. He had to start thinking about what would happen when he began to wind down his working life in twenty years. Should he take Linamar public so he could cash in and get his money out of the business? Alternatively, would it be better to keep it a private family company run by one of his two daughters?

As a first step, he spoke to Nancy and Linda, then twenty-two and nineteen, respectively. Nancy's interest had always been more toward the arts than business. She graduated in psychology and sociology at the University of Guelph, worked for a magazine, married, then stayed home, and no longer worked. Linda, who excelled in math and science, seemed a more likely candidate. He urged her to study engineering at university. "Dad never really wanted to push either Nancy or I into a career at Linamar. He wanted us to decide what we wanted to do and what we'd most like to do. So, he never pushed me into the idea of engineering. I think he was more hopeful than recommending," said Linda.

Linda chose instead to take honours chemistry at the University of Western Ontario in London. "In retrospect, I wish I had gone into engineering. No doubt I would have done well because I did have an aptitude for science and math. Given where I am today, it certainly would have been handy. But at the time, I didn't have aspirations of coming and working at Linamar. As a young person, you think you have all the answers and you know what direction you want. As young people, we should spend a little more time thinking and taking counsel from our parents and others about what options make sense."

With neither daughter interested in Linamar at the time, Frank had little choice but to take the company public. "If you have to sell a private company like ours, it would be very difficult," said Frank. "I needed a vehicle, so that if I wanted to cash in some shares, I could." If he had known that Linda would change her mind in five years and join the business, he would not have taken Linamar public. "But it was the right thing to do at the time. Hindsight is always 20/20."

There was also another road not taken at the time. "He had a few offers to sell before he went public and he didn't take them," said Bob Young, his accountant. "I don't remember who they were from but I do remember that the offers were enough that he could have retired." Frank had no interest in retiring. He enjoyed being in business too much.

⁓

For entrepreneurs, going public marks a major change in their business lives. On the one hand, individual and institutional investors are able to buy shares owned by the founder who at last receives a monetary reward for his years of hard work. On the other hand, a public company becomes beholden to shareholders and regulators, has to reveal on a quarterly basis financial results that had previously been kept out of the public eye, must appoint a board of directors, and files detailed information with various securities commissions.

From being your own boss, able to make all decisions with little reference to others, suddenly there are several new constituencies to please. Moreover, going public involves up to a year of intense effort. In addition to the many duties of a normal workday, the entrepreneur must spend hours preparing lengthy documents; meeting with underwriters, lawyers, and accountants; telling the company story to industry analysts; and convincing investors through a series of presentations to buy shares in your baby.

In the early 1980s, Ontario Premier William Davis had been encouraging the Toronto Stock Exchange to make it easier for small and medium-sized firms to become public companies. Davis wanted such companies to have better access to capital so they could grow and create more jobs. Walwyn Stodgell Cochran Murray Ltd., a Toronto-based brokerage firm, hired Rick Durst as an agent to beat the bushes, looking for likely corporate candidates. Durst passed half a dozen names along to Walwyn Senior Vice President David Allan, who in turn approached Frank. Frank's need for capital met the opportunity to raise money. "Frank's favourite phrase about himself at the time, was, 'I'm just a country boy' as if everything you told him was very complicated, but he understood perfectly well," said Allan. "In fact, he was incredibly wise. For somebody who was pretty distant from capital markets, he was enormously savvy and very relaxed about it. That's not something that you typically find when you're taking a company like that public."

A key part of any initial public offering (IPO) is what's called the "road show." In some cases, a company might make presentations right across Canada but Allan and Frank focused mainly on the Toronto investment community where they believed there would be the most interest. Attendees at the gatherings included two main groups. First, there were the institutional investors such as pension funds and mutual fund managers who would buy large blocks of stock for long-term holdings. Second, were the retail representatives and analysts from brokerage houses who, it was hoped, would encourage their individual clients to buy Linamar shares for their personal portfolios.

On such occasions, the jockey matters as much as the horse. The market likes a good story, a company with solid profits and excellent prospects, but the street also admires a leader who is passionate and a good communicator. Frank was just such a polished and entertaining performer who even told jokes, a rare trait among CEOs. During one presentation, when he showed photos of the M80 tanks for which Linamar was supplying treads, Frank pointed to the treads and quipped, "When I was in the Hungarian army and faced the Russians, this is where I would put the grenade." Once, when Allan tried to make a witty remark, Frank interrupted the proceedings and loudly admonished him, saying, "I tell the jokes around here." Said Allan, "He was very much at ease presenting to Bay Street."

Pricing the shares in an IPO is always crucial. The appropriate number is just below the perceived value so investors think they're getting a bargain. The best outcome occurs when there's more demand than supply, so that when the stock begins trading, those who were unable to obtain shares in the original allotment rush to buy shares from those who did. The resulting frenetic activity drives up the price.

For the brokerage firm, the higher the IPO price, the higher their fee. Walwyn suggested a price somewhere over $8. Frank believed that number was too high. He wanted everyone, including employees and Guelph residents who were interested in buying shares in the IPO, to see the share price go up when it began trading. "If you make a deal and it's not a good deal, the price will dive right away. I'd feel terrible," he said.

And so Linamar went public on January 16, 1986, at $6.75 a share using the stock symbol LNR. With 1,534,100 million shares sold, 58 percent of Linamar remained with Hasenfratz Investments Ltd., a holding company owned 55 percent by Frank and 45 percent by Margaret. The total amount raised was $10,355,175 of which $725,000 was Walwyn's fee, leaving $9,630,313 million for Linamar.

For Frank, going public meant that he now had a vehicle for the future, a way eventually to realize the value of his sweat equity since there was no second-generation successor. "He spoke forever about Linda and about his hopes and aspirations that she would come into the business," said Allan. Although he might not have had his first wish, Frank was consoled by the fact that a major payday had finally arrived. Of the $9.4 million raised, he received $2 million, which he took in the form of a dividend to reduce his taxes owing. Another $4 million went to pay down bank debt, including $2 million that Frank had guaranteed personally. The rest was invested in building the company's fifth plant, Emtol, to make diesel injectors for Cummins Engines.

The shares Frank continued to hold after the IPO were worth $14 million. Frank was not then, and is not now, a conspicuous consumer. He did not rush out to buy anything lavish with his newfound wealth. "My lifestyle didn't change. There was a year, 1998, when my total compensation, including options, was $21 million, and I didn't change then, either. I still have the same friends I had in 1986. They were all at my house last Saturday night."

~

As Frank had hoped would happen, Linamar's share price rose dramatically from the IPO's $6.75. Toronto architect Glenn Hadley almost doubled his investment in six weeks, selling the stock at $12. He told the *Globe and Mail* he'd made money faster on Linamar than on any other stock in twenty years of investing. His gains paid for his daughter's wedding. "She came to the church in a Rolls-Royce," he said.[4] Three months after the January IPO, share price reached $18.50, almost triple the original issue price, a rise that resulted in a two-for-one share split that November. Shares were split two-for-one again in 1993, and three-for-one in 1998 after peaking at $100 share.

Brokerage firm Richardson Greenshields conducted a survey that measured share price performance of the 105 new public companies created during 1986. The top gainer from date of issue in 1986 to April 1, 1987, was Linamar with a 336-percent increase. The average gain of the rest was 25.4 percent.

Share price rose because the company performed well. In the first year as a public company, revenue increased by 90 percent and profit rose 68 percent. Commentators took notice. "1980s-style entrepreneurs such as Hasenfratz, who've put their own money and life's work into their enterprises, view business through different glasses from the traditional Harvard M.B.A. whiz-kids who were the front runners of the 1970s. Too often, those M.B.A.s were taught to think numbers and systems first — and people last. By contrast, the self-taught entrepreneurs, the tool-and-die makers who've made it to the executive corner office from the shop floor, rank people up there with the rest," wrote Patrick Bloomfield in *The Financial Post* in 1987.

"They're a new breed of bread and butter executives with neither the time nor the inclination to adopt the fancy airs and personalized stationery of the big-city company executive. They're not sentimentalists. Most are, by definition, distinctly right of centre in their political attitudes. But they've learned from the school of hard knocks that a high-quality machine doesn't do a job any more efficiently than another piece of equipment unless the worker minding it has an incentive to get the most out of it," said Bloomfield."[5]

Linamar employees had such incentives; Frank kept everyone close. When Ken McDougall started at Linamar in 1987, his drafting table was near the door that Frank used to enter and exit the Ariss plant. Frank would regularly stop, look at what McDougall was doing, and urged him to look beyond his role as a tool designer. "Don't get lost, sitting at you desk. Get into the tool room and the plant. That's where things are happening," Frank told the recent graduate of Fanshawe College in London, Ontario.

McDougall followed his advice and was soon doing estimates aiming to land new business. McDougall, now president, Linamar Manufacturing Group Americas, vividly recalls the meeting with Frank in 1988 to review his estimate for an oil pump required by Detroit Diesel. Frank looked at the drawings McDougall had hung on the walls, asked a few questions, and studied the calculation sheets that led to McDougall's suggested sale price to the customer of $100 per pump.

Said Frank, "Eighty bucks is what they'll pay, not $100. Now, I think we should try to charge more, but I'm telling you that $80 is what they'll pay."

"We ended up getting the program for almost exactly what he said," said McDougall. If the bid had been any higher, a competitor would likely have undercut Linamar and won the business.

Frank continues to offer advice and counsel. McDougall accompanied Frank on a January 2012 trip to Linamar's plants in Mexico. "He's still got the rules of thumb in his head about costs. He's always calculating something; you can see it in his mind. My director of engineering was with us and he was writing down everything that Frank said during the entire flight," said McDougall. "Frank's got a fresh-eyes approach."

⁓

Shortly after Linamar went public, Dennis DesRosiers arranged an appointment with Frank. DesRosiers, who previously worked at the Automotive Parts Manufacturers' Association, had the previous year established his own firm, Dennis DesRosiers Automotive Consultants, the only consulting and market research company in Canada that specializes in the automotive sector.

When DesRosiers arrived for the meeting, Frank's secretary said Frank was in the plant and offered to take DesRosiers to him. They found Frank in greasy coveralls working on a disabled machine.

The two men moved into a side room and talked about a topic DesRosiers can no longer remember. What he has never forgotten is Frank's intimate involvement in the business. "If you have a successful owner crawling under a machine trying to figure out what's going wrong, then you've got a successful company. I've heard those stories from others and I experienced it." Although DesRosiers never did any project work for Linamar, he did buy shares in the company. "It did incredibly well. I had a quadruple. My broker talked me into selling and I've never forgiven him."

As part of the changed corporate structure, Linamar expanded its board of directors. Among the people Frank considered for directorships was Frank Stronach, whose auto-parts business making seats and panels was sufficiently different from Linamar's machined products that there would have been no conflict of interest. The meeting between the two men in Stronach's office north of Toronto got off to a rocky start. As Stronach ushered Frank in, he said, "So, why are you here?" when he knew full well that the offer of a directorship was on the agenda. Frank reminded Stronach that the meeting had been proposed by a Magna vice president. "Coffee or tea? I'm having tea," asked Stronach, as if there was no choice. Frank asked for coffee even though he didn't drink coffee just to keep pace in the game of repartee.

Stronach, a noted horse breeder, had an oil painting of a horse hanging in his office. Frank, who knew nothing about horses, walked over to the painting, looked at it closely, and announced, "That's a *mura*," a Hungarian workhorse. Stronach corrected him, but Frank was insistent. "That's a Hungarian *mura* if I ever I saw one."

"Oh, by the way," said Stronach, "we come from the same empire."

"Yes," replied Frank, "the Hungarian-Austro Empire."

Finally, Stronach asked, "Who is putting on who here?"

"Let's start all over again, okay?" said Hasenfratz. After the conversation settled down and became less like a fencing match, Stronach told Frank, "If I'm a director of Linamar, anything bad I do is a reflection on your company. Do you really want that? If you want something, call me, but I don't want to be a director."

Frank forgave Stronach his earlier remarks. "You have to understand an entrepreneur is an odd person, including myself. The entrepreneur doesn't see left or right, he believes in something and he doesn't give up. That's the reason why some of them go broke and why others are successful. Frank Stronach built a $25 billion company. It's unbelievable. The guy is very bright."

Frank looked elsewhere for additional directors. As a private company, the Linamar board of directors had previously consisted of three members: Frank, Larry Pearson, and local lawyer Hugh Guthrie. Two new independent directors were now added: Kaji Kado, vice president of PPD Technologies Inc., a Toronto-based plastics components manufacturer; and Robert Wilson, recently retired from his position as a purchasing manager at General Motors in Oshawa, Ontario. In 1990 William Harrison, president and CEO of Kenhar Products Inc., a global supplier of components for forklift makers, replaced Kado. "This business is about people, getting along with people, getting to know the right people, and dealing with them. Introductions are very important. The directors were very good for that," said Frank.

Once, when Frank was interviewing a potential candidate for director, the individual told Frank he was interested in the role but first he wanted Frank to resign. "The meeting's over," said Frank.

"Let me explain," said the candidate.

"There's nothing to explain," said Frank. For Frank, the candidate was typical of directors who don't properly understand their role. "They get carried away with themselves. It's not for the board to run the company. You don't control management; you work with management. The board advises us to make sure that our audit committee is correct, that our financials are right, that we don't cheat, and to look out for the other shareholders. You don't want to have a conflict within management and the board. If it becomes that, then you have to ask the board member to resign."

Two hundred shareholders, many of them local residents, plus analysts and investment dealers from Toronto, would attend the Linamar annual meetings held at the Holiday Inn in Guelph. In their speeches, CFO Larry Pearson talked about the financial results while Frank gave details about the company's growth and strategy.

During the question and answer part of the meeting, the same person would ask Frank the same question year after year: "Mr. Chairman, when will this company pay an annual dividend?" That shareholder was Margaret, herself a 45 percent shareholder in Hasenfratz Investments. Frank argued that shareholders should be happy because of the increase in share price and not need a dividend. In 1995, however, the running joke finally ended when Linamar paid its first quarterly dividend of 7 cents per share. The amount was raised to 10 cents in 1997, 16 cents in 1999, and is 32 cents per share today.

In 1992, the company changed its name from Linamar Machine Ltd. to Linamar Corp., thereby eliminating the "limited" status that Frank often joked about, in order to reflect the broader nature of products and sound more like the global player it hoped to become.

⁓

While ambitions might have been large in those early years, executive compensation was modest. The total amount paid to the top eight senior officers when Linamar went public was $700,000. Officers were granted 50,000 stock options, with a further 203,500 options issued to 471 employees — 432 shares for each employee. The value of each option was set at the same as the issue price, $6.75. After a year's wait, employees could exercise their options. Assuming share price had risen, part of the amount realized by selling the shares could be used to repay what was owed ($6.75 x 432 = $2,916) leaving the rest as a capital gain.

Frank was disappointed when most employees exercised their options and sold the shares as soon as they could to collect the cash rather than hold them as an investment. By his calculations, because of share splits, each parcel of 432 shares granted would have grown to be worth about $90,000 today at $16 a share.

Still, he understood their reasoning. "A lot of people who worked for us in those days were tool makers and machinists from Europe. They were very conservative. Their most important goal was to buy a house because they couldn't have one in Europe. So you can't blame them for selling the shares."

Frank also sold some of his own shares, in his case to diversify his investment portfolio so all his net worth wasn't tied up in Linamar. At the time of the IPO, he owned 58 percent of the company but within eight months, he held 42 percent. A year later, his ownership had fallen to 33 percent. At that level, a founder still retains control of the company. "Full control is 51 percent. Thirty-three percent is a safe region. With 33 percent, not much will get done without his permission," said Bob Young.

In one case, Frank traded a block of Linamar shares for the equivalent value in a mutual fund run by AGF. At the time, such tax-free rollovers were possible. As a result of the exchange, he owned a different investment in the full knowledge that AGF would hold the Linamar shares as part of that mutual fund's portfolio for the long term. "When you create a company that's successful and you generate wealth out of nothing, then you deserve to cash in on some of the benefit that you brought to other people," said Walwyn's Allan. "There are a number of equity funds that are quite happy when they make a new investment in a private company that puts money into the pockets of the founders as part of the process."

Frank also divested some of his shares outright. In a typical transaction, he sold 150,000 shares in 1986 for $1.6 million to a group of eight pension funds that included such diverse names as Hudson's Bay Co., Toronto Transit Commission, and York University. In another instance, in 1987, he sold 260,000 shares for $3.3 million to a group of institutional investors that included Imperial Life and Growth Equity Fund.

At one point in the 1990s, Frank's ownership fell to an all-time low of 19.5 percent because he continued to sell his shares, an investment strategy that Frank now regrets. "I have no idea why I did that. I didn't need the money. Selling the shares was not smart business. In the last few years, I keep buying back. I'm a strong believer in the company."

The Hasenfratz family now owns more than 30 percent of the company. Among institutional investors with shares in Linamar, the five top holders own about 17 percent. The largest is McLean Budden Ltd. with 5.4 million shares, or 8.3 percent of the company. The other four — BMO Asset Management, Howson Tattersall Investment Counsel, Dimensional Fund Advisors, and Tetrem Capital Management — each own between 1.3 million and 1.5 million shares. "As long as he's operated the business successfully, Frank's had a good following of people who will give their proxies to him," said Bob Young, his accountant. "People can control a public company through different ways. Frank has always done it by doing a good job. I think it's probably one of the better run companies. He can still protect the fact that what he's got will stay what he's got." For any business leader, that's about as close to eternal life as you can get.

12

FIRING ON ALL CYLINDERS

FOLLOWING UPON HIS SUCCESS with White Farm, Frank returned to the agricultural equipment business in 1989 when Linamar acquired some of the assets formerly associated with that company. He created Western Combine Corp., of Portage la Prairie, Manitoba, to build rotary combine harvesters for Massey-Ferguson. The machines were sold in North America under the Massey name. In the rest of the world, they went under the Western brand.

In the years since the 1981–82 recession many farm implement firms had merged and others had gone out of business. Under such conditions, Frank believed he was re-entering the market at exactly the right time. For him, the nation that held the most promise was the Soviet Union where about 35,000 combines were bought annually, most of them inefficient by North American standards. Not only were there problems with machines cutting the grain properly but also in carrying out the follow-on steps: drying, storing, and managing the crop. Total losses often ran to as much as one-third of the harvest. Western Combine promised to reduce that loss to 5 percent with a package deal that included combines, swathers, balers, grain dryers, and hands-on help from Russian-speaking Canadian farmers.

On his first trip to Russia following the acquisition, Frank was accompanied by Frank Pickersgill, president of Western Combine, and a farming neighbour from Ariss named Ed Thompson. To gauge the market potential of their harvest package, they flew to Chelyabinsk, a northern city near the Ural Mountains. Winter temperatures in Chelyabinsk reached minus fifty degrees Celsius, and soared to plus forty degrees Celsius in the summer when the sun shone twenty hours a day and produced bumper crops in as little as three months.

The Canadians stayed at a collective farm so they could deal directly with prospective end users. Frank knew from his childhood wartime experience that Russians acted in ways that could only be described as depraved, but even so, he was shocked by their living conditions. "They lived with goats in a one-room house that had a big brick stove with the bed on top. They were all heavy drinkers. For breakfast, they tried to be good hosts, so they served six to eight vodkas. I can only drink one and I am half-drunk. By noon, everybody was drunk. The whole scene scared the hell out of me."

As potential business partners, there were numerous other problems. Frank was well aware the Russians were notorious for not paying what was owed on the last shipment so, as an offset, he hiked prices in the early stages. To his surprise he also learned that he was expected to supply what the buyers called "service" vehicles, as if they planned to offer field assistance if combines broke down. In fact, the vehicles demanded were Jeep Grand Cherokees, complete with two-way radios. It was obvious that such high-class transport was nothing more than a personal payoff for the farm managers who signed contracts.

Despite all the possible ways this venture could go wrong, Frank believed there was a profitable future in exports to the Soviet Union. In 1991, he and Pickersgill returned to Chelyabinsk, this time accompanied by their wives, in the hopes of signing some deals. Frank quickly realized bringing their spouses was a mistake when they landed and found that all the bathroom fixtures at the airport had been stripped and stolen. The rule of law did not seem to exist; instead, anarchy reigned.

Local managers were anything but hospitable. They spent most of their time in business meetings behaving boorishly by harassing female translators. Social gatherings tended to disintegrate into drunkenness. Margaret tried to avoid the excessive toasts by drinking water and emptying any vodka she was given into a large glass she kept out of sight. Eventually, their hosts caught on and took away her water glass, leaving her with only the vodka. "She got it down but I thought she was going to faint," said Frank. During a dinner of lamb, served to everyone seated on carpets, as the guest of honour Frank was given the eyes to eat. He swallowed them whole. At 11:00 p.m., the hosts suggested they all strip and enjoy a late night sauna together. The Canadian party declined and thereafter spent as little time as possible socializing with their hosts.

Political instability only added to the travellers' woes. On the way home, the Canadians were staying in a Moscow hotel when senior officials launched a coup on August 19, 1991, to oust Soviet President Mikhail Gorbachev. With airports closed, communications disrupted, and chaos rampant in the streets, Frank considered hiring a car and driver so they could escape through Ukraine to Hungary. Boris Yeltsin, who that June became the first democratically elected president of Russia, led the resistance to the coup by delivering a speech while standing atop a tank outside the White House, the Russian parliament. Muscovites backed Yeltsin and the coup collapsed. Frank was then able to finalize the necessary arrangements to sell his combines and everyone flew home via scheduled airline. Gorbachev resigned, Yeltsin was in the ascendancy, and within a few months more than half a dozen new republics were created. The former Soviet Union was no more. Declared Margaret, "Never again do I want to see Russia."

~

Despite such fierce headwinds in the face of Western capitalism, farm equipment soon began contributing to Linamar's bottom line. In 1992, Western Combine flew 100 tons of farm equipment from Winnipeg to the former Soviet Union on a Russian-built Antonov transport with a seventy-three-metre wingspan chartered from Aeroflot. Aboard were combines, storage bins from Westeel, the Winnipeg division of Jannock Steel, a combine pickup from New Noble Services, and a grain dryer from IBEC, both of Alberta. As part of the package, Linamar also agreed to managed a 68,000-hectare collective farm involving 3,000 people.

That same year Linamar acquired Mezőgép Inc., based in Orosháza, Hungary, a producer of agricultural components for harvesting equipment founded by the former Communist government. Linamar had for three years been developing a North American market for the company's line of corn heads and decided to buy the 350-employee firm to increase Linamar's equipment sales in Europe and the former Soviet Union.

As a former revolutionary, Frank did not return to Hungary as an entrepreneurial owner for sentimental reasons. "Of course, it's a good feeling, but I went back because it made business sense. If it's a better deal in the Czech Republic and we made more money, I probably would have gone there. In business you can't have emotion."

Rather than simply rely on Hungary's low wages for success, Frank sought top managers. In his view, if management is honest, hard working, and properly compensated, they would hire good workers. Among the new managers was Frank's elder brother Marton and General Manager Janos Ivanics. "There was no favouritism. He had to work twice as hard as anyone else did. You cannot play favourites. Once you start then your subordinates want to play favourites and their subordinates follow suit. There is an expression in German: '*Arbeit ist arbeit und schnaps ist schnaps.*' Work is work, drinking is drinking or friendship is friendship. They are two different things. Don't mix the two."

To instill the best business instincts in Hungary's former totalitarian regime, Frank set up an incentive system that rewarded managers with profit sharing plus ownership positions if they reached certain goals. Two managers, including his brother, who was engineering manager, each ended up owning 3 percent of the company when it went public in 1997, the first Hungarian machinery manufacturer to become a public company.

Linamar also undertook a joint venture in 1993 with Russian interests to assemble combines in a former military plant. Because the Russians were unable to pay in hard currency, Frank set up a complicated procedure that included payment to Linamar of 30 percent of the grain saved through Linamar's more efficient methods. In turn, Linamar sold that grain to the Russian government in return for rubles and used those rubles to buy stainless steel that could then be exported to a Western nation and sold for hard currency.

Once he'd proved that Canadian harvesting machines and methods functioned well in Russia, Frank expanded sales to Kazakhstan, Ukraine, and Romania. Corruption and theft were rampant everywhere. In Romania, thirty combines arrived by barge at the Danube port of Braila. Officials declared that the combines contained hazardous material and refused permission to unload the cargo. Local Linamar representatives couldn't resolve the issue.

Frank flew to Braila only to discover that the so-called hazard was transmission oil. "Transmission oil? You can't run a machine without it," he said. Nevertheless, the regulations were clear: oil from foreign sources could be a pollutant.

Massey-Ferguson combine built by Linamar and sold throughout the world.

"What would it take not to be a polluter?"

"One hundred dollars." Frank paid while noting the irony that his plane ticket cost $3,000.

The toll gating in Romania continued. Frank hired security guards and drivers to deliver the machines. The convoy was stopped in the first village and ordered to pay a $100 permit fee for passage. Word spread and other villages en route adopted a similar charge. Each combine came with two boxes of spare parts chained to the chassis. By the time the convoy reached its destination, all the boxes had been pilfered. "There was such poverty in the country that people had to make a living somehow," said Frank.

Even senior officials didn't pay much attention to normal business practices. One elected official from Braila visited Canada to see the manufacturing operations and some of the combines in action on farms. Western Combine paid all his expenses including airfare and hotel. After staying five nights at the Westin Harbour Castle in Toronto, the official attended a dinner at the hotel with Frank, Pickersgill, Helm, and their wives. At the end of the evening, the visitor said he wanted to give his hosts gifts to thank them for their hospitality. He then handed over a bag filled with the contents of the mini-bar in his room. "The liquor is for the men," he said, "and the chocolate is for the ladies." Frank spoke to Pickersgill later and told him to return everything to the front desk so Western Combine wouldn't be charged.

Agricultural sales in Eastern Europe and Asia reached $24 million for the six-month period ended December 31, 1993, then fell to a disappointing $16 million in the twelve months of 1994. In neither period did sales cover production costs. Frank concluded that his idea to supply farm equipment in those parts of the world was not going to work. As a result, joint ventures were ended and Linamar sold its investments in Russia and Kazakhstan. The corn heads produced by Mezögép at Orosháza and Békéscsaba in Hungary were the only agricultural product that attained a decent market share. Operations in that country, now expanded to include auto parts, employ 2,500 today.

In 1996, Linamar sold its North American farm equipment assets for $25 million to AGCO Corp., of Duluth, Georgia, but retained production in Mezögép to ship the same parts to AGCO as it had previously supplied to Western Combine. "The amount of time and effort wasn't worth it. There's so much dishonesty. I like to make a sale, shake hands, and know it's a done deal," said Frank. "We wrote it all off." From one of the few to make a profit from farm equipment, Frank joined the throngs who lost money.

~~◌~~

Fortunately, Linamar had two other arrows in its production quiver, defence and automotive. Defence and aerospace contracts had filled Linamar's order book for years, comprising 55 percent of sales, with 25 percent in auto and the rest in heavy equipment and agriculture. As the Cold War escalated, arms production increased in the United States and the Soviet Union. "The military today is spending, or will spend, a lot more money on conventional equipment than they did a decade ago," Frank told the Toronto Society of Financial Analysts in 1988. He said he couldn't imagine a general giving up his $100 million budget. "It would kill his empire! They're all on an ego trip, those military people. I know, I went to military college."[6]

Serendipity also played a role. At a trade conference in Detroit in 1986, Frank struck up a conversation with a man named Gord Zettle who turned out to be a manufacturer's representative doing defence work. Was the connection happenstance, or was it because Frank was the outgoing type who met people easily? Whatever the reason, Linamar not only won a contract but also received a government grant to produce parts for the T-60 tank. "If it hadn't been for him, we wouldn't have progressed as fast as we did. It was a very good program for Linamar, but it was even better for the government. Because of the grant, over the next few years, we paid eight times as much as the grant in taxes," said Frank.

Linamar's other military contracts in 1986–87 included several deals in the $3 million to $4 million range for the turret drive and transmission parts in the Bradley Fighting Vehicle made by General Electric Ordnance in Pittsfield, Massachusetts. In 1987, Linamar bought Bata Engineering for $9.6 million. Renamed Invar Manufacturing Ltd., the two plants in Batawa, Ontario, employed 300 making specialized equipment and retrofit systems for military vehicles. In 1988, Invar won a $20 million contract from the Department of National Defence to make turrets for the M-113 armoured personnel carrier. But with Ronald Reagan and Mikhail Gorbachev winding down the Cold War as the 1980s ended, military orders began to wane. Because farm equipment sales were also falling, Linamar finally began to focus its main attention on the sector that would form and frame its future: high-volume precision-machined automotive parts.

Frank with, left, Joe Leman, and Ray Demers, checking the first shipment of tank wheels for the U.S. Army, 1979.

In January 1965, Prime Minister Lester Pearson of Canada and President Lyndon Johnson of the United States signed the Automotive Products Trade Agreement, commonly known as the Auto Pact. Previously, most of the parts used on Canadian assembly lines had been made in the U.S. The pact ended all customs tariffs on cars, trucks, buses, and auto parts. In return, the Big Three (GM, Ford, and Chrysler) agreed that for every new car sold in Canada a car would be built in Canada with 60 percent or more Canadian content.

The result was a bonanza for Canadian manufacturing that went well beyond the basics of the agreement. In 1964, only 7 percent of vehicles made in Canada were shipped to the U.S. By 1968, 60 percent of Canadian production was destined for export. Automotive became Ontario's largest industry. In 1964, there were less than 100,000 auto jobs; by the end of the century, there were 500,000 jobs, when one considers the ripple effect on suppliers, trades, construction, and services.

For Linamar, this updraft couldn't have come at a more propitious time. Linamar already had long-standing relationships with automakers. After all, Frank's first job was making oil pumps for Ford. Since then he'd expanded, bought the best equipment, and built a well-trained workforce. Moreover, the geographic location of Linamar in Guelph was fortuitous. Construction began in the 1960s on the new four-lane Highway 401 that swooped along the southern edge of the city and eventually stretched from Windsor, Ontario, to the Quebec border. As a result, Linamar was perfectly positioned halfway between General Motors to the east, the Big Three in Detroit to the west, and Oakville Ford in the middle.

Initially, however, major contracts were rare. Even two decades after the Auto Pact, automotive amounted to only 40 percent of Linamar's sales. Still, that's where the future lay. Defence orders for Linamar continued to be small volumes compared to the potential in automotive. "It's very difficult to grow a business making a hundred of this or a thousand of that. You cannot grow to a size of multi-billion dollars with low-volume jobs. We looked at automotive where vehicle production was 12 million a year and realized that while there were more than 100 models, there were only about seven or eight transmissions, so on average that's 1.5 million transmissions required," said Frank. "If I make a million parts a year, a million parts in 240 working days, and I have a thousand productive minutes a day, I've got to make four parts a minute. For that, you can set up a big production line and spend the $30 to $40 million required because your return will be good. If the job runs seven or eight years, you make big money." In contrast, those auto parts companies that made interiors, door assemblies, or stamped panels had to alter their tooling with each annual model makeover.

Linamar decided to target the "five Cs" — cylinder heads, cylinder blocks, camshafts, crankshafts, and connecting rods — parts that are not redesigned often. "Those are all critical parts of the engine," said Frank. "Today we are the biggest of the five C manufacturers. We probably produce twenty-five million camshafts a year. You've got to be highly skilled and you need a lot of capital. Small shops don't bother us too much."

∼

The final piece of the puzzle in moving out of defence into automotive was free trade between Canada and the United States — a topic the two nations had debated throughout the twentieth century. Canadians rejected reciprocity in the election of 1911, and Prime Minister Mackenzie King almost did a deal in the 1940s, but it wasn't until the election of Brian Mulroney in 1984 that a pact was finally possible.

Like most Canadian business leaders, Frank was a fan of free trade and made numerous speeches extolling the economic benefits. "Canada cannot prosper in the future without free trade with the U.S.A. We cannot isolate Canada and Canadian business from the trend that is in progress on this globe," he said in a speech delivered in Kitchener in 1987.

Frank foresaw five major trading regions: The European Common Market, communist countries, Pacific Rim nations, South America, and North America. "There is only one of those blocks where we fit, and that is with the U.S.A. We must strive to get a free trade agreement with the U.S.A. as soon as possible." He urged eliminating all tariff barriers, equal access to government procurement, and full competition in services, especially transportation and financial.

Frank viewed as "utter nonsense" any attempts to find new trading partners in Asia. "We spend millions on trade shows and trade trips in those countries, paid for by government, and we end up with a total export to those countries of less than we spend on the trips. Their culture, their working habits, their social structure, their values, and their needs are different. They do not make an ideal trading partner," he told audiences. To Frank, the ideal trading partner was the U.S., already home to 75 percent of Canada's total exports.

He also saw free trade as the best route to Canada's long-term prosperity. "If we can enter into a free trade agreement we will have new attitudes and entrepreneurial spirit will flourish. It will bring a higher standard of living and more opportunity for our young people," he said. Frank denounced those who feared a deal with the U.S. and cited President Franklin Delano Roosevelt's famous phrase, "The only thing we have to fear is fear itself." He also reminded listeners of Sir Wilfrid Laurier's 1904 prophecy that the twentieth century belonged to Canada. "I say, let's live up to Laurier's prediction and make it come true in what's left of this century and the next."

~

The 1988 federal election was fought on free trade. When Mulroney won his second majority government, public approval and political will combined to make possible the Canada-U.S. Free Trade agreement signed in 1989 by Mulroney and U.S. President George Bush.

Free trade solidified Linamar's future in automotive. Why bother with foolish forays such as Linamar had tried in the past by making a product such as plastics or combines and then try to find a market? Why not make and sell something for which there was a known demand? That's how the auto parts business worked. A member of the Big Three needed a steady supply of a particular part. Linamar signed a contract and then placed the work in an existing plant or built a new plant to fulfill the order in the full knowledge there was a committed buyer.

Moreover, the Big Three were fighting back against imports by making more fuel-efficient vehicles of higher quality than in the past. The combination of Linamar's new strategy and the changing market yielded a flurry of major auto parts deals: a $13 million contract in 1989 to build diesel engine gear cases and covers for Detroit Diesel; a $20 million, four-year deal to supply transmission gears to Ford; and $29 million over three years to make transmission supports for General Motors. A new plant, Quadrad

Manufacturing Ltd., was built to produce four-wheel drives for Chrysler mini-van assembly plants in Windsor, Ontario, and St. Louis, Missouri.

In 1992, Linamar signed its biggest contract ever, $100 million over five years to produce gear cases for Detroit Diesel Corp. And Rockwell International Corp., of Troy, Michigan, placed an order for 350,000 truck axle shafts annually, a five-year deal worth $40 million. For that contract, the largest Rockwell had ever outsourced, Linamar built another new plant, Traxle Mfg. Ltd.

In that instance, Linamar was the only Canadian company among twenty bidders. Product excellence, technical ability, and price clinched the deal, said Dave Blumenstein, Rockwell's vice president of procurement and business development. "You get to feel comfortable with a management style and their ability to deal with problems," he said. "There's a tremendous amount of pressure for performance. But when the market goes down, you're not being played off against other suppliers," Frank told the *Globe and Mail*.[7]

In 1990, Linamar had thirteen plants with annual sales of $129 million. The company planned to double sales to $250 million within five years, a healthy annual growth rate of 15 percent. "The street where [Linamar] is located is sometimes enviously referred to in Guelph as Hasenfratz Boulevard," declared *The Financial Post* in an article on November 13, 1990.

To further boost automotive production, Linamar plants began achieving difficult-to-get designations such as the General Motors Targets for Excellence, Ford's Q1 quality award, and Chrysler's Pentastar. Such achievements honoured a supplier's delivery, management, and product quality because parts could go straight to the assembly line without any incoming inspection. Suppliers who did not make the grade fell by the wayside. In 1992, Linamar won the Canada Award for Business Excellence in the Quality category from the Government of Canada. In 1994, *Ontario Business* named Frank named one of Ontario's Top 100 Entrepreneurs. He was also selected as Canadian Manufacturing Entrepreneur of the Year.

Linamar was designated by *Forbes* as one of the 100 fastest-growing and profitable small companies outside the U.S. By then, Linamar sales had increased fivefold since going public in 1986 with 83 percent of in the form of exports to the U.S. In 1987, automotive had been only 25 percent of Linamar's sales with defence at 55 percent. By 1991, auto parts had vaulted over defence to become 60 percent of annual sales.

Because of that burgeoning business, the recession of the early 1990s had little impact on Linamar. The company used the same techniques that had worked during the downturn of the early 1980s: cut back break time to increase productivity. "Our company's vital signs remain healthy," Frank told shareholders at the annual meeting in October 1990. "We are getting older, bigger and — I hope stronger."[8]

In 1990, even while overall vehicle sales in North America fell 10 percent, Linamar sales rose 13 percent. "The company forecasts another 48% leap this year in auto-industry contracts to $80 million — an astonishing record when you consider that more than 50 auto-parts firms in Canada have failed in the past year," said a 1991 article in *The Financial Times of Canada*. "So what's its secret? Paying attention to three basics: advanced manufacturing technology; financial probity; and a stable, flexible workforce that also happens to be non-union. And finally, there's Hasenfratz, a tool-and-die maker by training who abandoned his native Hungary in 1956 in the wake of the bloody revolution. A pioneer in the use of computer-aided machining techniques, Linamar invests $12 million annually — 9% of current sales — on new plants and equipment."[9] In 1992 Linamar reached the commanding heights of corporate hierarchy when the company joined the TSE 35, an index reserved for firms with long-term strength and sizable trading volumes.

Differential assemblies for transmissions await shipment to the customer.

The North American Free Trade Agreement, signed in 1993, assured closer ties among the three countries and more business for Linamar. Frank didn't fear free trade with a low-cost country like Mexico, pointing out that demand for Canadian goods would grow. "Free trade is cheaper than foreign aid," he said.[10] But Linamar had also begun to raise its sights beyond North America. In 1990, Linamar signed a $50 million, five-year deal with Steyr-Daimler-Puch of Austria to supply four-wheel drive powertrain components. In 1991 Linamar established a second global beachhead with a five-year $1.5-million-a-year contract to supply a Volkswagen plant in Puebla, Mexico.

By winning contracts abroad, Frank was going global to ensure continued growth. Thirty-five percent of the cars sold in Canada and the U.S. were imports or were made in North American plants owned by foreign firms. A further 20 percent of domestic production contained foreign content. As a result, as much as half the content of all vehicles sold in Canada and the U.S. was made elsewhere.

Wherever Linamar went outside Canada, Frank's methodology was always to hire local managers. "You don't send a German to sell in France and you don't send a Frenchman to sell in Germany. In the U.S., all our manufacturing reps are American. Americans like dealing with Americans and we should respect that. Canadians like to talk about how we're better than the Americans. We're not. Americans are go-getters, they work hard, and they're the easiest people to deal with. With Americans, if you make a deal, the deal goes through quickly. With some other nations, it drags on and on. I haven't got the patience for that."

Acquisitions also played a role in Linamar's expansion. In 1993, Linamar bought Saginaw Overseas Corp., a division of GM that made vacuum pumps in Saginaw, Michigan, then transferred production to Linamar's Mezögép site in Hungary. "To us, the market has never looked any better, and it really doesn't have anything to do with how many cars are being built in North America. It's that more components and sub-assemblies are being made outside the [major auto assemblers], and the fact that North American free trade has opened up a huge market for us in Mexico," said Frank at the time. Added David Allan, who had left Midland Walwyn and joined Yorkton Securities as director of research, "Linamar's products carry a huge value-added component. The pieces they machine are almost proprietary, so for almost all the contracts they win they are the sole supplier."[11] In some cases, the Big Three also supplied funds for tooling, often as much as half the total cash required. Defence-related production, once the company's mainstay, amounted to only 6 percent of sales. "In the automotive business we measure content per car sold in North America," said Frank. "At present every car that is sold, not just produced, we have an average of $135. That is the number we measure continuously and try to improve on."

~

But successful growth isn't just about more sales, it also involves working smarter to improve productivity. Increased efficiencies on the shop floor, including more parts produced on a just-in-time basis, freed up about one-third of the space in Linamar's plants. As a result, plants that had averaged $12 million in sales in 1989 were able to achieve $30 million in sales in 1994 using the same floor space. Thus positioned, Linamar set a daunting target for itself of $1 billion in sales by 2000, more than double 1994 sales of $431 million, itself a huge leap in the previous six years from $113 million in 1988.

By 1995, the automotive sector accounted for $546 million in sales or 87 percent of Linamar's total, up from 60 percent in just four years. Three major clients comprised 60 percent: GM with 33.8 percent of sales, Ford 14.7 percent, and Detroit Diesel at 11.5 percent. In 1996, Linamar landed its first orders with Honda and Toyota. Since then, it has made little headway with those companies. Sales to the Japanese carmakers remain minuscule, less than 5 percent of total sales today, because of a system called *keiretsu* whereby Japanese companies have interlocking business relationships with each other.

For their part, major automakers were spending money on production facilities in Canada, ensuring the industry's continued prominence in Ontario. Chrysler operations in Bramalea, GM in Oshawa, and Ford in Oakville all expanded in the 1990s thereby providing more work for Canadian parts makers such as A.G. Simpson, Automated Technology Systems, Magna, Woodbridge Foam, Ventra, and Linamar. "If you look over the entire sector, Linamar might be the best performer in the group," said Greg Thompson, a senior analyst at Midland Walwyn. Added Rich Morrow, an investment analyst with CIBC Wood Gundy Securities, "Twenty-per-cent growth in earnings and sales is certainly doable over a forecast period of, say, three years."[12]

But gaining and maintaining market share in the midst of such competition was expensive. In 1995, Linamar purchased new machines and precision tooling worth $63 million. Quadrad, Spinic, and Roctel were expanded at a cost of $1.5 million. Linamar also acquired leased premises and land and carried out refurbishing at Comtech and Vehcom for $3.8 million. After those expenditures, 1997 was a breakout year with sales up 27 percent to $771 million and profits 74 percent higher at $108 million. In that year, automotive became more than 90 percent of Linamar's sales.

By then, Linamar was making components for six of Ford's seven transmissions and four of GM's six transmissions. Linamar was also extending its reach beyond individual parts. Fully 36 percent of sales were related to assemblies — from simple two- or three-piece assemblies all the way to complete automotive engines.

In 1998 — two years ahead of the target set in 1994 — Linamar achieved the goal of $1 billion when annual revenue reached $998.3 million. By then, Linamar had 2.5 million square feet of manufacturing space in twenty-eight facilities in Guelph, Hungary, and Mexico. The total included several operations launched or acquired that year: a foundry in Windsor, Ontario, and a start-up business in Saginaw, Michigan, that machined, cleaned, and painted engine blocks; Eagle Manufacturing, a company that machined cylinder heads and connecting rods in Florence, Kentucky; and two plants in Saltillo and Torréon, in north central Mexico, that had contracts with Renault for machining engine components and assembling complete engines. Linamar was the only supplier in the world making a complete engine for an automotive OEM.

In 1998, Linamar employed 8,000, almost one-third of those workers outside Canada. The start-up in Frank's basement thirty-four years earlier had become a global business. For Linamar at least, Laurier's famous prediction about Canada had come true.

13

THE LINAMAR CULTURE

A TOUR OF HASTECH and Camtac, two of Linamar's plants, offers insight into the workings of the company, the foundations built by Frank Hasenfratz, and the vision of Linamar's current management. Everywhere the floors are scrubbed clean, litter-free, and well lit, with finished components carefully stacked in bins, clearly identified, and rarely stationary for long amid the constant whirr and whine of machinery. Like salmon swimming upriver to spawn, parts must keep moving, or paralysis ensues. Machines need to run fifty-two minutes out of every hour or profits shrivel. A visitor rarely sees an employee who's not busy. Overheard conversations aren't about last night's game, they're exchanges of relevant information. Walk around a corner and invariably everyone in sight is hard at work, milling, grinding, polishing, drilling, checking a computer screen, scrutinizing a part for problems, doing something, never nothing as the 450-member Hastech workforce produces transmission components for three different Ford models: Explorer, Mustang, and the F-150, North America's most popular pickup truck.

Linamar is like the United Nations. Employees speak a total of fifty-one languages. At Hastech, half the employees are from South-East Asia. "I don't care about their colour, if they want to work, they can work for me," says Hastech General Manager Frank Carpino, who also immigrated to Canada, in his case from Italy with his family, when he was twelve. Carpino dropped out of school after grade eight and first met Frank Hasenfratz while working for another Guelph firm. He brought a centre punch to Frank for sharpening; Frank did the job in three seconds and charged $2.50. As Carpino watched, he thought, "That's a mistake because now I've seen how he did it." Carpino ended up joining Linamar three years later in 1971.

In 1987, Carpino left Linamar to start his own business. "I don't want you to go," said Frank, "but you have to try it." Carpino lasted five years, until the recession of the early 1990s. Frank phoned and asked him to return. "I'm not ready to come back," said Carpino. Frank called again in three months. Carpino rejoined in 1992 as a supervisor, a lesser post than he'd previously held. Ten years later, he was named a general manager and is now a group general manager with 1,500 employees in four plants: Hastech, Spinic, Quadrad, and Vehcom. Each plant has more than $100 million in annual sales. He has also helped set up operations in Hungary and Mexico. "I learned everything at Linamar. It's like taking a course. Frank would work right with you," said Carpino.

Even when Carpino was overseeing the construction of Hastech, Frank was a regular visitor, making comments like, "You're leaving too much space between machines."

"What do you want me to do, build another Ariss?"

"Oh, we're going to build something that looks presentable," quipped Frank.

"Yes," said Carpino who stood his ground until Frank walked away, satisfied with Carpino's explanation.

"He's the most successful manager we've ever had and he worked his way up from the bottom. He's an example to me all the time, the way he does things," said Frank.

"Frank has a great mind and an incredible memory. He remembers everything. I still go to him for advice," said Carpino. "He is my boss but I consider him a friend. He's done a lot for me," said Carpino. "But it goes both ways. I've done a lot for him, too. I think we did well together over the years."

∽

Waheed Osman, who came to Canada in 1993 from Sudan, followed a similar upward path. Despite the fact that Osman was a graduate mechanical engineer from the University of Khartoum, and had a master's degree from California State University in Sacramento, he started at the bottom earning $8 an hour as a machinist at Roctel. Frank had instilled the ability to spot talent in others so effectively that Scott Zolnai, the production supervisor who hired Osman, said to him, "I'm your boss now, but one day I'll be working for you." Today Zolnai is an engineering technician and Osman is his general manager.

Shortly after Osman joined, Frank came through the plant and stopped to talk to him. "I want you to run a machine for a period of time. We'll see how good you are and then maybe move you up. But be patient." Osman was promoted to junior engineer, then project engineer, program manager, and engineering supervisor. "At Linamar there are no limits because of colour, strong accent like mine, or anything. As long as you can work and take responsibility, you will grow," said Osman.

When he was a new employee, Osman wondered why supervisors were always out of sight, hiding in their offices. As general manager, he moved the supervisors' desks onto the floor under large signs announcing their locations for mentoring, monitoring, and easy access when trouble arose. He also pays cash for employee ideas that improve productivity or reduce costs. Last year at Camtac, Osman paid $67,000, at $100 a time, for good ideas. Put into practice, those 670 ideas saved more than $3 million. "You'd be surprised what good ideas employees come up with. You listen to them and make sure it happens. It might just be something simple like making the height of a table adjustable or putting a rubber mat on the floor to make someone more comfortable," said Frank.

"As a manager, you've got to be able to talk to the guy on the floor. You don't ask everybody to adjust to you; you adjust to everybody. With certain employees, you have to be firm. Others will be very touchy, so you speak to them in a different way. Managers can no longer be rigid. Those days are gone."

Osman has worked closely with countless employees. Typical was Ashraf Mulla who began work at Camtac in 2005 with no skills. Osman spotted his innate talent, made sure he was taught machining, and sent him on a set-up course. Mulla is now an engineering assistant because Osman believed in him and Mulla was eager to succeed, a combination that never fails.

Osman has also added industrial robots that heft and turn the 700-pound cylinder heads they make for Caterpillar. One robot in a protective cage does the work of seven people. "That means we can make it cheaper, get more growth, and hire more people. We've got to compete with Asia," said Osman. None of the seven workers lost their jobs — they moved to other roles where human hands, sharp eyes, and professional judgment were needed.

The Linamar culture is built on pride in accomplishments. Osman likes to tell the story about the dubious Caterpillar officials who stood outside on the frozen ground on Valentine's Day 2003 as foundation work was begun for Camtac. Gary L. Bevilacqua, Caterpillar's global purchasing officer in Mossville, Illinois, looked around, shook his head, and wagered Osman $10 the plant couldn't possibly be open by May 31 as planned. In fact, Camtac was not only built but also had $100 million worth of machinery installed that was up and running with time to spare. The $10 bill Osman won in the bet is framed and hanging in the plant lobby. "I lost this bet and as I said back in February, this will be the best $10 I ever spent," reads the accompanying letter signed by Bevilacqua. "Not only were the first machines installed and powered up by the end of May, Camtac accelerated production to meet our demand to a level of 3,000 heads during the month of September." In February 2011, Camtac made its one-millionth cylinder head for Caterpillar.

Of all the places in the world he could possibly be, Frank by far prefers the plant floor. "I love to go on the floor. I teach, but as I go from plant to plant, I learn a lot too. When I'm at a plant, maybe I see how they're handling a particular situation. I go to the next plant and I say, 'I saw something recently. Here's a good way of doing it.' Now, is it my idea? No, but you learn, you remember, and you pass it on. Whenever you go into a plant, you learn something or you teach something. If you don't do either of those, it was a waste of time."

For Frank, the shop floor is the pulse of his business, a place that stimulates ideas about cost reduction, propels solutions to problems, and provides conversation time with people who might also rise up as he did from machinist to manager. "Look at our management, almost all came from the bottom. If you never worked on the floor, you don't know how they think. Linamar has a unique culture, built from the bottom up. Up to the manager level, the best people come from the bottom because the culture is so ingrained; if an outsider comes in, it's overwhelming. It's different when we get to the executive level. There, we've got a lot of help from the outside, bringing in new people, and learning from them."

According to Frank, Linamar's biggest mistake in the area of personnel has been promoting people too quickly. "A good supervisor doesn't necessarily make a good general supervisor. A good machinist doesn't necessarily make a good foreman. Don't promote people beyond their capabilities. If you do, he fails in front of his family, his friends, and our clients. You had a great supervisor and you destroyed him. Now he's leaving.

"A better approach is to keep people in their current job a little longer rather than promote them too soon. "If you have a good supervisor and he stays a little bit underemployed he will do great things because he can do the job inside out and he can also make changes. If you have to promote somebody, do it temporarily, for six months. Now, if he fails, he is not embarrassed in front of his family and friends. He's not unhappy, he goes back to his old job, and we didn't lose a good man."

As part of his role as general manager, Waheed Osman has trained many others to run operations such as Roctel in Guelph and Wuxi in China. "General managers need to have a sense of urgency, good team work, and we need to communicate. If you talk to Mr. H., he will say, 'Tell me how you're going to do it, don't tell me how you can't,'" said Osman. "There are some guidelines and as long as you are within those guidelines, if you're willing to work extra hours and have new ideas, you're free to do whatever you want. That's what makes the difference at Linamar. Everybody is responsible for their area and there is no bureaucracy."

Every general manager has a plant operating committee that usually meets for a daily update as well as for a more extended session each month about long-term issues. Succession planning is part of the agenda. Managers constantly look for people who can be promoted or need encouragement to get a high school degree so they are better placed for the future.

Managers are expected to know all of their employees personally. "That's good for morale because people feel like a team. It also means you can work with each employee individually," said Frank. "I tell my managers that no one has it made. The day you start to think that, your life will get black because there are always competitors out there."

One unusual leadership trait exhibited by Frank is his apparent desire to keep people off balance. Rather than start a conversation with something humdrum like, "Hello, how are you?" he will often make a comment that seems aimed at making an employee wonder what he had done wrong or how he can improve.

Typical was this encounter with Brian Wade, now vice president of operations, when Wade was a plant manager. Wade was working late, alone in his office, when Frank strode in, saying, "I saw you sitting down," as if that would somehow affect his managerial performance.

"I wasn't sitting down," said Wade,

"I saw you sitting down," insisted Frank.

"No, I wasn't," repeated Wade with equal force.

"Well, that's good," said Frank, then headed for the plant floor to make certain that everyone else was on his or her toes, too.

On one occasion, Frank crept up behind a co-op student, Leigh Copp, and asked, "Do you know what you're doing?" Startled, Copp whirled around and nearly took off Frank's eyebrows with the oxyacetylene torch he was holding. Frank didn't flinch. "As long as you know what you're doing," he said, then turned and walked away. Frank once asked Ray Wagner, two years after he joined Linamar as a young man, "Are you tired at the end of the day?"

Wagner responded, "No, not really. I'm only twenty years old."

Frank shot back, "Then you're not working hard enough."

If Frank asks, "Do you know what you're doing?" and an employee replies, "No, not really," Frank will say, "Are you getting paid for it?" When the employee tells him, "Yes," he'll say, "Well, that's good isn't it?" Or Frank will come upon someone who is slacking off and say, "Do you work for me?" When he or she replies, "Yes," he'll counter, "It doesn't look like it," and keep on walking while the employee scrambles to become productive again.

Frank's demanding nature affects anyone in his path. One day, he noticed two new employees in the accounting department. They didn't seem occupied, so he asked one of them to create a spreadsheet. After handing over a sheaf of papers and explaining what he needed, Frank asked, "Do you understand what I want?" The man said he did. Frank added there was a noon deadline and left him to it. At noon the man presented the work as requested.

Larry Pearson saw the individual leave Frank's office and asked, "What was all that about?"

"Those two new employees weren't very busy. I gave one of them a job and I have to say he seems to know what he's doing," said Frank.

"They don't work for us," said Pearson. "They're from Revenue Canada."

People helped by Frank remain loyal all their lives. When Rance Oosterveld, who trained as an apprentice under Frank at Sheepbridge, left to set up his own machining operation, Frank helped him choose the lathe he bought and agreed to send Oosterveld business. "You have to earn the work, but I'll help you any way I can, providing you can do the job," Oosterveld recalls Frank saying. "He was always considerate. If I had an issue, he would always listen. He always told me, be the best at whatever you do."

～〇

If there is one word that captures the corporate culture of Linamar, that word would be "entrepreneurial." The 1994 annual report featured a short essay on the topic. "An entrepreneur is defined as someone who runs a business at his own financial risk." Clearly, the creation of Linamar in 1964 by Frank meets this definition. Since that time, the company has continued to grow and flourish through its ongoing commitment to the entrepreneurial spirit.

"With direction from Frank Hasenfratz, the concept of running a business as if it was your own, and the taking of some controlled financial risks has been entrusted to Linamar's subsidiary general managers. Throughout the organization, we encourage individual initiative and decision making to stimulate growth and continuous improvement in our business processes."

Frank has his own definition. "To be an entrepreneur, you've got to believe, follow through, and never give up. A lot of entrepreneurs fail because they don't recognize when it's time to change," he said. "You can teach someone to be an entrepreneur by teaching them to truly believe in themselves. But the problem is when you believe in yourself so much you come across as being cocky. If you ask me what did I do wrong in my life, I'd have to think about it. I can find it in the archives somewhere, but I don't harp on it, it happened, it's done, let's move on. I don't get headaches, I give headaches."

As "entrepreneurs," general managers are treated as though they have their own money at risk. They receive 40 percent of their annual compensation in salary with the other 60 percent in the form of a bonus that depends on a variety of measurements including productivity and performance by themselves and their employees. General managers can earn $150,000 to $400,000 annually depending on how many plants they oversee.

Linamar has its own program to train prospective managers. Courses cover a broad range of topics from leadership to metallurgy but the first requirement for any leader is to be a people person. "Whatever you don't know about management, you can learn, as long as you are ambitious. We have jobs where you don't have to be a people person, but if you want to lead people, you better lead by example. In the army, I could order soldiers to do things and they did them. Here, it doesn't work like that," said Frank. "If a worker does something wrong, as a leader you don't step on him. Most people get something wrong once in a while."

Rising stars require an inborn ability to work with people. "I cannot teach you how to be a people person. If you look down on people you cannot be successful," said Frank. "If you don't have people skills, you can be the most intelligent person, but you will be a bad leader. Because you're a good engineer, doesn't mean you're going to be a good manager."

Being in the trenches is crucial. "You have to be with your people every day. You cannot just say, 'Do this, do that,' if you're not willing to do it yourself, if you're not there on the line with them. Don't push them; lead them. If you don't like people, people know. You can fake it for a week or two, but you cannot fake it for long."

To create skilled workers, Linamar runs its own apprenticeship program in conjunction with Conestoga, a local community college. The company also operates a co-op program for grade eleven and grade twelve students who work at Linamar two and a half days a week. According to Frank, many parents don't want their children to become blue-collar workers. In the past, most skilled workers were immigrants. Most parents want their offspring to become doctors, lawyers, or members of other professions.

As a result of those views at home, young people are no longer drawn to the automotive sector as they once were. "The days of the automotive industry being sexy are gone. They can go work at Walmart," said Ken McDougall, president, Linamar Manufacturing Group Americas. "It's not so much about making the money any more. Look in our parking lots. We've got some kids driving BMWs and living at home. My first car was a 1972 Pinto that I bought from my grandfather for $400. We want more and better things for our kids, but they should still have the work ethic. There seems to be a sense of entitlement that 'You need to respect me for who I am and then I'll figure out whether I work for you or not.'"

According to Frank, government support for apprenticeship programs would benefit society. "It's a job multiplier. For every two workers on the shop floor at Linamar, we have another worker in the office. And there are two employees working at other firms — suppliers and services — who wouldn't have a job without that Linamar job."

In his view, Canadians have it soft. "We could expand twice as fast if we had the skilled labour available. A generation of Canadians grew up with a relatively easy life; they know nothing or little about war. We are comfortable. We know all our rights but know little about the other side of the equation called responsibilities. If we are going to succeed on the world market, we must understand the free enterprise system. Wealth is not to live on, but to build on, to invest, and create more wealth."

Recent photo of Frank Hasenfratz in a Linamar plant. (Guelph Mercury)

⁓

Linamar has the usual grandly worded mission statement posted on the wall, but Frank's philosophy is much simpler: "The business is out there; go and get it." To do so he has a two-pronged approach, seek exports and use advanced technology to be competitive globally. Those who become successful exporters must first have achieved success in their home markets, if they are to be able to compete against the Germans, Italians, or Japanese. "Profit is not a dirty word," he told the Fergus-Elora Rotary Club in 1993. "Profit should be admired and enjoyed. We must have self-discipline, sustained hard work, and work smart. Lenin once said, 'Let the capitalists live, prosper ... let them get comfortable and lazy and they will choke on their own fat.' Let this not happen to us Canadians."[13]

Once those capitalist elements are in place, the key is always to have a goal. "Many times it's not a straight line and many times you have to make detours to reach your goal, but if you stay focused and keep your eye on the goal, you'll get there." All along the way, Frank carefully measures everything or nothing gets done. "If you're going to run a marathon, you've got to measure it and you want to do better the next time. I always aimed as high as I could and, when I was getting close, I moved the target higher. And don't say 'I reached my goal' because what's the sense in living?"

For Frank, daily accomplishment is his most treasured possession and what drives him onward to more success. "I enjoy making money but my desires are not great. Making money is a lot easier than retaining money. I've seen too many people make a lot of money and then blow it." More enjoyable is the actual doing. "I love it when I do something and I see the results. I can't wait to do it tomorrow and do it better."

Doing it better does not necessarily mean smooth sailing. In fact, Frank recommends a state of alarm from the moment a plant signs a contract. "I always say, 'Don't panic when you have to ship the parts, panic when you get the order.' Set out a timeline immediately, and then try to stay ahead. Don't think you're going to catch up tomorrow, because tomorrow's another day and sure to bring another problem. If you wait until shipping time, you'll have to hire more manpower to catch up. Now you've got a premium shipment that's costing you money because you're shipping every two hours."

Any entrepreneur needs help to succeed. "How do you get people to work with you and pull on the same end of the rope? Sometimes it's by accident," he said. Frank was recently at an event in Detroit and — as he always does — began talking to the man standing next to him. When the man learned what business Frank was in, he asked, "Do you do any work for John Deere?"

No, said Frank, so his newfound friend set up a lunch with the president of John Deere Canada where Frank could make a pitch. A similar conversation occurred recently in the Shanghai airport. "I started talking to a guy from Brazil. When I asked 'What do you do?' it turned out he was in a similar business as ours. We are trying to go to Brazil; now we've got a contact man."

Such contacts and the corporate reputation lead to new business, and that's when Linamar's loyal and committed employees make a difference in the marketplace. Typical is Ray Wagner who joined in 1979 after finishing high school at a time when two other brothers, Doug and Gary, were already working at Linamar. Doug has since left, but two more brothers, Kevin and Dennis, have joined. In addition, Doug's son Joel works at Linamar. In all, the Wagners have a total of more than 125 years of experience at Linamar.

Ray Wagner started by doing deburring, then worked on lathes, CNC programming, and is now a manufacturing engineer at Hastech. "I feel like a blue-collar guy. I don't have any aspirations of becoming manager. I'm just not into the complications, red tape, and the bureaucracy. Just give me a machine and I'll make you a part," said Wagner.

His role includes improving current jobs, cutting costs, and troubleshooting at Hastech as well as half a dozen other plants when they need help. Recently he was part of large group cobbled together to get a new line working to make a complicated, high-volume part for Ford after the previous supplier had suddenly been unable to produce. Any other parts supplier would have taken a year to tool up for such a job; Linamar promised Ford they'd could produce parts in a month. "It was chaotic, it was crazy, but at LPC they had the floor space and the machines just kept coming in the door daily. People from half a dozen different Linamar plants were crawling all over these machines — all the best manufacturing engineers, set-up men, operators, maintenance people, and inspectors — they just threw everything they needed at it," said Wagner. "We worked liked dogs, sixty, seventy, eighty hours a week to get the line up and running. That's the way things happen at Linamar. They'll promise what most of us will consider ridiculous start-up times. But people get down to business and the job gets done." Not only did Linamar fill in the urgent gap in Ford's production schedule, they won the job on a permanent basis.

～

While Linamar relies on people, numbers matter, too. Frank follows several rules of thumb. For example, every $1 of capital spending must produce $2 of revenue after two years in production. He also likes to keep debt around 25 percent of equity and not spend more on expansion annually than was earned in cash flow (net income plus depreciation on equipment) in the previous year.

Depreciation follows a very specific path on the books. During the first two years, there are no maintenance costs because a machine is under warranty. Beginning in the third year, maintenance costs run counter to depreciation. As depreciation falls, maintenance rises. Taking into account all machines across the company, the average maintenance cost as a percentage of revenue runs about 3.5 percent of sales. "If you buy a $1 million machine and it depreciates 20 percent a year, after six or seven years, it's all paid for. We don't have many machines that are over nine years old. You let your competitors have them — at a cheap price — with the guarantee they're going to use them," said Frank.

For every dollar of sales, Linamar aims to make a profit of 7 percent and a 20 percent return on shareholder equity. "We don't want to be rigid, we can deviate from those numbers, but you need to show me how you're going to get a return on shareholder's equity. You want to have rules, but you also need some flexibility because two and two isn't always four. Sometimes it's five; sometimes it's three," said Frank.

Such careful measurements come into play when considering new plant locations. Linamar has four plants in Mexico because that's where the company's long-time clients are now operating and because shipping parts to them from Canada makes no sense. Linamar's philosophy is that plants in other countries don't compete with Linamar's plants in Guelph for the same business, so manufacturing is carried out in the country of consumption.

The philosophy also makes sense from the points of view of cost and customer needs. "They want just-in-time delivery so if there's a snowstorm in Kentucky the truck is hung up for two days. Secondly, that means we have a lot of inventory on the road. A truck takes a week for the round trip." If a truck carrying 50,000 pounds of parts costs $4,800 to cover the distance, that's about 10 cents a pound. Linamar sells parts at the equivalent of $1.40 a pound, so already the company has lost 10 cents a pound because of shipping, or about a 7 percent reduction. Better to be located nearby and have minimal shipping costs.

Of the four Mexican plants, two are profitable and two are not. In Canada, it takes up to two and a half years for a plant to be profitable. In Mexico, it can take twice as long. "In Mexico the problem is not with the skilled labour, it's the bureaucracy in management. We had some very good Mexican managers but we had to let a lot of them go. They didn't see the urgency," said Frank. Even with those changes, the average machine in Mexico runs for less than fifty minutes an hour instead of the fifty-plus minutes typical in Canada.

Such a rigorous approach does not mean Frank blindly hews to rules. "If you're going to do everything the way the book tells you, you're just another company. You can make a living, but that's not the idea — just to make a living. The idea is to create something. You have a lot of people and if you want to keep the good people, you have to grow so you can promote them. If you cannot promote them, they're going to leave you. As result, we grow at an average of 15 percent a year compounded so we can keep our good people and let them help us keep growing."

Over the years, Linamar has reduced its operating costs by accepting money from a variety of government programs. However, Frank doesn't see such funding as the foundation of corporate success. "When you get a grant or a tax break, do not sign a production contract because of the grant. To rely on government assistance and build a business on it, you're going to go bankrupt sooner or later because governments change and policies change. We apply and if we can get the money, fine, but the truth is, we would sign a contract without it. The job has to stand on its own feet to make a profit, but grants helped our growth tremendously."

People who know Frank well say he possesses some particular qualities that are not present in most business leaders. "What sets Frank apart as a business-man are his knowledge and his drive," said accountant Bob Young. "Frank worked six days a week. I don't think he would know all the employees now, but back in the early days of one, two, and three plants he would know them all and treat them well." Frank is also decisive. "If Frank wants to get some-thing done, he'll get it done as quickly as possible. On the floor, where he's watching the work, he's very quick to make a decision," said Young.

One of Frank's most enduring traits is his willingness to share know-ledge. When Rance Oosterveld was in sales with Stackpole Ltd., a powertrain supplier, he would run into Frank in Detroit when they were both visiting GM headquarters. "He was never one to sit back and keep things to himself. He'd always be saying, 'Let me show you this,' or 'Here's what we're going to do.' He's a very confident person. He always had this vision that he was going to show people that he had more credibility than they gave him credit for at that time. To this day, I feel honoured that he remembers me, has patience and time for me, and calls every once in a while to talk."

For Frank, such friendships are a natural outcome of his leadership style and the culture he has created. "I like to achieve things, I like to work at things, and I like to know that I can do it. And, I like to pass knowledge on to others." Above all, never believe a problem, an issue, or a competitor can beat you. "I've had to change course, but I've never been defeated." And always, there's the sharing. As the visitor leaves the plant, another group arrives, invited by Frank to take a good look around at whatever they want.

14

STARTING AT THE BOTTOM

W HEN NANCY AND LINDA Hasenfratz were growing up their father rarely talked at the dinner table about the business he'd founded, but both daughters were well aware of Linamar, what it meant to the family, and the value of hard work. "He and my mother both instilled a good work ethic in us and an appreciation for the value of a dollar. They encouraged us to get out into the working world when we were teenagers," said Linda. "From the time I was fourteen I always had a part-time job. I liked to earn a little money."

Linda's first job was making popcorn and selling candy at the Three Star Cinemas, a ten-minute bicycle ride from home. At sixteen, she started work at Suzy Shier, a ladies' wear store in the Stone Road Mall on the other side of the city. She clerked during summer holidays and on weekends while attending Guelph Collegiate Vocational Institute where she was a member of athletic council, and played basketball, badminton, and volleyball. Linda graduated in the top three of her class in 1985 and was designated an Ontario Scholar, an honour given only to those students with an average of 80 percent or higher.

Frank and Margaret hoped Linda would join the family business. "She is very, very intelligent and she has the drive that her father had — to do better, to do more. The drive to succeed is very important to both of them," said Margaret in an interview with the *Guelph Mercury*. "The company was something he started from scratch and he felt he wanted somebody in the family to carry it on. We felt Linda was very capable. But we didn't want to force her."[14]

Instead, Linda took a four-year honours Bachelor of Science course at the University of Western Ontario in London, Ontario, and worked summers in Guelph for two different pharmaceutical companies, Hart Chemicals and McNeil Products. After graduation in 1989, Linda joined Servier Canada, the French pharmaceutical firm, as a sales rep. Her job, calling on physicians in Toronto's downtown and east end to tell them about the company's products, paid well: $35,000 a year with a car provided.

In 1990, after working at Servier for a year, Linda decided to join the family business. "Suddenly the light bulb went off. I don't think it was anything specific. Maybe I proved to myself that I could succeed on my own, that I didn't need to have a job from my dad in order to be a success. It was also the realization that Dad had created something that I shouldn't turn my back on. I was enjoying business. I liked being a part of a business, and being

The Hasenfratz family celebrates Linamar's twenty-fifth anniversary with Frank's first lathe, 1989. From left: Nancy, Margaret, Frank, and Linda.

a businessperson. I realized that I was interested in learning more about other areas of running a business, seeing what we were doing at Linamar, and finding out what the opportunities were for me," she said.

Her parents happened to be on a ski holiday in Colorado so Linda phoned and asked when they were coming home. Sunday, they replied. She said she had something important to tell them when they got back. They asked her to reveal her news right then but Linda insisted she wanted to talk in person. After they hung up, Frank and Margaret concluded there could only be two reasons for such a call, either Linda was ill or she was pregnant.

When Linda met her parents at Toronto's Pearson Airport she said, "I want to come into the business. I think it will be a really good opportunity for me to come back to Guelph. If I work well and play my cards right, I might be running the company one day." Her parents' eyes welled up with tears as they heard the welcome news and embraced their daughter.

When Linda and Frank met at his office a few days later, Frank told her, "There's only one job you start at the top and that's when you're digging a hole. And guess where you end up? In the hole. So, you'll start on the bottom and work your way up. I did the same thing. I learned everything on the floor, finances and everything else, as I went along. I want you to put on boots and run a machine. It will take you eight years to come into head office."

As the discussion continued, Frank told Linda, "You've got to learn how to run each machine, but *you've* got to do it, not just when you're beside another guy. I want to make sure you can produce as many parts as he can, then you'll understand. You've got to measure yourself. Without measurement, nothing gets done. You want to know: Can you produce as much as the other guy?"

At the time, recalled Frank, "My wife thought I was crazy. But if you ask Linda today, she'll tell you that she knows the people and how they think because she did it. Linda is very capable, she's well liked, and she knows how to talk to the people on the floor."

The complete eight-year plan was not fully laid out at the beginning but there was a general agreement that the first few years would involve working on the shop floor followed by roles in quality control, engineering, and production that would give her an understanding of the basics of the business. Because Linamar was growing quickly, they knew openings would occur, as she became ready for them.

At twenty-four, Linda's first job, in July 1990, was machining steering knuckles on a Boehringer VDF-250 lathe at Hastech. She wore jeans, a shirt, safety glasses, and safety boots. "I think I crashed the machine a few times," she said. "It's not an easy job. I have a lot of respect for those who do it. As time went on, I learned how to be efficient and to keep the machine running. If it's not running, it's not making money. I learned the terminology, the processes, the materials, and the different parts. I learned how to measure parts, what the different gauges were called, and how to use them. There was a lot to learn."

Relationships with her fellow employees required careful attention. "In any of the positions that I stepped into there was always a period of time where you had to win the respect of the people around you. Obviously, people's first instinct when the boss's daughter gets put into the department is, 'Oh, great, now I'm going to need to carry her.' So it always took some time to win people over and show them that I wasn't there for a free ride, that I was willing to put in the hours, that I was capable, intelligent, and wanted to do a good job. You can't walk in and say, 'Respect me,' you have to earn it," said Linda. "That happened with every position, not just on the shop floor. The people on the floor were really supportive. They were happy to teach me and maybe endured a few more visits from the boss than they might normally have had because my dad was out there quite a lot."

After a month working on the lathe, where the part being machined rotates at high speed, Linda moved to a vertical machining centre so she could learn the second basic type of machining: milling. In that case, the part is held stationary while the tool moves. Next, Linda worked on an Urawa UB75 jig-boring mill in an environmentally controlled room making high-value parts for a helicopter project. "When I was working on the lathe, I was doing high-volume automotive work. It was precision machining, still within a certain tolerance, but it wasn't like the tight tolerances they were doing in the jig bore room. I was working with skilled people who would do the set-up so I could see how the set-up was done. Once the set-up's done, you're still running parts like on the other high-volume job, but it's more precise. As a result, there was more gauging because the cost of the materials in those products was very high," said Linda. "Not that scrap is ever acceptable but typically we see scrap levels of half a percent to 1 percent on an automotive high-volume line, but on very high value parts, you can't afford to scrap even one part. You're doing a lot more offsets, tool changes, and adjustments, so that was very interesting."

Beyond the specific techniques, Linda learned a broader lesson. "I think it's critical for anyone in business to get a good understanding of the nuts and bolts of what they make. It was an opportunity for me to see first-hand what it was like to work on the shop floor, to understand a little more about the machining process, and what was important in the manufacture of the products at each of those stages. I learned the importance of quality and consistency of production — and keeping production levels high — to the success of the business. I had an opportunity to meet a lot of great people who are still with the company that I can call on for support. I liked working my way up and starting at a point where I could really learn the basics of our business."

After those shop floor roles, Linda spent a few months in the quality lab. Whenever a part is set up on a machine for the first time, a sample is sent to the quality lab for a full workup to ensure that the part precisely matches the blueprint created by the client. Once approved, the machine is given a "first off" or okayed to run.

Linda then spent time in engineering, doing computer-aided design and learning how to program machines. "She was very down to earth, very easy to get along with," said Ray Wagner, a manufacturing engineer who trained Linda on the CAD/CAM system that generated the first process drawings at Linamar. Frank happened to come through the plant, stopped to look at one of the drawings on the computer screen, and asked, "Did you do that?"

"Yes," said Linda, "I just finished it."

"No, you didn't make that."

"Yes, I did," insisted Linda, who laughed, made a printed copy, and handed it to Frank, saying, "Here, do want to take it home and put it on the fridge?"

Next, Linda went to production control, the department where work is scheduled. There she measured the output from the equipment on the factory floor and worked with suppliers and customers so the shop had the correct material, in the right amounts, on hand to keep the line running. "I had spent a lot of time learning what we were doing technically and now I was learning more about the business side and how to manage that," said Linda. "How do you move from the order to getting it scheduled in the shop, lining up the materials, and keeping the customers informed. It was good to see the whole process." By then, Frank knew that he'd made the right decision to let her join the business and slowly work her way up. "After a year, I knew she was going to be okay," he said. Succession was assured.

~~~

In September 1991, Linda left Hastech to be materials manager at Traxle, a new plant built to produce axle shafts for Rockwell International. Linamar had bought the equipment from a Rockwell plant in Pennsylvania and moved the machines to Guelph. As materials manager, Linda oversaw two employees and worked with suppliers to schedule production of the 200 different axle shafts Traxle was making for four different Rockwell plants.

After two years as materials manager, Linda replaced the Traxle accounting manager who took a ten-month maternity leave. That role meant she managed three employees on the financial side of the business, overseeing income statements, balance sheets, accounts payable, and receivables. When the accounting manager returned, Linda moved to marketing for five months. "The strategy all along had been — assuming that I could handle each successive level of responsibility — that I would work my way up to be CEO one day. There was a good understanding between my father and myself that if either of us felt we weren't comfortable with the next move, then we wouldn't make that next move."

Despite the smooth flow of roles with greater responsibilities, there were frustrations about being the boss's daughter who constantly had to prove herself to a new group of people. "I got a little weary of that. I'd change jobs and have to do that all over again. I'd think, 'Oh, what a pain, why can't you talk to the people that I just worked with.' I couldn't believe I had another set of people who thought that I'm not smart, I'm not going to work hard, and I'm just here for a free ride. But once I got past that stage then it was all good again."

~~~

In January 1995, Linda was appointed operations manager at Comtech, another new plant. She was responsible for hiring and managing the individual leaders in several departments including quality control, materials, finance, engineering, and human relations. Linda reported to Comtech general manager Jim Jarrell. Linda and Jarrell would rise through the ranks together. Jarrell had grown up in London, Ontario, where his father was an executive at General Motors. Jarrell worked at GM during the summers in sales and marketing while taking a general arts degree at the University of Western Ontario. After graduation, he joined GM full-time but soon concluded that the company was too bureaucratic for his taste.

He was hired at Unimatic, one of the Magna plants in Toronto, working on the shop floor, then moved through roles in sales, marketing, production, and operations in different Magna plants. After five years at Magna, he left to start a small business, Ultramat, in Breslau, Ontario. "I used to get there in the morning, set up a die, handle the cash receivables, get the people on the floor oriented, jump in the truck, drive the parts to one of our customers, give out some cigars to the people on the floor, and then put my tie on, go around the front to the purchasing office, do some sales calls, draw up a quote, and then go back to the Ultramat plant to start the whole routine again."

Jarrell joined Linamar in 1991 in sales and marketing. Ten months later, Frank asked him to become general manager of Hastech, which was losing money. "They really didn't have enough business, the jobs were not priced right, and the cost structure was out of control," said Jarrell. As is his custom, Frank was demanding. On Jarrell's first day, Frank dropped in to say, "I hope everything's going well." On the second day, Frank visited again and asked, "Are you making any money?"

Within six months, Jarrell had added sufficient new business from GM and Ford for the plant to be profitable — all under Frank's watchful eye. "He's been my mentor day in and day out ever since. He knows business and he knows machining. I bounced ideas off him and he would give me guidance," said Jarrell. "I probably talked to him every day, including Saturday. I'd ask for advice or he'd give it unsolicited. That sounding board was really helpful."

Topics covered included putting together a quote, purchasing a machine tool, or improving cash flow. "Frank knows how to eliminate waste and make sure you're adding value. If you have a technical cost issue, there's no better person to go to. A general manager today probably does not have the same connection to Frank as I had the luxury of having," said Jarrell.

Once Hastech was profitable, Vehcom and Comtech were added to Jarrell's duties and he named Linda as operations manager of both. Each plant had about 300 employees and annual revenue of $60 million. Linamar grew by building such plants when the company had a new contract, unlike Magna, which built a plant every three months whether there was an order or not. "Linda and I had a good relationship from day one," said Jarrell. "We never really had a really major blowout. I think we complemented each other. We're both aligned on the way to run a business, set up systems, have a process to follow up, and to be on top of issues. I had philosophies on meetings, systems, and quality and she was great on implementing that with the folks there."

Their success as a team was immediate. "An OEM [original equipment manufacturer] needed someone to produce transmission cases for them for six months, a part never before outsourced to a supplier. We jumped on the opportunity," said Linda. "Within a matter of two or three days we had purchased all the machining centres that we needed for what was a very complex job. It's not run-of-the-mill work. To put it in context, an OEM would probably spend two years from the start of planning to bring in a line, get it approved, and get it into production. We did it in two months."

Almost twenty years later, Comtech is still producing 400 transmission cases a day for that customer. "We can boast of being one of maybe two suppliers globally with years of experience in machining transmission cases which we can lever off for further growth," she said.

Throughout the process of being promoted, Linda always felt ready for the next position. "Dad didn't want to set me up for failure. He wanted to make sure I had all the ingredients for success and that I had the opportunity to learn in each of these jobs before he ever suggested that I take on a management or leadership role," said Linda. "I couldn't have been a materials manager if I hadn't spent nine months in production control working for a materials manager and learning what that job was all about. And it would be hard to be an operations manager if you hadn't been a materials manager. I ran the accounting department so I saw how the plant operating committee worked. As a result, I was in a good position to step in and be an operations manager because I'd been part of the team below it. You've always got to have that succession plan if you want to be successful."

While other general managers ran one, two, or maybe three plants, Jim Jarrell was soon in charge of six plants in Guelph: Hastech, Comtech,

Vehcom, Diversa Cast, Roctel, and LPP, where Linamar made gas engines, a business bought in 1997 from Onan Engine. Because Linda reported to Jarrell, she had the opportunity to work with an unusually large number of leaders in all of his plants and observe a wide variety of management styles. "You have to learn to deal with all kinds of different personalities and different management styles," she said. "The more different styles that you have the experience of working for and with, the better you're able to develop your own management and leadership style. I worked under a very technical manager who came from an engineering background who had a different style of management to a guy like Jim who was much more sales focused and entrepreneurial, and looking to build the business from a sales perspective. Another general manager I worked with had come from a shop floor background so it was really interesting to see the different management styles and the strengths of each as I developed my own leadership profile."

Linda came to realize there was no one leadership type. "You can be a good leader whether you're an outgoing, enthusiastic person or a more quiet, thoughtful, introspective person. You just engage people in a different way. There are lots of examples of leaders who have acted in completely different ways. Martin Luther King was fiery and made inspirational speeches in a completely different way than Gandhi, who was more quiet and introspective but equally inspirational. I'm definitely more on the passionate side than the introspective type."

Among all the possible leadership role models, Linda also watched her father's winning ways. "You've got to have strong leadership, you cannot try to please everybody," said Frank. "You shouldn't look for *who* is right or who is wrong, you should look for *what* is right and what is wrong. What is right is strong leadership to run the company for the best profit. I don't try to please everybody. A social director's going to please everybody, kiss all the babies, and so on. I haven't got time for that. Our family owns one-third of the company. Why would we make a decision that's not good for the entire company?"

In such an environment, a manager could do multiple jobs, but there are better ways to use managerial time and talent. "You're going to manage 200 people, so if you can do four jobs, and 200 people are watching you do it, you're not getting anywhere. You want to delegate, not to do," he said. Another relevant element of the role is how a leader treats people. "If you don't treat people well, they will do the job well while you watch them, but you can't watch them twenty-four hours a day. So you have to convince them what's important, and why we have to produce it like that, and everything works a lot better."

Ethical behaviour is essential. Bribes or gifts are outright refused. Once, Frank was negotiating the price on a machine and the manufacturer offered him two first-class airline tickets to the country where the machine was made. "How much does that cost?" asked Frank. "Seven thousand each," came the reply. "Okay, take $14,000 off the price," said Frank. "Nobody's ever done this before," said the vendor who reduced the price as Frank demanded.

Leadership by example is the best, according to Frank. "Words help, but actions count the most. When people have to work until midnight because we've got to get things out, I don't go home and play cards. Even if I cannot help, the least I can do is I drop in just to show I acknowledge that they are there. When I hear one of our financial guys say, 'Well, I cannot help with anything,' yes, you can. Buy donuts and coffee and take them in at three in the morning. Jim Jarrell does that all the time. It's very important. People want to be acknowledged."

Caring about people is one of the many leadership lessons that Linda learned along the way. "You have to remember them, remember something about them, and make them feel important because they *are* important. It's not about *creating* that feeling, you have to really care about that person, and how they are. A leader who is that way creates a great deal of allegiance and respect. You want to follow somebody that you respect and who cares about you, because then you know that they're going to lead you on the right path."

As for her own leadership style, Linda describes herself as team focused. "I'm a big believer in sharing information with my whole team and getting their input on decisions. I'm not somebody who looks for consensus. I'm more comfortable making the decision myself, but I do like to get input from a variety of perspectives. I like people, I like interacting with people, and I like to create an environment where you know each other well and feel comfortable talking about things. I encourage people to be open about their ideas, good or bad. I recognize I don't always have all the answers. Sometimes I'll come up with an idea that's not a good one so I appreciate it if somebody gives me some feedback and says, 'That might not be the best thing for us to do because of this, this, and that,' instead of just blindly following me and doing it."

Linda is the first to admit she is opinionated. "I do have strong opinions and it can be plainly laid out for people. I don't think there's ever a question as to where I might stand on a particular topic. For some people, that's harder to accept than others, but once you work with people they become comfortable with that."

Linda's education in maths and sciences has also made her an analytical leader. "I like to dig into the numbers and understand what's going on underneath instead of just on the surface. I'm a big believer in data-driven decision-making that's not just emotional. Gut instinct is really important, but I also think — where time permits — the best way to make a tough decision is to lay it out, look at all the facts, then make a decision."

Leadership is also about trust. "People have to earn your trust. I'm probably too trusting of people right off the bat. Overall, I think you give people a little and see what they do with it. If you can see that they've maintained that confidence, then you give a little bit more. The longer that you work with somebody, obviously the more comfortable you're going to be and the more you'll trust them and value their opinion."

Negotiations with outsiders are a different matter. There, you rely entirely on the signed contract. "There are lots of strategies that might be played on that side of the table that you're employing as well. You're certainly not going to take everything that's being said at face value. You need to be savvy about what somebody's saying and what makes sense," said Linda. "At the same time, understanding their position really helps you to know where your leverage is and where you can take something. What's always key is knowing how badly they want something compared to how badly you want it. You should always not want it that badly; if you do then you're going to compromise somewhere on the price or on some terms. So, as difficult as it may be, you need to be disciplined and willing to walk away — even from something that's strategic — if you can't get the terms that you think are necessary. That said, you don't want to walk away from a great opportunity for something inconsequential, so you need to understand going in what are your non-negotiables so that you're clear on where you're willing to go — but not beyond. If you're prepared ahead of time, then it makes the negotiation easier because you know you're willing to give over here, but not on something else."

Despite the best intentions, deals can go sour. "I recall one particular deal that appeared to a very good opportunity for us to grow the business and tap into some unique talents that this person had. He was a very good sales person, appeared very competent, and very trustworthy. We entered into this agreement eyes wide open without having done enough homework and background checking on the individual," said Linda. "It ended up that this person was not quite as honest as we may have liked and was a little more self-serving than was really appropriate. We ended up with somebody that we really didn't want to be in bed with. That was a huge lesson for me. You don't enter into a business arrangement with somebody unless you do enough background checks and really understand who you're dealing with."

In such cases, a company's strength can also be its biggest weakness. "We're a great operations company, so we're very tactical. We can move much more quickly on contracts than many other companies, but you can't allow that to creep into the strategy side of your business. You need to be much more thoughtful and spend a lot more time thinking about and evaluating a decision that has long-term impact. If it's something that has an impact lasting only hours or days, then you can spend minutes making that decision. But if it's a matter that could impact you for a decade, then spend several months on the decision. I think we all need to be a little more disciplined in that regard."

Companies that don't get decision-making right can suffer. "There are companies that do a great job of spending lots of time thinking about the long-term strategic decisions but haven't learned to be swift on the operational, short-term stuff. You also see small companies that become top heavy with bureaucracy; they haven't learned how to maintain their nimbleness as they've grown. Similarly, there are large companies where you see the exact opposite. Getting that balance is really important." For Linda, a good work-life balance, thought by some to be impossible for women in leadership roles, would prove to be just as do-able.

15

THE FAMILY WAY

As if running both Comtech and Vehcom weren't enough on her plate, at the same time Linda and her husband Ed Newton were thinking about starting a family. She had also been considering the two-year executive M.B.A. program offered by the Ivey School of Business at the University of Western Ontario. The two-year course required two weeks of classes in London at the start of each school year, two days a week in the classroom every other week, plus innumerable hours of study, preparation, and assignments. Linda asked Frank, "Ed and I want to start a family and I want to do my M.B.A. What do you think I should do first?" "Do both," he said. "I thought, 'What the hell?' So I did," said Linda.

Linda and Ed Newton's first meeting couldn't have been more serendipitous. He's from New Zealand where many young people travel abroad for a year or two once they finish school. London, England, is often the first stop so Newton headed there as a young man of twenty, worked at odd jobs, then decided he'd like to learn to ski. He'd heard about a man in Klosters, Switzerland, who'd lived in New Zealand and had a soft spot for Kiwis, as natives of New Zealand are known, so he went to Klosters in hopes of getting work from him to help pay for ski lessons. Newton made the connection and landed a job stacking wood and shovelling snow.

One day while skiing during a terrible storm, he took refuge in a kiosk

where he met another Kiwi, Steve Oliver. They became friends and both
returned to London where Oliver was a carpenter. Newton learned the trade
from Oliver and they spent four years together renovating houses. Oliver
went to New Zealand for a holiday and, although he lived on the North
Island, happened to be travelling on the South Island where he picked up
two Canadian hitchhikers, Julie Morrell and Keren Adderley, who were high
school friends of Linda.

Steve and Julie immediately fell in love. She took off for London with
him, abandoning Keren who returned to Guelph on her own. After Steve and
Julie were married, they moved to Guelph. Meanwhile, Newton had gone
back to New Zealand, worked for a while with his brother, but decided to
return to London. En route, he stopped in Guelph to visit Steve Oliver in the
summer of 1992 and while there met Linda. "The heavens had to align for
that one," said Linda. "If he hadn't chosen to go to Switzerland, if he hadn't
gone skiing that day, if Julie and Keren weren't hitchhiking, if Steve didn't
happen to be travelling there."

Ed Newton stayed in Guelph and started his own construction business. He and Linda were married in 1994. Newton's company, Kiwi-
Newton Construction Ltd., has numerous clients in the Guelph area and
has done some work for Linamar. All contracts for new plant construction at Linamar are put out to tender with the awarding process over-
seen by Terry Reidel, an independent director who chairs the board's
Human Resources and Corporate Governance Committee. As a result,
Kiwi-Newton has no inside track on Linamar projects. "Everything is fully
disclosed. We're very careful about that and we're very careful to ensure
that anything he's doing for us is market tested so that we know it's the
best price," said Linda. "He's also our secret weapon for foreign expansion. When we build overseas, the instinct is for it to be overdesigned and
overbuilt. They see big wealthy foreign companies coming in and they rub
their hands. He will ensure that the specifications are appropriate to what
we want and then he'll negotiate the price for us. He's saved us millions."

In addition to starting a family, Linda also followed Frank's advice
about her M.B.A. When their first child, Katie, was born in March 1996,
Linda was in her first year of the M.B.A. program as well as in the midst of
a two-year renovation to their house. Following Katie's birth, Linda took
three months off, returned to work half time in June, and was back full-time

by August. "I thought, no matter what I ever do, it'll be easy compared to all this."

M.B.A. classes were held in Markham, Ontario, with other students gathered in Calgary and Edmonton, all participating via video conferencing with their professors in London. "Once you got used to the technology, it worked very well, and I really got a lot out of the program. I found it very informative and really a great complement to the more practical education that I was gaining while working in the plant as operations manager and general manager. I was learning things at school that I could literally come to work and do the next day. I still have the binders and pulled them out just recently to have a look at something."

At one point during Linda's studies, a female executive addressing the students told them, "You can't have it all. You need to choose between family and career." As an example of someone who was doing both, Linda was upset by the declaration. "At the time I was about seven months pregnant with my second child, starting up my second plant at Linamar, and managing to squeeze in an M.B.A. I remember being angry with her for discouraging others from having both elements in their lives just because she had chosen to follow a different path. She made the choice that was right for her, and was happy with that, but why discourage others from making a different choice? You *can* have it all if you want. My philosophy is to live every moment of your life. Live more, laugh more, do more."

Linda graduated in May 1997 and Emily was born in July. After three months off, she returned to work full-time in October, and at thirty-one was named chief operating officer (COO), replacing Larry Pearson, who took early retirement. Initially, Bay Street analysts were not impressed by her appointment, and their negative comments drove share price down 6 percent on the day Linda's new role was announced.

Most of the senior managers at Linamar welcomed her promotion, but not all. "To me, it wasn't an issue, whereas some of the guys that are no longer here couldn't adapt," said Jim Jarrell. "I knew Linda well, so I knew she was very capable and very bright. I knew Frank wasn't going to jeopardize the company; it's not his way. His way is that family is important, but this is his business. We're not going to screw up the business. I think the family culture concept in the business is good. You try to keep that ingrained in the culture. I looked at it as totally natural and I think it's proven itself out."

The promotion to COO meant that Linda went from running three plants to seventeen plants with four senior executives reporting to her: chief financial officer, as well as the heads of sales and marketing, operations, and human resources. In addition, Linda had several vice presidents who were in charge of more than one plant, and all the other plant managers reporting to her, about fifteen reports in all. "Would it have been better to build up to that responsibility than make such a leap? Of course, but you can't be afraid to give it a go and work it out," Linda said in a speech to the Women of Influence in 2010. "I asked a lot of questions, relied on some great people and made it work. I will never regret that."

Shortly after becoming COO, Linda was pregnant again. The couple's third child, Tommy, was born in November of 1998 and Olivia came along two years later. In each case, Linda worked from home during a brief maternity leave then returned to work full-time as Linamar grew in three years from seventeen plants to twenty-eight plants. "Although we already had one facility in Europe, we were very Guelph-centric before. Now we were expanding into new countries while building new plants in Guelph. We had a lot of growth all at once which really took its toll in terms of start-up costs and just managing the new complexity of the organization," said Linda. "Because we were Guelph-centric, everybody knew what was going on so you didn't have to work very hard at communication. But when we started to expand internationally, it became more and more difficult to manage that without a few rules while not losing the individuality and entrepreneurship of the plants."

With plants in Guelph, Hungary, the United States, and Mexico, Linda reorganized the company on a more formal basis in order to standardize new procedures. She took large groups of plants where one person oversaw as many as seven facilities and reduced the number to three or four with a group vice president in charge. She also eliminated the standard practice manual, a binder that had grown too thick over the years and included too many detailed descriptions of every activity from how to quote a job through setting-up machines to quality control. "There were so many procedures that nobody was following them. They were too specific and went into too much detail. We went through them all, slimmed down the manual, and replaced items with simplified procedures," said Linda. The eventual outcome was the Global Operating System Playbook, a minimalist description of activities common to all. Linda also decided that all plants should attain QS9000, a quality standard developed by the Big Three automakers and since adopted by most suppliers. In that one move, 100 procedures for quality were replaced by only one: QS9000.

In April 1999, Linda was named president, nine years after joining Linamar as a lathe operator. Frank was delegated to reveal her new role at the annual meeting but forgot, leaving Linda to deliver the news. "My father was supposed to announce this, but he didn't, so I did," she told the assembled shareholders. To replace herself in the COO role, Linda picked Jim Jarrell, who by then was running ten plants, the most ever by any general manager at Linamar. Jim took charge of all the plants, leaving Linda with five senior officers reporting to her.

At no time on the way up did she feel hampered because she was a woman in a male-dominated business. "I think it's all about your attitude. If you go into a meeting with men expecting to be treated differently, you will be. I just go in and do my job, and am happy to be judged on that. I don't go in expecting respect, that's when you get disappointment," said Linda.

In her first annual report commentary, Linda showed shareholders that she'd embraced her father's belief in measuring progress. She noted that annual sales per employee rose 12.8 percent to $203,610 and annual sales per square foot rose from $539 to $596, an increase of 10.5 percent. Total lost time per employee was 4.7 days a year compared to the national average of 10.6 days. There was specific praise for performance at LPP Manufacturing, Linamar's first dedicated assembly plant. "This engine assembly plant broke all records by producing their first engine eighty-eight days after ground was broken to build the facility, an event occurring just three weeks after signing the purchase agreement," she said.

The most significant change under Linda and Jim Jarrell was to change what had been short-term thinking into long-term goals. Under a plan called Vision 2020, they established a target of $10 billion in sales by 2020, an ambitious level that required growth of 15 percent a year.

In addition to numerical goals, the strategy, launched in 1999, comprised six core values that included balancing customer, employee, and financial satisfaction; inherent responsiveness to stakeholders; fostering an environment of opportunity and mutual respect; innovative use of technology; intense entrepreneurship; and unsurpassed work ethic. They also established a core purpose: Linamar would do what it already did, but better.

At that point, Linda went to Frank — who had not been involved in the process — and told him, "We've been going through this exercise, trying to identify who we are, and where we're going as a company. If you think back to when you started the business, why did you do that? What was your purpose?"

Replied Frank, "I guess I thought I could do better."

"Perfect," said Linda. "We got that one right."

Frank with his Knight's Cross of the Order of Merit awarded by the Republic of Hungary in 2006. (Guelph Mercury)

~⌒

The final step in Linda's long climb to the top took place in August 2002 when, at 36, she was appointed chief executive officer. "Would Linda have been CEO of Linamar if she hadn't been my daughter? No. I wouldn't have known her. I wouldn't have given her the chance to learn. But Linda is my daughter and she was willing to do what I asked her to do. Any other graduate with an honours degree in chemistry and an M.B.A. would not do that," said Frank. "We are the largest shareholders, so if you're going to hang on to this business and grow it, we decided she would join and learn. Is there nepotism? When all things are equal, of course there is. Nepotism's a real problem for many companies. A big percentage of second-generation leaders fail and almost all of the third-generation leaders fail. But the opportunity was there for her because I gave her the opportunity. Beyond that, she proved herself and is proving herself every day," said Frank.

A few Bay Street analysts griped one last time about nepotism, but their concerns soon died down. "I didn't hear much after the first year or two. As in anything, people will make assumptions when they don't know you, your capability, or what you're willing to put into a job. Whether those assumptions are around nepotism, male-female, or young-old, they are quickly put to rest once somebody's had an opportunity to get to know you and learn that you are capable, that you're going to put in the time and effort, and that you've got the ability to do the job. It always takes some time to win over the crowd," said Linda.

Before Linda agreed to be CEO, she wanted to make sure the position was not just window-dressing. "You want me to be CEO, but what's that going to mean to you? What are you going to do differently? I don't want to become CEO and not have the reins. We need to agree on what you're going to do," she said to her father.

Frank told her that in addition to serving as chairman of the board, he wanted to lead cost-cutting exercises, conduct audits in the plants, and negotiate the purchase and disposal of capital equipment. "I loved those ideas because they tapped into all the things that he had so much knowledge about, things that we could all really learn and benefit from," said Linda. "Nobody can purchase capital equipment better than my father. Nobody can get more for it at the time of sale than him. Nobody's better positioned to do cost-cutting or audits because he's had fifty years of manufacturing knowledge and managed to retain every single fact that he's ever learned, particularly if there's a dollar sign in front of it."

There was no need to make a list of Linda's responsibilities. She was in charge of everything else. She wrote his four duties on a piece of paper and had him sign the document that she continues to keep in the top drawer of her desk. To date, there's been no need to produce the list or remind him of his agreed-upon role. "We've got a very good relationship. We'll have a discussion about topics and come out of it with something that we're comfortable with. He doesn't try to force his way. He's more than willing to give his opinion, solicited or not, but he's never been one to insist that it be his way. He's always been good with saying, 'It's your decision.' Obviously, if he's strongly against something, then I'm going to pause before I go down that road and make sure that it really is the right thing."

One of the decisions on which they agreed to disagree was opening a plant in China in 2005. "Linda's vision is totally different than mine, much more progressive, and she proved me wrong a few times," said Frank. "I would have never gone into China that early. I would have taken my time, but she looked at it and she analyzed it and she said we should be there. Today it's one of our most profitable plants."

For Linda, the opportunity presented by China was too great not to take. "He's an entrepreneur and entrepreneurs by nature are risk takers. But he'll take risks that he knows, risks that he feels more comfortable about. When it came to expansion into China, he's not as comfortable there because he feels the risk level is high. For me and the rest of the team we felt there's just so much opportunity that for us to not be part of it would be a huge mistake and really short change our potential of where we could take the company," said Linda.

Initially, Linamar had eyed Korea for its first Asia-Pacific plant. Ken McDougall and General Counsel Roger Fulton travelled to Korea to talk to government officials, conduct site assessments, and arrange for business licences. They soon realized, after meeting with potential customers, that China looked like a better location for expansion.

Negotiations continued off and on for nine months at which point Linamar appeared to have all the necessary approvals. McDougall and

Fulton returned to Guelph on a weekend only to hear by email that final authorization would take several more months. On Monday, McDougall and Fulton flew back to China and obtained approval within forty-eight hours. "See, you learned a lesson," said the official with whom they dealt. "In China we do business with our face."

That ability to be decisive means that Linamar can outmanoeuvre rivals but it can also be an Achilles heel. "Our swiftness in decision making has led us to jump too quickly into important strategic decisions, joint ventures where we did not adequately research our partners, or acquisitions that didn't fit our business model," said Linda. "These were costly lessons but I certainly learned from them and now take time to fully understand a strategic opportunity, get lots of opinion and advice, run the analysis from a few perspectives, and make sure that the decision is the best possible one for us."

One such lesson had its beginnings in 1999. Linda took Linamar into a joint venture called Weslin Industries with auto-parts firm Wescast Industries Inc. of Brantford, Ontario, to make machined exhaust manifolds in Hungary for the European automotive market. "Having a partnership with a company is never easy. It's like a marriage. It can't always be one way and it can't always be the other way," said Linda. "The more time that you spend making sure that your values and culture are aligned, the more likely that you'll have success. Linamar and Wescast were just too different in terms of our cultures and how we got things done. I have a huge amount of respect for Wescast and all that they've achieved. Dick LeVan was a fantastic entrepreneur who built a business that was wildly successful. They just managed things differently than us and it was just too difficult for us to be able to continue in business together." The joint venture ended in 2004 when Linamar sold its 50 percent interest to Wescast.

∼

When Linda was appointed CEO, Linamar had $1.2 billion in sales; employed 8,000 in twenty-eight plants; one research and development centre; and four sales offices in Canada, the United States, Mexico, Germany, Hungary, and Japan. In an interview conducted at the time, Linda said she was taking on the role for the long haul, not just the usual three-to-five year term of the average CEO. "What can you do in three years? You can't do anything in three years if you want to effect change. I have thirty years to make my plans happen," she told Gord Pitts of the *Globe and Mail.*

Several articles compared Linda's appointment with the naming the previous year by Frank Stronach of his daughter Belinda as CEO at Magna. But Belinda was promoted to the top with far less training than Linda had. Still, both appointments were unusual in a nation where only a handful of the 100 largest companies are run by women. Nancy Southern, another daughter of a founder, is CEO at ATCO Ltd., the Edmonton-based conglomerate. Southern also served a long apprenticeship, starting as a teenager when ATCO was making trailers for construction sites. One of the few other female CEOs, also based in Guelph and appointed in 2002, was Kathy Bardswick, of Co-operators General Insurance Co. American subsidiaries tend to be more likely to name a woman to head their Canadian operations. Examples include Bobbie Gaunt at Ford Motor Co. of Canada and Maureen Kempston Darkes, of General Motors of Canada.

With the specifics of their roles settled, Frank launched Cost Attack Teams (CAT). Under CAT, Frank visits each plant at least once a year and works with the executive team and employees studying everything, tool by tool, operation by operation, to find ways to reduce manufacturing costs, typically by about 3 percent. In any given year, Frank finds $15 to $20 million in savings across the company. In 2008, he found $27 million. "I've never had a CAT that I don't save at least $200,000 a year on an annualized basis," he said.

If Frank thinks he can make a difference on a specific item, he'll call a supplier in the middle of a CAT meeting. "Frank carries a lot of weight. When Frank Hasenfratz is calling the supplier, generally they sit up and take notice," said Ray Wagner, a manufacturing engineer at Hastech. "He's a very shrewd negotiator."

In one case, Linamar was using a shipper to send two containers a week, 104 containers in a year. Frank decided to ask for a price reduction in return for which Linamar would agree to a two-year contract. He called, negotiations ensued, and the shipper agreed to lower the fee, thereby saving Linamar more than $80,000 on its annual costs.

The savings come can also come from small changes. In one plant, for example, employees were using glue to bond two items together. The glue came in a litre bottle but there always seemed to be glue left on the bottom when the bottle was discarded. Someone suggested getting a larger container, resting the bottles upside down on the edge, and letting all the glue drain into the larger container for use. Costs for the glue dropped 10 percent.

In another case, a pump was used to pour water on a machine to cool it. By shutting the pump off sooner, the cooling process was not affected, but electricity costs were reduced. "The pump will use 5 horsepower, that's roughly 4 kilowatt hours, so at 9 cents a kilowatt hour that's 36 cents an hour. If we run it 6,000 hours, that's $18,000. If we can shut that pump off earlier, because we need it only half the time, we save $9,000. Pennies add up." Cycle time is very important, said Frank. "Our cost is $60 an hour — that's $1 a minute or 1.6 cents a second — so if I can save ten seconds on the production line that's 16 cents on a million parts for a savings of $160,000. Every little thing counts."

According to Wagner, another way Frank's experience can reduce costs during a CAT is by knowing how much another plant is paying for the same item. "He might say, 'You're paying $8 for that item, I know a guy over at Ariss or Roctel or another plant that's paying $7.30, you should talk to them.'"

Frank also remembers everything he ever saw in any plant. "He'll call me and ask about something that we used fifteen years ago on a line that's exactly what he wants for another job. More times than not it's in the junk pile, but he remembers it," said Wagner. "He's got a memory like an elephant. He never forgets anything."

Each CAT Frank runs lasts a minimum of four hours but can go on for several days. "People are very nervous when he comes in, especially in Asia and in Mexico. When I was running the German facilities, and he came over to do a CAT, I prepped them. The Germans were very meticulous and methodical. Their whole goal was to be so transparent and say that he will never find anything," said Brian Wade, vice president of the driveline group. "He always lightens it up with some jokes. If he's getting upset with somebody, he'll get upset with the top guy, never with the engineer who is giving the wrong answer, so people get comfortable very quickly. About two hours into his first meeting with the German team they said, 'He is one of the smartest people we've met. He understands what we're saying to him.' The savings at that session amounted to €600,000."

In China, where they are less comfortable speaking in English, there is additional pressure. "It's a lot harder for him to do a CAT there because everyone's trying to speak English and trying to make sure they're saying the right thing. But he doesn't want you to say the right thing, he wants you to tell how it is," said Wade. "At the end of the day, everyone's worn out but we saved hundreds of thousands of dollars."

Frank was impressed by the first CAT in China. "They were so anxious to learn. When I told them, we do things this way, the engineers got excited, saying, 'We can do this.' It was very tiring, but in four days, on an annualized basis, we found a little bit over a million dollars in improvements," said Frank. "They are very hard-working people and they look after their families."

Beyond the immediate savings, CATs have a lasting effect. The sessions create a way of thinking that penetrates deep into the organization. "I always say, if you make a million parts, and you save a penny a piece, that's $10,000 a year. So let's start with every cent," said Frank. "Guys come back and say, 'Gee, remember, five years ago you showed me how to do this? I'm still doing it.' You know, it's a good feeling."

Rare is the business leader who pays such attention to detail. "I don't know of any other organization that does that," said Glen Hutchison. "And I don't know anybody else except a person like Frank who could do it. That's because he is so intimately involved in having worked and run the machines on the floor. It wasn't too many years ago, when there would be a disaster at one of the plants, and Frank would go in and run the machines. He was prepared to put on dirty clothes and run that damn machine just the same as any workman. He knows the running of everything, and the price of everything, and he has that street sense of how do I get it better and how do I get people to do it my way,"

Watching the founder in person and learning his methods first hand is the best way to build a corporate culture. "CAT gives so much value to the company from the standpoint of taking waste out, reducing cost, and training people," said Jim Jarrell. "Employees see the passion of the founder and that creates that culture of elimination of waste. CAT is a tailored program for Frank and for the future of the company to keep that culture alive."

In addition to CAT, which is program-based, in 2003 Frank launched PAT, the Paper Audit Trail, which is document-based. He regularly visits each plant and randomly focuses on specific documents such as all the cheques that were written the previous month. He'll look at each cheque one by one and match it with the related purchase order, invoice, and packing slip looking for mistakes such as a currency error where the purchase order was in Canadian dollars but the invoice was in U.S. dollars. "All kinds of things pop up in the PAT," said Linda. "We've found purchasing opportunities where somebody was paying more for something than they needed to and we've found simple clerical errors, so he's looking for all kinds of cost-saving opportunities."

On one occasion, a few employees had a little fun with Frank's tight-wad ways. They left two pennies on the plant floor in a place where they knew Frank would see them. He did, and when he bent down to pick them up, he discovered that they had been glued in place. Everyone laughed, including Frank.

16

THE UPS AND DOWNS OF SKYJACK

THE TELEPHONE CALL TO Frank Hasenfratz one spring day in 2001 from Wolf Haessler was just like hearing from a neighbour. Haessler, a fellow entrepreneur, had started a machine shop in 1969 that had become Skyjack Inc. Successful growth in the years since meant the company had manufacturing facilities in Canada, the U.S., and Germany, as well as sales and service offices in the U.K. and the Netherlands. Skyjack had two plants in Guelph, both of which were near the Linamar head office on Speedvale Avenue. Skyjack had 1,200 employees and annual sales of more than $200 million but the firm had run into some financial trouble. Could Frank help him out?

Born in Germany, Haessler moved to Canada in 1952 as a boy of nine with his family. He graduated from the University of Guelph and obtained his master's degree in mechanical engineering from the University of Western Ontario. He wanted to start his own company but worked at DuPont of Canada before opening a machine shop in Brampton, Ontario. For the first few years, Haessler built custom equipment but then in the 1980s he began thinking about building Bobcats, the dexterous mobile diggers used on tight construction sites. For market research, he talked to equipment dealers in the area and learned there was another item for which there was greater demand and fewer manufacturers. They urged him to build self-propelled scissor-lift elevating work platforms that could raise a worker high into the air for warehouse operations, window cleaning, and construction sites — anywhere an alternative was needed to scaffolding. Haessler took a few lifts apart, decided he could improve on the design, signed up some dealers to buy his production, and began manufacturing lifts in 1985.

By 1989, Skyjack had a 40,000-square-foot plant in Brampton, eighty employees, and $10 million in annual sales. The company had a bank line of credit but was limited by how much it could borrow and needed more money to grow. Through his local Royal Bank branch, Haessler met Barrie Laver, a vice president at Toronto-based Royal Bank Capital Corp., the venture capital arm of the bank.

Laver arranged for $1.5 million in funds, part debt and part equity, in return for a 30 percent ownership interest in the company. "What I liked about Wolf from day one was that he had a good head on his shoulders, an interesting story, and he was honest and straightforward," said Laver who joined the Skyjack board of directors in 1990 while continuing in his venture capital role. "He was rough around the edges in some respects in the sense that he was not financially sophisticated. But a lot of entrepreneurs, Frank Hasenfratz being one of them, are not really interested in spending time with accountants and lawyers,"

Skyjack moved its manufacturing operations to a 150,000-square-foot plant in Guelph in 1989. By 1994, the company was making fifteen different models of scissor lifts that could send platforms as high as fifty feet. Skyjack had $41 million in annual sales but continued to need money for expansion so the company went public in May 1994 at $5.40 a share.

For the next two years, Skyjack was the darling among all the new issues on the Toronto Stock Exchange, much like Linamar had been almost ten years earlier. Share price hit $49.60 in June 1996, a meteoric rise that was six times better than the increase in the TSE 300 Index during the same period. From 1989 to 1996 Skyjack's annual profit rose from less than $1 million to $13 million while employment grew tenfold to more than 800.

But Skyjack's market was beginning to change. Equipment dealers were no longer mom and pop operations; consolidation in the sector intensified competition and pushed down prices. "In the space of two years we were losing one customer per week to these consolidators," said Haessler. "At one time I had 150 dealers in the United States, most of whom I knew personally and could speak with at any time. Suddenly it all caved in and I ended up with maybe five customers."

New, larger agencies such as United Rentals had more clout and drove a harder bargain, so Skyjack's profits shrivelled. Bankers were getting nervous about their loans to such a financially stretched firm. With all the bad news, by April 1997 share price had fallen to $17.

In spite of the challenges, Skyjack sales continued to grow so the company opened a second Guelph plant in 1999, a 150,000-square-foot building next to the existing 220,000-square-foot facility. That year, the company sold its fifty thousandth scissor lift and reached $262 million in sales — six times more than when the firm went public in 1994. "Our sales didn't start going down until later on in 1999," said Haessler. "The consolidators didn't have the experience or the insight that the owner-operators did. The industry was run by hired people and it was harder to get good information on the market so we could plan ahead. We probably overexpanded."

In 2000, serious financial trouble arrived. The economy had soured, the construction sector slowed, and demand for Skyjack lifts fell precipitously. The company lost $22 million in 2000 then barely broke even the following year. At $126 million, bank debt was far too high. Production of some lines was halted and a plant in Iowa was closed. "It became clear we needed new leadership at the top," said director Barrie Laver. As far as the board was concerned, the founder had become a major part of the problem. "It was mostly a matter of an entrepreneur and an inventor who found himself presiding over a business that had got to the dimensions that it was beyond his reach," said Frank Potter, a Toronto-based corporate director and former executive director at the World Bank who joined the Skyjack board in 2000. "At one time I was the hero and suddenly the board had some doubts about me," said Haessler.

Haessler continued in the role of chairman but the board replaced him as president and CEO with Jos Wintermans, formerly a senior executive at Canadian Tire Acceptance Ltd. and Rogers Cablesystems Ltd. In turn, Wintermans recruited his own senior team of half a dozen new executives. "Some of the costs were shed and we tried to get out of some facilities but the company was still under-financed. It's a very cyclical industry," said Laver. "In the upswing, sales would go up by multiples. In the downside, sales might drop by 40 percent. If you're levered [by debt], 40 percent hurts. We were going through one of those cycles."

The board might not have been happy with Haessler's performance, but as far as he was concerned, there was plenty of blame to go around. As his discomfort grew, Haessler sought a way out for himself. That's when he called Frank. The two men met that weekend in the Linamar boardroom. After hearing his story, Frank warned him, "Wolf, you better watch it. You're losing your business."

But Haessler had come ready to sell his 48.5-percent stake in the company. "He realized the nature of the problem I was having with my board and with the industry. I realized that the thing was slipping out of my hands. I talked to Frank about buying and we were already on the same wavelength. There wasn't much arm twisting," said Haessler.

Among his many worries, Haessler was unhappy with Skyjack's strategic direction. "He was concerned about what he saw happening in the market and felt that the board and existing management were not approaching the market appropriately, and were not running the business the way he felt it should be run. That's what made him come to us to talk about buying his shares," said Linda, who was by then president of Linamar. "We quite liked the idea because we'd already started down the road of wanting to diversify our business. Although it wasn't really machining based, it was more fabrication based, Skyjack shared a lot of the same challenges as Linamar from a purchasing, manufacturing, and assembly perspective."

From Linamar's vantage point, Skyjack's products resembled the vehicles for which Linamar already made parts. Linamar saw other parallels. Just as the automotive sector consisted of a few large players, the equipment rental business had also become dominated by three firms: United Rentals, RSC Equipment Rental, and Canadian Equipment. Observed Linda, "We saw some similarities in that regard as well, and felt that our experience and knowledge when it came to lean manufacturing and efficient purchasing would be a huge asset to bring to Skyjack. In doing so we could create quite a bit of profit and opportunity."

Skyjack also offered an entirely new type of manufacturing that was far different from what Linamar had been used to, a way of stretching the company in a new direction. Until then, Linamar had been little more than an order taker. One of the Big Three automakers would offer a contract for a machined part, Linamar would look at the plans supplied, quote a price, and sign a deal. "Quite frankly, we used to be a blueprint machine," said Linamar COO Jim Jarrell. "You do the blueprint, I'll make that, and that's all we did." By contrast, Skyjack offered Linamar a broad product line that required a far fuller scope: design, production, assembly, an understanding of the potential demand, a marketing plan, a sales team, and follow-up including repair and warranty work.

Frank discussed the possibility of buying Haessler's control position with Jarrell during a business trip on Linamar's recently acquired eight-passenger corporate jet. On the trial flight, Frank had asked Jarrell for his opinion about buying the Citation Excel. In response, Jarrell stood up and demonstrated how he had to duck because at six foot two he was too tall for the interior. "I don't fit," he said. Frank also stood up, found there was plenty of room for his five-foot-eight frame, and commented, "Doesn't matter. The calibration gauge fits."

As the two men soared high in the sky talking about Skyjack, Frank scrawled some numbers on a napkin, showing how an acquisition might be structured to fit well with Linamar. "I thought that it was a pretty bold, strategic concept, and very entrepreneurial. I thought it was a great idea," said Jarrell. Linamar approached various possible investment partners including the Ontario Teachers' Pension Plan and the Ontario Municipal Employees Retirement System (OMERS) but there was no interest, so in June 2001 Linamar went ahead on its own and bought Haessler's 4,018,757 million Skyjack shares — 48.5 percent of the company — for $22 million. The price per share, $5.42, was a 13-percent premium over the average of Skyjack's share price in the twenty days before the transaction. "Frank has a very good knowledge about his main business, the machining of parts. He knows the business inside out. He started by making parts himself so has very good knowledge," said Haessler. "But there's another factor. He's a very smooth, practical, and straightforward person who could see opportunities where other people couldn't see them — especially with regard to producing parts at a faster rate and a lower cost. He had a good understanding of the environment in which he had to compete. The auto industry is a very competitive industry. He learned that and applied that to Skyjack and made Skyjack very profitable. Looking back, I'm quite happy I did the deal."

Linamar's new vision wasn't obvious to everyone. Analysts at the broker-age firms who followed Linamar were leery that the company might not be able to make the leap to this more multi-layered way of doing business. "I don't think they liked it because it didn't fit the Linamar profile," said Jarrell. "We were automotive, you could fit us into this bucket. They said, 'Wait a minute, now you're going over here.' Part of our strategy was you don't want to be in just one bucket, you want to have some diversification."

~

Once Linamar acquired Haessler's shares in June 2001, Wintermans departed and was replaced as CEO by James Hacking, a former Linamar executive and president of IMT Corp., of Ingersoll. Frank, Linda, and Jim Jarrell joined the Skyjack board. Laver and Potter remained as independent directors; in November, Frank took over as chairman from Haessler who resigned from the board. "I didn't know Frank and Linda well but certainly Linamar was a Canadian success story, now a global success story. For me it was an opportunity to get to know them a little bit better. I believed Skyjack had a bright future," said Laver. "Frank was always very hands on. As soon as he could, he was in there on the shop floor trying to figure out ways to save money. Clearly, he's bright and has accomplished a lot. He's very much salt of the earth. Linda obviously has more education. She took that opportunity and has done a good job. I enjoyed dealing with both of them."

Linda had an opportunity to take a close look at Skyjack's operations when the CBC-TV business program *Venture* approached her to participate in *Back to the Floor*, a segment of the show where a business leader spends a week in the factory to get an employee-eye view of the business. "I'd already worked on the floor at Linamar, so been there, done that. I thought the show presented a great opportunity to learn about the nuts and bolts of the Skyjack business, so I spent my week at Skyjack, which was a great experience," said Linda. "I worked on a variety of spots on the assembly line, right from the start to the end. It was great, seeing how it all came together, how we worked up a shop floor, and the efficiency of our operations. It was a good opportunity to meet some folks at Skyjack and get to know them a little bit better."

Frank also spent time at Skyjack, in his case with no cameras present. "When they took over Skyjack, Frank said, 'I want you to take that particular unit apart and put every part on the floor.' He went through and said, 'Where did we get that? How much did we pay for it?' He cut the prices on the machines," said his accountant Bob Young. "It worked very well. Skyjack became profitable when it wasn't. The machine that he took apart, he picked up a lot of work that Linamar could do. He knew how to do it in house. That's a businessman," said Young.

However, while the acquisition may have made long-term sense, there were short-term problems. "When we first got Skyjack, it was like a stone in the water. Sales dropped overnight and got worse very quickly," said Jarrell. "We were scrambling and spent a lot of time on cost reduction and consolidation." As the economy continued to deteriorate, the aerial platform business was heading into one of its down cycles where two bad years follow five good

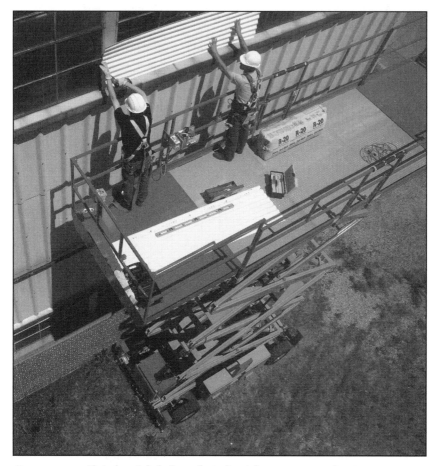

Contractors use Skyjack aerial platforms for industrial construction and maintenance.

years. After breaking even in 2001, Skyjack lost $34 million the following year. Skyjack plants were shut down for more than three months and employment cut by about half to 530. Plants were closed in Kansas and Germany with production consolidated at the two facilities in Guelph as well as one in Iowa.

Progress was made on refinancing the heavy debt load. Skyjack lined up $65 million in working capital from Congress Financial Corp. as well as a $22.5 million loan from GATX Capital Canada Inc. Most of the new money went to pay off a $55 million bank loan. But within a few months, in the face of worsening economic conditions, Skyjack failed to meet the requirements of its new debt arrangements. With the stock down to $4.65 and shareholders becoming restive, it was clear Skyjack needed still more financial help. Linamar loaned Skyjack $10 million in February 2002.

Hopes for increased sales in Europe — only 16 percent of the company's total revenue — had failed to meet expectations. Ongoing consolidation in the marketplace and low demand continued to squeeze profits. For the fiscal year ending March 31, 2002, sales fell to $117 million from $245 million in the previous year, and the company lost $34 million.

Because Linamar owned slightly less than 50 percent of Skyjack, Linamar could not appoint a majority of the directors. Frank felt hobbled, unable to carry out all the changes he wanted to make. As a result, in his role as Skyjack chair. Frank told the board in March 2002 that Linamar was not interested in selling its stake but he asked the directors to establish an independent committee that would place a value on the company and seek new investors who would inject additional money. Frank also told the board to be prepared to consider any offer Linamar might make.

The Skyjack board named the two independent directors, Barrie Laver and Frank Potter, to function as that independent committee. In turn, they retained financial advice from Calcap Valuation Services Ltd. of Toronto and hired as legal counsel James Baillie, a securities lawyer at the Toronto law firm of Torys. In April, Laver and Potter told the Skyjack board that Calcap's initial view was that the value of Skyjack shares was in the $1.70 to $1.90 range, a far cry from the $5.42 Linamar had paid Haessler only ten months earlier. The committee also sought investment alternatives but could find neither a new partner nor new financing.

In May, on behalf of Linamar, Linda made a verbal offer of $1.75 a share for the rest of Skyjack. Shortly after, as part of its due diligence, Linamar discovered there were tax recoveries possible at Skyjack that increased the value of the company. As a result of that new financial information, Calcap revised its estimate of the per share value upward to the $2.00 to $2.25 range.

In June, Linamar told the committee it was prepared to pay $2.13 a share for Skyjack. The effect of such a purchase was to take the company private by buying out all of the remaining shareholders. In turn, the committee recommended that the Skyjack board accept Linamar's bid and Linamar made a formal offer in July. "When you looked at the intrinsic health of the business, it needed deeper pockets, and Linamar had those deeper pockets. Skyjack was not going to survive on its own. We had run out of access to credit and Frank was willing to take it over," said Potter. "We salvaged a company that was not going to survive. That seems to me to be the essence of what we should do as directors. We were not in a strong bargaining position." Shareholders voted to approve the offer in August, the same month as Linda was appointed CEO of Linamar. Linamar paid $10.6 million for the 51.5 percent of Skyjack it did not own for a total acquisition cost of $33 million.

In addition to shrinking the number of facilities, Linamar improved efficiency at Skyjack and was able to recoup all of its acquisition costs within eighteen months. By 2004, as the economy rebounded, Skyjack's profits and sales doubled from the previous year. Skyjack became part of the Industrial Division that also included European fabrication, the energy group, and consumer products such as trailers. In 2007, sales for the Industrial Division peaked at $518 million or 21 percent of Linamar's revenue. "We could have sold Skyjack for $500 million," said Frank. "The investment dealers were all over us. We kept Skyjack because it fits our company, it's independent, and has a good marketing group. It was a very good acquisition for Linamar." Added Jarrell, "We could have sold it, but that's just not the style we are. That's not why we got into it. We're not venture capitalists to milk it and off we go. We look at it as a solid product line that gives you that flexibility to keep yourself diversified."

Since 2002, Skyjack scissor lifts have been produced for the European market by Linamar's Hungary division while the Linamar plants in Guelph provide machined components and axles for North American production. In 2002, Linamar named Lloyd Spalding, former senior vice president of marketing at Linamar, as president of the Industrial Group. When Spalding retired in 2008, his second-in-command Ken McDougall replaced him until

2009 when he was named group president, Powertrain Mexico. Today, the president is Brad Buehler.

Skyjack has moved beyond the core business of scissor-lift platforms by introducing the boom lift line and in 2007 acquiring Carelift Equipment Ltd, of Breslau, Ontario, a manufacturer of rough terrain forklifts (known as "telehandlers") under the name Zoom Boom. The total annual market for such products is huge, US$3.5 billion. The telehandler lineup was completed in 2008 with the acquisition of Volvo's materials handling business based in Shippensburg, Pennsylvania. Skyjack now has three manufacturing facilities, two development centres, and six sales and service offices in Canada, the United States, Hungary, Germany, China, Sweden, and the U.K. The business, however, remains cyclical. During the global economic crisis that began in 2008, Skyjack suffered along with everyone else. Sales fell because the construction industry was idled and rental firms ceased buying new equipment. From $444 million in 2008 annual sales declined by almost two-thirds to $161 million in 2009 with a loss that year of $40 million.

Ontario Premier Dalton McGuinty with Frank and Linda during a project partnership announcement in 2006. (Guelph Mercury)

That cyclicality is worse for Skyjack's equipment rental business than for Linamar's production of machined auto parts. "When you shut off the tap on automotive, you're talking a 30 percent reduction. When you shut the tap off on Skyjack, you're talking an 80 to 90 percent reduction for a period of time. So you've got to have more market and more independent dealers, not just the big rental companies," said Jarrell. "That's something we've worked on over the last few years that has gotten better, but certainly still needs work because the independents are not like the big guys who turn the tap on and off. They need product when they get a contract; they're more like local guys."

But Skyjack remains an integral part of Linamar's future. Skyjack sales are projected to make up $1 billion of Linamar's $10 billion sales target in 2020. Skyjack has more than sixty customers in North America, with plans to add more in other countries. For Linamar, Skyjack's eleven different product lines are examples of the company's ability to develop, design, and manufacture sophisticated and highly engineered products and then bring those products successfully to market. "Skyjack has added a lot of value intrinsically to Linamar to be able to be a full-module system product builder. Because it's a full product, you've got warranty and all those types of things to look after," said Jarrell. "You want to create your own mousetrap versus being subservient. You want to do those things that we do, like machining, but you also want to actually create that mousetrap that you can sell versus having customers say, 'Hey, just make this,' and then beat you down to the lowest cost anyway. There are a lot of people who have said, 'Why do you guys stay in it?' Well, we think it's a good business for us long-term."

Along the way, Linamar and Skyjack have helped each other. "We've been able to share lessons learned at Skyjack and plants that do the painting and vice versa. We've been able to take machining over to Skyjack and help them on that. On welding they've been able to help us, so that integration of all the process capabilities has been good," said Jarrell.

"It's still going through cycles. It's coming out of one now," said Wolf Haessler. "But Linamar's already made good money with it and they're about to do so again."

17

HER OWN STAMP

W HILE FRANK, LINDA, AND Jim might all have agreed on the good sense of buying Skyjack, the difference between how Frank and Linda performed in their respective roles of chief executive officer was like the sound of a one-man band versus a symphony orchestra. "All of us have learned that we can't be a top-down autocratic organization. The more we grow the more important that influential leadership becomes in terms of getting feedback and buy-in from our team or the next layer and the next layer beyond that," said Linda. "We try not to say, 'This is the strategy; everybody go and do it.' We say, 'This is what we're thinking about. What are your thoughts?' We're not looking for consensus, but it's critical to get feedback. You're not going to get that with an autocratic dictatorship. You're going to get that through influential leadership. That's something that I've learned along the way."

Of course, the lessons from her father also continue. "He taught me by example to ask sales people whenever I see them: 'Did you get an order today?'" To build influence and buy-in, early during her time in office Linda improved internal communications. Linamar also launched Linamar Vision, a global employee news magazine, and created LINUS, an employee intranet site. Linda instituted the President's Forum, small groups of employees who met with her over lunch, so they could offer ideas and hear first-hand about corporate strategy in a relaxed venue. She also launched new training and development programs that focused on technical skills, leadership, quality systems, succession planning, and communications at all levels in the organization.

Cost Attack Teams, the cost-reduction sessions run by Frank, is just one of the ways Linamar tackles waste. A broader method Jim Jarrell put in place starting in 2002 was the lean manufacturing philosophy known as the Linamar Production System, a program that yields the best quality, lowest cost, and shortest lead-time through the elimination of waste. "Being competitive means vigilance around eliminating waste, a dedication to innovation, and the ability to move with speed," said Linda. "In order to keep driving costs down you must be dedicated to constantly improving and changing the way you do things to eliminate inefficiencies and waste and drive improved productivity. You don't do a lean exercise just once. We've been doing them for years, each and every day."

The point of the program is to turn employees from problem solvers to problem preventers with a focus on planning, purchasing, and labour costs. In 2004, the first full year of operation, the Linamar Production System reduced inventory by 12 percent and direct labour costs by 18 percent. Use of space was increased by 17 percent and internal scrap reduced by 30 percent. "We, like so many companies, felt we were very efficient in managing our operations. We were wrong. Today we look for waste every day and every day we find it. There is always something you can do better," said Linda. "It's a never-ending journey."

The new system was also applied to the important task of approving capital. The previous system had worked well when Linamar was small. Frank would always be involved because he instinctively knew what prices, costs, and capital amounts made sense. "He had his own way of doing things which was great when you're smaller, but as we grew, it became harder and harder to have those less-than-formal systems for assessing your potential return. I felt we really needed something a little more formal. We ended up splitting the process into two parts. The first, the Process Review Board (PRB), still involves my father."

There is hardly a machine at Linamar with which Frank hasn't been involved. As recently as December 2010, he bought four used Walter Helitronic tool grinders. Frank got them dirt-cheap from a company that had gone bankrupt, paying $41,000 for all four. One new version of the same grinder would cost $1 million.

To be sure, the machines were bought in "as is" condition and needed major repair. Employees at the previous shop, angered by losing their livelihoods, had done some damage. Linamar created a team at Camtac, and within two months, they had two machines up and running and the other two almost running. For those two months, Frank phoned twice a week to see how the crew was doing. When he wasn't calling the floor, he was chasing the general manager.

Why was he so interested? Because those four machines now do all the tool grinding work that the two dozen Linamar plants in Guelph had been sending to an outside firm. Annual savings for Linamar will be $2 million. In addition, Camtac will offer faster service and will make a profit of $400,000 on the business.

Such intimate knowledge made Frank a natural to be involved in the Process Review Board gathering information prior to the purchase of new equipment, whether it's available in house or needs to be bought, and if so, which brand, from what supplier, and at what price. Once that review is complete, the proposal goes to the Financial Review Board (FRB), made up of Linda and Jim Jarrell. "Previously we didn't have a very good process for analysis of project returns. We did have a very robust quotations spreadsheet so we had a sense for what the process should be, what the cost should be, and the budget associated with capital, but we weren't taking it a step farther to do an in-depth return on investment," said Linda. "We developed a spreadsheet built right off of the estimation worksheet so we could use the very same sheet to do the FRB analysis. By looking at the cash outlay and when the money was being spent we can do an internal rate of return analysis to make sure it meets a hurdle rate of 20 percent pre-interest, pre-tax, on total investment."

⁓

As part of her rise to the role of CEO, in 1998, Linda was appointed to the Linamar board of directors. Two other directors joined at the same time: John Jarrell, a retired GM executive and father of Jim Jarrell, and David Buehlow, who spent thirty-seven years as an accountant with PricewaterhouseCoopers.

In 1999, Mark Stoddart, then director of sales and marketing for Linamar and the husband of Nancy Hasenfratz, joined the board.

In May 2003, in order to comply with new corporate governance rules that required additional independent directors, Jarrell and long-time director Hugh Guthrie — who were deemed to be inside directors — stepped down and were replaced by Terry Reidel, a chartered accountant and president and COO of Kuntz Electroplating Inc., of Kitchener. The third independent director, William Harrison, chair and chief executive officer of Lift Technologies Inc., had been appointed in 1990. The board also implemented a formal director-orientation program and became more involved in the company's strategic planning process. The two board committees are both chaired by independent directors. Reidel chairs the Human Resources and Corporate Governance Committee; Buehlow chairs the Audit Committee.

In 2011, Linamar took another step toward improved governance by replacing slate voting for directors — when shareholders can only vote for directors on an all-or-none basis — to a majority voting policy, which allows shareholders to pass judgment on individual members of the board.

Directors know their roles and Linamar maintains a skills matrix to ensure board members cover all necessary talents. "Corporate governance is something that we take seriously. Every two years we'll take a day off site to go through our governance, review our mandate, the approval and oversight guidelines, as well as expectations of the board — including tenure — to make sure they still reflect shareholder needs," said Linda. "We also look at outside interpretations of our governance. For instance, the *Globe and Mail* does a survey once a year on board governance. We look at that in detail, what our score was and why we scored what we did to see if there is something that our shareholders care about that we think is an appropriate change."

~∽

Of all the new programs Linda and Jim have instituted, however, the one with the most lasting impact has been the Stepping Stool of Success, a system of measuring performance in each plant on an individual basis as well as providing a way of comparing that plant with all the others. When Linda first moved into head office, each plant reported monthly performance information, but every plant used a different method. No one in any of the plants knew where they stood compared to other facilities.

The situation was placed into stark relief during a senior executive meeting when George Sims, then chief financial officer, told the group about a conversation he'd had with the accountant at one of the plants. Sims had asked, "Why can't you have the same performance as Transgear?" Replied the accountant, "We could have quality performance just as good as Transgear, but we wouldn't be making as much money." In fact, Sims knew that Transgear was not only the best performer based on quality, it was also among the most profitable. "It made us realize that our plants didn't know who the benchmark was in terms of being the best in a variety of areas. We needed a measurement system that would allow our plants to see how they ranked," said Linda.

Jim Jarrell told the group about a program he'd put in place, first at Hastech, then at the other plants he headed. The program's genesis came from a brief conversation Jarrell had with Frank Stronach when Jarrell worked at Magna. Stronach told him, "Just don't screw up the customer, the employee, or the financial side." Said Jarrell, "That stayed with me forever."

Jarrell created a performance measurement based on satisfying those three groups and used it at Hastech, Comtech, and Vehcom when he ran the three plants. Just when he was about to extend the system across his ten plants, he was named chief operating officer. Linda decided to expand Jarrell's program and take it company wide. The idea of balancing financial, customer, and employee satisfaction — three goals — lent itself to being described as three-legged, thus the name: Stepping Stool of Success. Begun in 1999, the program uses a simple visual of a colour-coded stool based on the traffic light, in each plant. A green light means targets have been met or surpassed, yellow shows the plant is on track, and red indicates that targets have not been met. As Jarrell puts it, "If you're red, you're dead."

A points system was devised for each of the three legs. In the case of the employee leg, for example, key measurements include turnover, absenteeism, and sales per square foot. The financial leg follows return on net investment, earnings growth, and the cost of manufacturing items, among other criteria. Customer concerns include warranties, quality, and on-time delivery.

The resulting report card not only identifies problem areas but also creates a lively company-wide competition. Twice a year, an animated film presents each plant's position relative to the others as trucks in a race. "Stepping Stool was a great way to organize reporting and allows us to easily spot issues, whether they were company-wide issues or plant-specific. You could see right away who is red and jump in to address that problem," said Linda.

Stepping Stool pays bonuses to employees and the executive team in plants that are declared green. "We saw it as self-funding. If you meet the objectives then it's paying for itself because the company's getting success from employees, customers, and financial," said Jarrell. "Stepping Stool is a foundation to the company and the leader. You need all three legs." Stepping Stool, which ranks employees as highly as customers and shareholders, is one of the reasons that none of the Linamar plants is unionized. "Employees feel involved and engaged in running the business. There's no need for third-party representation," said Linda.

With the average annual salary of employees about $50,000, good results from Stepping Stool can add another $1,500 a year to their pay. Members of the plant operating committee (plant manager, quality control manager, accounting manager, and operations manager) can earn as much as 15 percent of their salaries if their plant is green. Top winners are announced at a celebration held in Guelph with other regions participating by WebEx, an Internet conferencing system. To date, Linamar has paid a total of $57 million in bonuses. "Stepping Stool has become an essential part of our culture that emotionally ties people to strive for performance in the areas in which we wish to excel," said Linda. "We have a link between creating an emotion, driving performance — and ultimately — prosperity."

~

The evolution of Stepping Stool demonstrates how Linda and Jim Jarrell, who in 2004 added the title of president to chief operating officer, have become a strong leadership duo. "As you grow into and through a role you recognize where your strengths and weaknesses are and the importance of having a team around you that complements your strengths," said Linda. "Jim and I are very complementary and that's been a huge part of our collective success. You learn over time that you don't have to be the one to do everything, that maybe you're better off if you have somebody with more skill and experience in one area doing that piece and somebody else doing another piece. I help tie it together and provide some vision and strategy," said Linda.

A major cause of the change in management style, of course, is the much larger size of Linamar. "Linda definitely has a touch with everything but she is not as hands-on as her father was," said Ken McDougall, who oversees seventeen plants as president, Linamar Manufacturing Group Americas. "When I started in 1987, annual sales were around $80 million. Today there are individual plants doing over $100 million a year so it isn't physically possible to go in and micro-manage the way Frank would do. But she's definitely a chip off the old block. She's extremely intelligent and has a vision for longer-term strategy."

Since becoming CEO, Linda has also rebranded Linamar. "Your brand tells people who you are, where you are going, what they can expect from you, and what they perceive you to be. It sums up your culture, your strength, and your aspirations," said Linda. "It is critical for any company to have a consistent message to their customers, employees, and shareholders. This is particularly true for a company extending its global reach. In many areas of the world, Asia being a notable example, customers almost care more about how you approach business than what your business is. Your brand helps you explain that to them. It is your brand that drives people to make decisions about which company they want to work for, invest in, buy from, or support."

As part of the rebranding, Linda had a new corporate logo created in 2007. The previous version showed the word Linamar in a green box. In the new version, the original slogan, "Power to Perform," was retained but the box disappeared in order to declare the company's ability to think outside the box. The typeface was changed to bold capitalized letters in metal grey to reflect the company's history of metallic product manufacturing. Completing the picture was a diamond icon with a grid pattern in copper-orange that represents cutting tools, the products made by the company, and the autonomous yet collaborative nature of employees.

As the company has grown under Linda so has the number of employees per plant. "I think we're pushing the envelope a little bit at 300 to 500 employees. Instead of having four, five, or eight product lines, you might have twenty, thirty, or forty product lines. Some plants are large but with just one product line, a very large job for one customer. But more often you're going to have a series of, $5, $10, $20 million jobs, so the bigger the plant, the more complex the operation you're trying to run," said Linda.

If a plant gets too big, the relationship with employees can become stretched. "Once you get over 300 to 400 employees, it's very difficult to maintain the kind of relationship that we want between management and the shop floor. We want people to know each other by first name and feel comfortable talking to each other about concerns, issues, or ideas for improvement," said Linda. "If we get past the 300 to 400 employee level, that close relationship becomes increasingly difficult. At 500 to 800 employees in a plant, the chances of management knowing all of those people are slim. We'd rather have a more collaborative approach because there's no one who knows how to improve operations better than the people on the shop floor."

～～

Despite all the transformation by Linda, one immutable element remains. Linamar's corporate culture continues to thrive on the entrepreneurial spirit that was originally instilled by Frank. "I think we have a very strong and unique culture at Linamar with a solid grounding in an entrepreneurial approach to business with a top-line and bottom-line focus that flows right from my dad and his drive for success and growth. As an entrepreneur, he has a huge amount of respect for every person in this organization and the role that they play. Our culture is also about hard work, being responsive and innovative, and a balanced approach to customers, employees, and shareholders. It's what's made us successful and what we want to continue into the future."

For Frank, one of the most vital aspects of the Linamar culture is handpicking the right people as leaders. Linda has continued that crucial approach. "A leader who shows they care will have people follow them anywhere," she said. "We look for six leadership behaviours: people who are passionate, who are good planners, who can execute on that plan, have sufficient edge and acumen necessary to make tough decisions, who care about their people and their responsibilities, and who do a good job of communicating, both internally to their people and externally to customers, suppliers, investors, and our community."

A Linamar employee inspects an industrial application cylinder head for quality standards.

To create such leaders at all levels, Linda divided training into streams of interest. First, there's apprenticeship training for machinists and millwrights. Second, there's a management stream that includes succession planning and a mentorship program. The third element in the leadership evolution is the STAR performance management system, where STAR stands for Setting Targets, Achieving Results. The basic premise of STAR is the evaluation of an employee's performance as a blend of the results they achieve and how they attain those results. "The STAR system assesses each salaried employee's performance based on their behaviour as defined by our core values, leadership behaviours, and performance to goals. Outstanding performance nets you a larger salary increase and lands you in our succession planning program," said Linda. Today, about 140 of the most promising employees are enrolled in a development program aimed at getting them ready for a series of successful career moves.

STAR, begun in 2006 for executives and rolled out for everyone else over subsequent years, uncovers a person's greatest strength and areas requiring improvement, while providing helpful commentary. STAR had its beginnings when Linda read Jack Welch's book, *Jack: Straight From the Gut*, in which he describes evaluating people at General Electric. GE uses a similar grid system that assesses behaviour and performance, but what Linda put in place is totally customized for Linamar. Linda also gained a lot from a book by Jim Collins, called *Good to Great*, and her M.B.A. program. "Exposure to other leaders and other leadership styles is crucial. Every person you meet, every speech you hear, every book and every magazine article you read influences you. You might find something that's interesting, a way to motivate somebody, or a way to evaluate someone or a situation. There are always opportunities to learn."

Linamar's STAR system uses the company's twelve elements — six core values and six leadership behaviours — to measure individuals in their annual review. "STAR is not just a poster on the wall that says these are our core values and this is what we like to look for in leaders," said Linda. "If they reach a certain level of performance on the STAR review we put them in the succession program. High performance on the STAR also means you get the most opportunity for the highest wage increase. It's how we find who our STARs are."

Despite Linamar's growth, the company's core values remain constant, according to Dale Schneider, who started at the company as a co-op student in 1990, joined full-time in 1993, and is now chief financial officer. "It amazes me that we've been able to continue that intense entrepreneurship, mutual respect, and the solid foundation work ethic to build a company this size," he said. "We have adapted over the last twenty years. The plant you want to talk to is no longer down the road. You have to manage at a distance and motivate people at a distance."

Key to handling the changed perspective has been Linda's capacity for leadership. "Linda is definitely her father's daughter. What Linda has brought to the organization is an overall long-term vision of where we want to go. She's helped reinforce the culture of Linamar. It's through her that the core values of the company are well-known and understood," said Schneider.

According to Jim Jarrell, STAR ranks among Linda's best ideas as CEO. "The STAR system was a really good idea to cement a more formal system for progress reports with people. That was and will be one of the key things for the future of the company," he said. By creating programs such as STAR and Stepping Stool, Linda has made Linamar a more formal organization. "I've tried to provide more structure and more formality around communication, people development, and the systems that I think are critical for us to be successful globally. I've also been careful to allow enough innovation and ingenuity at the plant level and at the group level so we can have fantastic performance and great ideas. At the same time there has to be enough commonality in terms of systems, how we manage a new project, and how we approve a capital budget for a new program in order to mitigate the risk that can come from pushing too much control out to the plants."

Spreading the word about Linamar and its culture to the company's various constituencies is a major part of Linda's job. "The keys to developing and nurturing a strong culture are simple — communicate, demonstrate, and reward. People need to hear often about your culture, they need to see it demonstrated by every level from the CEO on down, and they must be rewarded for following that culture," she said. "Showing you care about your people, and treating them with respect, is an important element in staying connected. Visit the shop floor, talk to people, and see who meets your eye and who does not. Walking through a plant where our people don't want to meet my eye is a sure sign we have a management problem in that plant."

Like Frank, Linda is not only good with people but also with numbers. "The breadth of detail she can remember is amazing. She has an inherent sense to want to know everything that's going on," said Dale Schneider. Shortly after Roger Fulton joined Linamar as general counsel, he and Schneider, then director of financial analysis and planning, decided to have some fun during the legal department's budget approval process. There were six members of the executive but only five reserved parking spots in front of head office. As part of the budget, Fulton asked for a parking spot for himself. The two convinced Ed Newton to produce an official Kiwi-Newton drawing showing the additional spot as well as work required that included moving a large tree and a transformer.

Schneider sat with Linda on one side of the table, and Fulton sat across from them, presenting various items. "She's got a great sense of humour, otherwise Roger and I would never have pulled that stunt. We knew it would drive her nuts to have that drawing rolled up on the table and she took the bait."

Linda asked several times about the drawing. Fulton stalled by claiming that he wanted to present other matters first. Finally, Linda could wait no longer and demanded to see the drawing. Fulton spread it on the table and explained the need for a sixth parking spot.

"Well, how much will it cost?"

"It's only $50,000," said Fulton.

"Fifty thousand! Are you serious?"

He assured Linda that, yes, he was serious. By this time, Linda was flailing her arms and sputtering about the exorbitant cost. Schneider and Fulton let her vent for a while, then came clean, and everyone had a good laugh. No sixth parking spot was created.

For Linda, stringent oversight of corporate culture matters not only in the workplace but also in aspects of life in general. "We teach our children about the values to use in living their lives, to be respectful of people, to work hard, to be self-confident, polite, and well-behaved. We emphasize these values with our children every day, in our actions, in the behaviour we reward, and in the lessons we teach them. Creating a set of values in a company and then living by them is the same exercise. We as leaders need to live the values in our own actions, reward those that do likewise, and coach those that need to learn more."

Linamar's culture is very different from Magna, Canada's biggest auto parts company. "Both companies are very entrepreneurial, growth oriented, fast, creative, and innovative, but the one key difference that I saw when I worked at Magna is that it is more self-serving than the Linamar culture," said Jarrell. "At Magna, it's all about how do I benefit 'the me' versus benefit the company or the whole. I'm not saying that that formula is bad or not appropriate to drive entrepreneurism, but I think you've got to be on a team. At Linamar, we all wear the Linamar sweater. It's a unique culture."

As part of maintaining that culture at Linamar, bureaucracy remains at a minimum, just as it was when Frank ran the company. "If I need something, I can call a general manager in Asia at eight o'clock at night and that guy will help me," said Brian Wade. "And it's the same with Jim. When you have a problem, Jim jumps in and says, 'What do you need?' He doesn't tell us why didn't we do it, he tells us what we're going to do to fix it. We all want to solve the problem."

Transferring the Linamar culture to some countries remains a challenge. For example, the Linamar culture is difficult to export to Mexico where Linamar's four plants feed the Big Three, Caterpillar, and many other customers. Of the nine managers from Mexico brought to Guelph to learn the Linamar system, only one remains. Sending people from Guelph fared better but problems persist. "You can put expat people in there but you're never really going to make the Guelph culture work in Saltillo, Mexico. That's not the way they're built. You want to make sure that they understand the system that we have and what's really important. You also want them to understand how you get ahead in this business and who fits and who doesn't fit," said Jarrell. "Expats need to impart the general knowledge of how Linamar works, what's important, and what the expectations are but then tell them to use those in their own society to make things happen."

Linamar also uses CATs and the global operating system for its plants in Saltillo, Torréon, Nuevo Laredo, and Coahuila. Still, uptime in the plants — the amount of time machines are running — is not quite as good as in Guelph, so profits are slightly lower. "You're not going to change a Mexican guy to be like a Guelph guy. It's just not in their nature. They could have the house burning down and still say 'We don't need any help, thanks very much for coming, and off you go,'" said Jarrell. "That's their culture, they don't want to have conflict, and they don't want to have failure because they're proud people. You've got to adapt to that. The expat people who know us here are teaching there and making sure their systems are aligned to our culture."

⁓

Since taking over as CEO in 2002, Linda has more than doubled the size of the company. As part of that updraft, in 2005 Linamar became the world's largest supplier of camshafts with fifteen separate programs representing 24 million camshafts a years and more than $150 million in sales. More than two-thirds of all new business won in 2005 was in core products including $60 million of annualized sales in gears, $120 million in cylinder heads, and $60 million in transmission shafts and clutch models. The engine group also performed well with $260 million in new business. In the Industrial Group, sales jumped 75 percent. Skyjack became the largest scissor lift producer in North America with a market share of more than 30 percent.

By 2006, Linamar was also the largest producer of machined cylinder heads in the world as well as the largest producer of machined transmission shafts in North America. At the same time, parts were becoming more complex with more value added. New business wins in 2006 were up 34 percent over the previous best year, 2005. "I think Linda has opened up the eyes of the entire industry to her capability," said Dennis DesRosiers, of DesRosiers Automotive Consultants Inc. "She's proven to be the most capable person we have operating a parts supplier in Canada. I think that surprised some because of the female factor and the nepotism factor. But nonetheless, she was able to pull it off and that is incredible."

Linamar's revenue remains diversified. Linamar's four largest customers — Ford, Chrysler, GM, and Caterpillar — comprise about two-thirds of Linamar's total sales. Linamar doesn't want any customer to be more than 20 percent of its business and no powertrain platform should represent more than 5 percent of sales.

Green programs are also gaining traction. "We must increase focus on reducing CO_2 emissions in our atmosphere, and improving our environment. We have developed technologies for cylinder heads and camshaft designs that reduce emissions by up to 15 percent," said Linda. "These products meet a key need of our customers, and their customers, and will be important in increasing our market share and sales. There is also cost savings available in being more environmentally conscious. If we can reduce energy consumption, we help the environment and reduce costs for a win-win scenario. There is green in being green."

18

RECOVERING FROM THE CRISIS

T HE 2008 FINANCIAL CRISIS that began in the faraway trading rooms of Wall Street investment banks had a serious impact on Linamar. As the contagion from mysterious financial instruments such as derivatives spread around the globe, an implosion in consumer confidence sent North American vehicle production plummeting from 15.4 million vehicles in 2007 to 8.7 million in 2009. As a result, Linamar's annual revenue dropped by one-quarter and the company lost money for the first time since going public in 1986. In response, Linamar slashed dividends in half, grounded the corporate jet, reduced Skyjack operations to just three days a week, closed two plants, and cut overhead by $60 million. Jim Jarrell closely monitored cash flow and signed every cheque.

Linamar also reduced overall employment from 12,000 to 7,000. In order to maintain some of the more skilled employees for an eventual recall when conditions improved, about 2,000 of the 5,000 employees let go were placed on temporary layoff. "That was the worst part, dealing with the people issues. There would be a wife laid off at one plant, then the husband laid off at another plant, and that was difficult," said Jarrell. "We set a very objective standard, not subjective. Because when you're in a recession like that you've got to try and take the personal out of it."

Sales provided the objective benchmark that was used to decide the level of employment. For every employee there had to be $210,000 in sales or

$140,000 in what's called value-added sales, which is total sales less the cost of the materials, services, and taxes. As sales shrank, employment at Linamar had to come down, too. And when jobs were lost at Linamar, there was a collateral impact on the rest of the economy, since the each manufacturing job creates three-to-four more jobs in other companies supplying tools, materials, goods, and services.

Employee salaries were reduced across the board by 5 percent, management salaries by 10 percent. Executive compensation was reduced even more dramatically. Frank, Linda, and Jim Jarrell also voluntarily gave up all options and share appreciation rights they had recently received. All three had been granted 333,333 share options in both 2007 and 2008, 666,666 share options each, and those options evaporated.

Letting people go during the recession was personally difficult for Linda. "The massive upheaval of the economic recession on our organization from top to bottom also caused difficult days for the people that we had to let go to ensure our survival," she said. "It's tough to do that and try to keep a positive attitude when there was so much uncertainty."

In Linda's mind, communications was the top priority. "We quite consciously ramped communication and did plant visits to make sure employees knew we were still alive and well, had a plan, and were going to get through this. We told them, 'Tough times don't last but tough teams do and we're one tough team.' We cut costs, conserved cash, grew the business, sought opportunities, and kept our people motivated. We knew if we did all that successfully we were not just going to get through it, but get through it bigger and stronger and better than we ever were."

At one point Linamar was sending employees memos almost daily and holding conferences via WebExes monthly rather than quarterly. "There was so much uncertainty about the economy in general and the automotive industry in particular. GM and Chrysler were clearly on the edge so there was a lot of fear. The day that GM declared Chapter 11 bankruptcy we put a note out to all employees saying here's what happened, here's what it means to us, and here's what it means to you. We tried to stop the fear before it got too acute so that people understood and felt comfortable that we had put risk mitigation in place," she said.

The combined total of receivables greater than twenty days with both GM and Chrysler was less than $30 million, only about 9 percent of all receivables.

"We were able to say to our employees, GM has declared Chapter 11, here's how much receivable money we have at risk, it is not a material amount, it will not affect our ability to continue to operate as a company, it's not something you have to be worried about," said Linda. "GM is shutting down for a month. We will shut down in accordance with them. As they come back into production, we will resume as well. We did the same with Chrysler. It was important to get that message out because we were in a very good position. The level of business that we did with GM and Chrysler was less than some people had expected. Chrysler, for example, was only 9 percent of sales at that time." Ford was in a stronger position. It did not receive any government bailout money, and it has replaced GM as Linamar's biggest customer.

Keeping employees motivated was a problem, admitted Jarrell. "People are sitting there in a state of frenzy. 'Am I going to have my job? Am I not going to have my job?' How do you motivate people when they're not sure they're going to have a job and, second, what do you motivate them with? If you don't have money, you do it through good will, you do it through being very communicative, more than you typically would," he said. "You try and take it a little more lightly. We did some of the WebExes in the form of David Letterman top ten lists but it was tough because people were a bit freaked out. All you can do is recognize you're in a crisis, be very up front about it, and get yourself on offence versus sitting there feeling like a whipped puppy. You've got to get the leaders out there and carry that flag forward."

⁓

As part of the survival and turnaround effort, Linda took the lead in public by urging that governments offer auto-parts companies financial help, just as they had with GM and Chrysler. "We will see fewer OEMs and fewer suppliers either as a result of irreparable financial distress or for some as a result of a strategic shift out of the automotive industry," she said in a speech to the Automotive News World Congress in Detroit in January 2009. "The immediate future is a fairly gloomy place."[15] The Canadian government agreed to provide insurance on receivables through the Export Development Corp. in order to backstop possible losses. Like other firms in the sector, Linamar purchased those policies that were not normally available. In the end, the insurance was unnecessary because everybody came out of Chapter 11 and paid what they owed to suppliers and others.

Frank and Linda also sought to promote investor confidence in Linamar by buying more than $7 million worth of shares on the open market with their own money. During the downturn, Linamar's share price tumbled from a peak of $20.60 in January 2008, to a low of $2 in March 2009. Frank bought 250,000 shares in July 2008 at $12.58 and 100,000 shares in November 2008 at $6.69. Linda bought one million shares in December 2008 at $3.70.

Analysts who followed Linamar expressed concern about the amount of cash the company had on hand. "It was almost like they were feeding rumour rather than following fact, claiming that the banks would no longer allow us to draw on their credit facility," said Dale Schneider, who was then corporate controller. "We kept explaining to them that our credit facility was fully committed but for some reason the analysts weren't listening and this became a bigger and bigger issue."

To solve the dilemma, Linamar used bank credit to prepay some private placement notes six months before they were due. "Right after that our stock price started jumping through the roof because the analysts' cash concerns

Frank inducted into the Canadian Manufacturing Hall of Fame by Perrin Beatty, CEO of Canadian Manufacturers & Exporters, 2007. (Vern Harvey Photography)

had been 'alleviated' even though we'd been telling them for months that there wasn't any problem," said Schneider.

From 2008 to 2011, Linamar's cumulative total return increased by 295 percent and has remained above the TSX 300 Stock Index in four out of the past five years, assuming reinvestment of all dividends. At one point during the downturn, Linda and Frank considered taking the company private but decided against that course of action. "If you make a going private bid, you're basically putting yourself into play. You're creating the opportunity for somebody else to come in and make a counter bid for the company. I felt that was a real risk given the very low valuation that the market was giving us at the time. Secondly, even if your valuation is low, you are going to incur quite a bit of debt in order to take on that bid," said Linda. "Given the uncertain economic times I decided that taking on significant debt when there was such a lack of economic clarity was a high-risk scenario. We're now launching almost $2 billion worth of work and that requires $1 billion in capital. If we had tied up all of our debt capacity with money to go private, then that would impact our ability to grow. So we decided going private was the wrong route for us."

Once the general recovery began, and North American vehicle production bounced back to 12.1 million units in 2010, Linamar returned to profitability and started hiring again. Linamar first called back those employees who were on temporary layoff then started hiring again. By July 2010, the company's workforce had increased from by 3,000 to 10,000 — half in Guelph, the rest in other countries. Salaries were restored to previous levels and bonuses reinstated. In addition to base salary, Jarrell receives a bonus of 1 percent of Linamar's pre-tax profit, Linda receives 1.25 percent, and Frank 1.5 percent. Shareholder dividends were also restored to their previous levels. According to Jarrell, "We're out of the mess we were in and I do believe that we're on a slower growth pace which I think is actually better for business long-term. I don't think most businesses could take a 'hockey stick' uptick right now. We can't get the people, we don't have the equipment, and a lot of suppliers went away."

That disappearance of competitors means opportunities for Linamar. In 2009, the company won $400 million in "takeover" business, orders that customers needed on an urgent basis because their previous supplier was suddenly no longer able to fulfill a contract. Forty percent of that business was launched in 2009, the rest in 2010. Said Linda, "Some of our customers have told us we're the 911 of the automotive industry."

By 2011, employment had risen beyond pre-crisis days to 15,000. Most of those who'd been terminated during the downturn had found other work. "That made it much more challenging because we had a huge number of brand new, green people who didn't know the business and required a lot more training, development, and orientation," Linda said.

~

The return to better economic health caused Skyjack's annual sales, which had languished at $111 million in 2010, to rise by 150 percent in 2011. Sales of machined parts at Linamar rose by 25 percent. "We've had so much uplift coming out of the recession that I've been hiring from anywhere I can," said Brian Wade. "A few people have left Magna and come to work with us, but our technical staff is not keeping up to our growth right now. We have a training program in place for CNC set-up but it takes eighteen months to get somebody through it. Plus our customer demands are exceeding our capacity so everyone's running seven days and week and that stretches you."

The fact of fewer competitors has altered the landscape. Numerous smaller firms, those with sales under $200 million, went out of business. As a result, they no longer compete with Linamar by undercutting prices on specific jobs, selling lower quality goods, and eating into Linamar's revenue. For Frank, the recession was a good adjustment. "Governments made money on the bailouts and consumers benefited. If Chrysler and GM hadn't been bailed out car prices would have gone up because there would have been fewer manufacturers." Automotive consultant Dennis DesRosiers attributes Linamar's success to its strategic place in comparison to the competition. "Their true brilliance was getting into a manufacturing process that suits a developed economy like Ontario perfectly. They concentrate on the highest value added products in the marketplace. Low value added is very mobile. As it's become global, it has become a commodity. High value added requires high skill and a lot of technology," he said. "Linamar has been able to survive on an Ontario base where a few hundred other auto suppliers have disappeared. The simple stampers, injection moulders, low value added guys have fallen by the wayside. You can count the number of truly global companies in Ontario on your fingers.

Once you get beyond Magna, Linamar, Wescast, and the odd other company, you don't need very many fingers. Linamar's in that category because of the amount of technology in their processes."

For Jim Jarrell, another positive outcome of the recession was that Linamar no longer so readily gives in when the Big Three demand rollbacks on signed contracts. "You've got to manage your business. A lot of suppliers just rolled over. Big bad Ford's coming in, big bad GM is saying, 'You will give me.' Some suppliers say, 'We'll give it.' Well, I'll give it if I can," he said. "That's why the diversification play is so critical to Linamar. Because if a supplier works with just one customer, he's done like dinner."

⁓

As economic conditions returned to normal in 2010, Linamar reviewed the Vision 2020 target of $10 billion in sales by 2020. "We went back and forth on that and asked ourselves 'Are we truly going to invest?' and 'Are we truly going to grow the company?' because that's a long-term thing, not short-term," said Jarrell. "In the short-term you can act like a venture capitalist and just milk the company. But if you want to get to $10 billion, you've got to invest in the process, in people, and in infrastructure. We've got good strategies for global growth through acquisitions and greenfield projects. I feel confident that we've got a good roadmap. I think we can reach $5 billion by 2015 and have a line of sight for $10 billion in sales and $1 billion in operating profit in 2020."

Such a major investment in plant and people may mean lower profits and more employees than might otherwise be necessary because some employees are being trained for future expansion. "I wanted to make really sure Frank and Linda were committed as the family-based major shareholders," said Jarrell. "If we're walking through a plant and we see an extra supervisor who's being trained for growth, that's a good thing, but that changes the messaging. I don't expect Frank not to say, 'Why is that guy standing around?' I expect him to be right in my face about that every time and we'd better have a reason why the guy's there. And if I ask the question, I expect the supervisor to be able to answer. If I just get a deer-in-the-headlights stare, that's not a good answer. I want that acid test; I want that pressure. I want that because you should be able to answer the question. That's the bottom line."

In 2011, for example, Brian Wade launched a new $120 million program in an existing 400,000-square-foot plant in Mexico that will employ 1,200 to supply Getrag, a German transmission maker. In preparation for production beginning in 2012, he brought twelve engineers to Guelph for a year of training. "It's an expense that will pay off," Wade said. "A lot of the people haven't worked elsewhere. The Mexicans have mainly worked in Mexico, the Germans in Germany. But we are getting more cross-functional training now. I brought some Germans over to China to work, I brought some Canadians over to China, and some of the Chinese have come to Guelph, so we're doing more of that."

The advantage to the extra effort required to operate in Mexico was demonstrated by vehicle production figures following the global financial crisis of 2008–09. In 2010, vehicle production in Mexico quickly rebounded to a record 2.3 million vehicles, better than Canada's output of 2.1 million. The growth was caused by the worldwide popularity of smaller cars made in Mexico such as the VW Beetle, Ford Fiesta, and Nissan Versa. Popular cars are made in Canada, too, such as the Toyota Corolla and Honda Civic, but total production in 2010 was still below pre-crisis levels of 2.5 million vehicles.

As Linamar expands, the firm intends to maintain plants at the 150,000-square-foot size with 400 to 500 employees in each plant. The first plant in Wuxi, China, is larger, but the second one will be about 150,000 square feet. Other plants that are 300,000 square feet in size, such as Camtac and North Carolina, have to be that big because they make big parts with big machines. The workforce is still in the 400 to 500 range, the optimal number needed to maintain excellent employee relations.

That smaller scale has been a keystone throughout Frank's business life. "Frank's been successful because he remembers everything and he knows the four walls of almost every plant," said Wade. "When the plants get too big you start to lose focus on the small things and that drives your costs up. You focus on the big cost driver and you may not have that low-hanging fruit where you can eliminate it. So when I walk in, or Frank, or Linda, or Jim walks in as a fresh set of eyes, we'll say, 'Why are you doing that?' And they'll say, 'Wow, I never saw that.' Because they're focusing on the big stuff. But you'll find five or six small things that add up to more than that one big item. That's the only issue when the plant gets too big."

The number of plants will likely double to eighty by 2020. New global locations are crucial because the cost is too great to ship parts from Canada to other countries where Linamar's long-time customers have operations. If Linamar wants to maintain business ties with those traditional clients, the company has to stay close geographically. For example, the plant in Wuxi, an industrial city near Shanghai, began modestly in 2006 with a 10,000-square-foot facility leased from the Chinese government making valve bodies for a customer in China with whom Linamar already had a relationship in North America.

Once Linamar was established in China, more work followed after other potential customers saw that Linamar was committed to manufacturing there. By 2007, Wuxi had been enlarged to a 150,000-square-foot plant making components for a six-speed transmission program in Asia as well as other chassis and engine components and modules. "Once you're there, you're there, and then people say, 'They're not bullshitting, they're here.' There are a lot of suppliers who say, 'Give us lots of business, and we'll come.' But that's not the way it works," said Jarrell. "You get business once you've got people on the ground, and actually have infrastructure. It doesn't have to be big, but you're there."

Wuxi is now making transmission, driveline, and engine components in a 300,000-square-foot factory. Linamar brings workers to the plant by bus from pick-up points because they can't get there by themselves, then feeds them and supplies uniforms. The managing director of China spent several years in Guelph before going home to run the plant at Wuxi. "He is Chinese and his family lives an hour from the factory. He came back as a leader so he looks good in the eyes of his culture. Things like that help," said Jarrell. "The key is to try and get contracts with customers we know and build those relationships, then you can start to look at dealing with local Chinese companies. Going into a new setting is tough enough. A new customer is difficult because you don't know them. This way, we know the people we deal with," said Jarrell.

Customers in Asia include old friends such as Daewoo, General Motors, Delphi, Bosch, Caterpillar, and Cummins. Linamar is building two more plants in China and by 2020 could have as many as eight factories in Asia that might also include operations in India and Thailand. The company has a warehouse in South Korea but has no current plans to build factories in that country.

Linamar also recently won a job to produce parts in Mexico for shipment to Brazil. That new business could lead to more work in Brazil at which point Linamar might open a plant in that country. For the moment, shipping parts from Mexico to Brazil makes more sense than shipping from Canada because Mexico and Brazil have a treaty that reduces the tariffs between the two countries. Canada and Brazil do not have a similar trade relationship.

~

Given the many issues at play in Guelph and around the globe, stress and sleepless nights are part and parcel of being a CEO. "Anything that is difficult to do can be stressful. You achieve your goals by breaking them into a bunch of little steps," said Linda. "As a result, you're not climbing the mountain today, you're going to climb ten feet today and tomorrow you're going to do another ten feet. When you break a big task down into a whole bunch of little ones the job seems so much more achievable than looking all the way up to the summit. I certainly have nights where I've been kept up worrying and thinking about something, but you can't let it impact you to the level that it's affecting your health and your ability to have a clear mind. You do need to separate yourself a little bit but the higher you are in an organization the more difficult it is. I'm never away from this business. I might walk out the door, but I'm not really ever away from it. I'm pretty good at turning it off for a little while."

For relaxation, Ed, Linda, and their children visit his native New Zealand once a year and spend weekends at a cottage near Meaford, Ontario. Linda also has staff at home — two full-time and one part-time — who clean, do laundry, shop, prepare meals, and drive the four children to appointments and events. "That's the bonus, as you get higher up in an organization you have the ability to hire the staff at home to help you manage. When I'm not working, I can just spend time with my kids, help them with their homework, and have a relationship with them. I probably see more of my children than most working mothers."

That ability "to have it all" has applied throughout Linda's career. "On the way up you just need to find a way to make it work. I've heard other women, who are successful in business and also have family, say that they didn't necessarily wait for approval from somebody to leave early to pick up their kids. They knew they had a job to do and they had to get that job done. You've got twenty-four hours in a day in which to do it, so, you take control over that situation and say to your boss, 'I have to pick up my daughter. I've got this, this, and this done. I'm taking this home and I'm going to have that done tomorrow morning.' As long as you're doing a great job and you're getting everything done, then how can they ever question your capability, your dedication, or your ability to do that job or the next one."

In order to get to that next station in life, the only thing that's permanent is change. In 2010, Linda altered roles among her executive group, combining human resources and legal affairs under Roger Fulton, and giving Jim Jarrell responsibility for operations, new business, and product development. "Jim's role is integral to our success. With his focus on execution, I can spend a lot more time on external relationships and putting in place a strategy for the future. I told Jim I think of it as if I'm steering the canoe while he's shooting the ducks. He and I have a great relationship. He is fantastic at operations and sales, he's wonderful with customers, and a great team player," she said.

At the same time, Linamar reorganized into self-sustaining groups each with their own sales, marketing, product development, and human relations functions rather than share such administrative services as Linamar did in the past. Global vice presidents were named in functional areas to create a matrix-type of organization where the whole team is responsible for collective success. "The global vice presidents can highlight areas of concern to Jim so that they're addressed quickly and efficiently. They can also share best-in-practice ideas and make sure common required processes are being properly rolled out across the organization," said Linda. "That's a shift for us, to have that type of matrix structure where you have two bosses, a primary boss and a line boss."

Still, she notes that there needs to be a balance between independence and intervention. "Ideally you want them to be able to learn from their own mistakes just like you do with your own children. But you can't let them make a fatal error so you need to know when to step in. Nor can you just unleash somebody without any preparation, and that's where the leadership training and development comes in. They need to be armed with some knowledge and some skills."

In fact, it was the growth of the company that dictated the need for a change in approach. "Once you get past a certain size one person can't know everything that's going on. With 12,000, 15,000, or 20,000 employees and forty, sixty, or eighty locations, you can't possibly have enough knowledge to make a decision on everything. You've got to rely on others to make those decisions. If you want the right decisions then you have to train those leaders to think the way that you think. You have to make sure they're very clear on the strategy and then hold them accountable. You need to provide them with the support to meet those goals and that's where this matrix structure comes into play," said Linda.

As a result, Linamar's culture is also maturing, according to Brian Wade, vice president of operations. "In the 90s, Linamar was part of everybody's blood. If you needed something, each guy would work seven days a

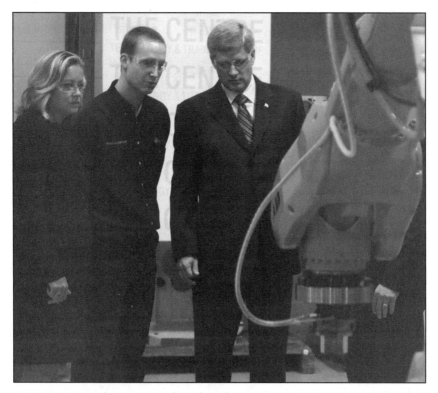

Prime Minister Stephen Harper with Linda and automation technician Ralph O'Brien at the official opening of the Centre of Excellence, 2009. (Waterloo Region Record)

week. They'd cancel things; they'd really go to bat. Although taking care of family was important, people weren't that worried about a balanced life. As we expanded and became global, we started putting much more emphasis on ensuring we had more robust quality systems in place. We're also getting a lot more diversified from a nationality standpoint and we're getting more professional diversity. In the past, we just grew guys like me. You came to the company, worked your way through, and got promoted. Now we're bringing more people from the outside so that brings a different look to the company."

These outsiders are more educated, come from a broad array of professional backgrounds, and often have worked for the Big Three. "We are trying to be one team, which is different than how it is at the OEMs where the political infighting is unbelievable," said Wade. "Here we don't have that. It's an open door policy. You might have some disagreements, but they last about a minute and then it's, 'How are we going to fix it?'" Even with this most recent transformation, everyone's still wearing the Linamar sweater.

19

ROOTS AND WINGS

ROGER FULTON HARDLY LOOKED like someone from head office. No dress shirt and tie for him on this occasion. His jeans, golf shirt, and relaxed manner made him seem more like one of the gathered group rather than a Linamar senior officer carrying the title of executive vice president, general counsel, and corporate secretary.

As closing speaker at the weeklong Linamar Leadership Development Program (LLDP), he told the assembled that even during the cost-cutting caused by the recent economic downturn, the one program that did not suffer was leadership development. "So that tells you the importance we attach to this program," Fulton said, and then asked each participant to tell him his or her "takeaway," the one thought that captured what they had learned in the week of study. "Follow-up," was the first response. "Watch my body language," said another participant. "Listen," said the next. "Actively," someone interjected to laughter all around. The takeaways continued: People are different so treat them differently; set realistic objectives; inspire people to change; manage conflict; provide clear, specific, and attainable direction; be considerate; lead every day by example; learn to adjust to conflict styles; and feedback is the number one motivator. "All of those are very people-focused," says Fulton. "I love to hear that. In the old days if we needed an accounting manager, we just automatically hired an accountant. We can't operate that way anymore. You have to be a good accountant but you also have to be very good with people. It's not good enough anymore to be good at one and not at the other."

This twenty-five-member LLDP study group, made up of managers and supervisors who lead front-line employees in plants in Canada and the U.S., met in the Hungary Room, one of half a dozen conference rooms at the Frank Hasenfratz Centre of Excellence in Guelph. They'd been at the centre all week but were still paying rapt attention even as the program entered its final few minutes. As of September 2011 about 600 of the 700 managers, supervisors, and executives at Linamar — including Linda and Jim Jarrell — had taken the mandatory fundamentals program. By early 2012, all 700 had completed the course.

In the basic program each group spent nine hours a day — plus homework in the evening — studying six themes set out by Valerie Beckett, corporate organizational development trainer: leadership effectiveness, performance management, managing change, dealing with conflict, communication, and coaching. The overarching message was that leadership is getting things done through others. Key questions discussed included, "What's the difference between managing and leading?" and "What makes some leaders stand out while others fail?"

The Friday closing session included a question-and-answer period with Fulton. The questions were submitted to him the previous day so the teacher did some homework, too, preparing his answers. One member of the executive — Fulton, Linda, Jim Jarrell, Mark Stoddart, or Chief Financial Officer Dale Schneider — open and close each weeklong gathering. Such participation underlines the importance the company places on the program and gives the employees direct access to thinking at the top. Attendees go through a follow-up session four months after the conclusion of the course to make sure lessons have been learned and put into practice. This course also leads to other leadership development programs in quality, safety, and finance.

The first question from the group was about Fulton's career and his initial role at Linamar. After working at as a general manager of human resources and legal affairs at Stelco, he joined Linamar in 2003 as general counsel, added corporate secretary along the way, and recently took on human resources as well. For him, leadership is all about being transparent and delegating. "It's really important to explain where you're going and why, and then let people do their job. As long as they understand the what and why, they're the experts and will do the how."

The next question was about Linamar's goal of $10 billion in sales by 2020. "Are we on track?"

"Yes," came the firm reply. "We'll be $5 billion in 2015. We certainly have a very clear runway to that figure."

Reaching the $10 billion goal will, however, require continuing effort because of the high cost of launching plants in Germany, North Carolina, Mexico, and China in 2012.

Such continued expansion will mean even more training and development with an emphasis on retaining top workers. "None of this happens unless you have the right people here as well as the right people who want to come here. It can be exciting work; it can be rewarding work." Fulton also predicted a further maturation of systems already in place including a new global operating system that will be both more rigorous and yet simpler at the same time.

Although the average supervisor oversees forty people, a questioner noted that some supervisors are in charge of fifty or more employees and wondered what tips Fulton had for those circumstances. Appoint team leaders or lead hands to help, he suggested. Both are positions where you can test potential leaders. "Putting in the effort up front will pay off down the road. If you're applying the techniques you've learned here with your people, your team will become used to how you're leading, how you're delegating. You'll see them respond and you'll have to do less and less of that over time. With help from lead hands, you'll have time to plan, not just run around like chickens with your heads cut off."

How do employees get the tools they need to achieve their goals? "We're a cost-conscious company and will remain so, but simply to just say 'no' on the basis of money is not an acceptable answer. One of the principal jobs of a leader is to provide the tools for those people who are working for us. If they're not getting those tools, it's a leadership issue." A recent engagement survey conducted at Linamar showed that 70 percent of all employees have worked at more than one plant. Such statistics should encourage general managers to have people take more training so they can switch roles, learn new skills, and have a broader knowledge about the company. "It makes you more valuable and makes the company better because you're better."

When information is communicated to management, how is it transmitted to people on the plant floor? "I think we do a fairly good job of flowing information out, but our concern has been to make sure that it gets all the way down and that's not always been the case," said Fulton. He cited a change in methodology that began with the quarterly WebEx held two weeks earlier. Plant operating committees were charged with cascading the ten most important slides to all employees. "I'm hoping that's what you're seeing. Has anyone seen that presentation?" No one had. "I'll take that back," said Fulton.

Are Linamar's wages and benefits truly competitive with the market? "I personally think we can start by improving some of our benefits. Our wages are very competitive. Last year, we reset our wage bands after three or four years of not moving the band. Our wage bands for skilled workers are very competitive against most companies. You'll get the odd outlier who will pay a lot more. Toyota blows everybody away, but if you're at the top of the wage band, you're being paid in the eightieth or ninetieth percentile. Can you get more somewhere else? If you're at the top of your wage band that's not going to be easy. Trying to tweak the benefits is the probably the best way to help increase the package."

The final question focused on Linamar employees who don't communicate well in English. Why doesn't Linamar have an English as a Second Language (ESL) program? Fulton noted that Linamar partnered with Conestoga College in a course called Pathways to Essential Skills that was launched in 2010. The course used online resources to train employees at the Frank Hasenfratz Centre of Excellence as well as at three Linamar plants in such skills as reading, writing, numeracy, working with others, and computer and communications skills. "That's been very successful and very well received. We're going to grow that."

He said the company had begun thinking about an ESL program after the engagement survey showed that English was not the first language of 65 percent of employees. "English-speaking workers are in the minority at Linamar. I think ESL is something that will fall out of the engagement survey as a pretty obvious issue that has to be addressed."

Said Fulton in his wrap up, "Go back and use the concepts you've learned here." Added Valerie Beckett, who thanked Fulton and organized the weeklong program, "Go forth and lead in your organization."

The Frank Hasenfratz Centre of Excellence in Manufacturing, where the course was held, officially opened on Woodlawn Road in Guelph in September 2009 with the help of a $44.5 million grant from the Ontario government. "This centre is a testament to who we are as a company, but it is also a tribute to where we came from. It is a company founded by an inspirational man with a vision to build a business, Frank Hasenfratz," said Linda at the opening ceremony. "He once famously said when he started Linamar he had a vision of having a business employing twenty or thirty people, a vision that clearly did not come true considering the 9,000 people we employ globally at Linamar. This centre is a testament not only to our history, but to the man who inspired it all and remains a driving force behind our prosperity and success."

Prime Minister Stephen Harper also attended and committed up to $54.8 million in the form of a loan for Linamar's Green and Fuel Efficient Powertrain Projects. "Our government is investing in research and development as part of our long-term commitment to the auto sector, and particularly, skilled labour and suppliers," Harper told the gathering. "We are seizing the opportunities that will get us through these tough times, ensuring our country emerges stronger than ever, and creating high-quality jobs in communities like Guelph."

The 80,000-square-foot centre houses training and development as well as product testing, design, tooling, and automation development. "We try to take advantage of any government funding that we can," said Linda. "There are several programs from the provincial and the federal perspective that we have tapped into and continue to take advantage of. These are very import-ant programs to help us afford to continue to invest in product, process, and people development that help us achieve our growth goals. The fact that the money was given to us here means that we commit to doing that work locally. That obviously creates skilled and semi-skilled jobs so it helps the economy in Ontario and Canada."

Linamar also benefits from government programs in other countries. In Germany, for example, the government pays up to 30 percent of capital expenditures through a cash subsidy. In Hungary, tax incentives are available.

The Centre of Excellence, erected by Kiwi-Newton Construction, is LEED (Leadership in Energy and Environmental Design) certified. The design brings indirect natural light into the building, thereby reducing the need for electric lighting and connecting people to the outdoors. To achieve this, there's a twelve-foot by forty-foot automated skylight in the ceiling of the 10,000-square-foot technology hall. The tech hall also features carpets made of recycled fibres and a "green wall" containing two tall pillars of plants that absorb carbon dioxide. In the spring and fall, a glass curtain wall on the front of the building opens to let in fresh air that has flowed over a pond. A control system automatically dims lights to low levels during daylight hours to save power. In the office and amenity areas, motion sensors automatically turn off the lights when there is no movement. Solar collectors on the roof produce power that is sold to the provincial grid. Concrete floors from the previous office and plant on the site were used as a granular base under the parking lot, thereby reducing truck traffic and landfill.

Initially, the centre housed projects such as gear development, making key prototypes, process development, and equipment testing. Since then, other divisions have been added including centralized purchasing. The equivalent of three-quarters of Linamar's annual sales comes in the form of some type of purchase and has the power to make or break the company, according to Linda. "At Linamar that means more than $1.5 billion in purchasing. Purchasing is an art. It is so much more than just getting three quotes. It is about really understanding the manufacturing costs around the product you are buying, using common sense in what to buy from where, understanding total cost including logistics, supplier management and quality, and being absolutely focused on every detail. You can do everything else right, but if you don't buy right you will not thrive," she said.

The centre opened just as the economy was going into a swoon. "Our original plan was for advanced tooling and automation but we put some production in there because we didn't want it to be a total cost centre," said Jarrell. "Now we really don't want to do production, we want to go back to the innovation side of the tooling, products, and processes. There's still limited production but it's become more of a support mechanism for the company's growth."

Production currently carried out in the centre will be phased out in 2012 in favour of prototype testing. "The centre had a vision, but it didn't have a clear vision," said Brian Wade, who ran it for a year. "When I went in we set some clear visions to make sure Linamar's going to have sustainable people and processes as well as the right product — not today, but in 2013, 2015, and 2020. The number one goal was to get leaner and more cost competitive on fixture building. Secondly, we started to put in the CNC set-up training systems so we've got people for the future. Thirdly, we created a team that was qualified cross-functionally so it was able to troubleshoot or help a quick launch. It can go anywhere in the world and help."

Brian Wade is typical of the today's leaders. He started at Linamar in the 1970s as part of Linamar's co-op program while he was a student at Guelph Collegiate Vocational Institute. He joined Linamar full-time in 1981 and was able to complete the three-and-a-half year apprenticeship program in two years because he was already a high school graduate. He learned programming as well as how to run many types of machines including milling, grinding, and turning. Among the eight apprentices in his group, Wade received particular mentoring by Ariss Plant Manager Ernest Severa, a tool-and-die maker from Austria. Frank also mentored Wade. "Almost from the first day, Frank would come and talk to me, give me some advice, or correct something I was doing."

Frank Hasenfratz Centre of Excellence in Guelph.

The close relationship continues to this day. "Recently I was trying to get some capital for a new job and Frank called asking, 'Do you need my help?' He made some phone calls, found some machines, and called me back. When he does jump in, you usually get your solution within twenty-four hours."

In the early years, Wade often worked seven days a week. "There were lots of postings to move into higher paying jobs, like supervisor or set-up, but I never took them. I really liked to learn. Every department I went into I stayed there until I'd learned it fully," said Wade. "I never asked for more money because Ernest didn't like to give it. I just took what I got, kept going along, and they treated me well."

Wade became lead hand at Cemtol then left Linamar in 1988 for Magna where he worked for two years in CNC programming while taking a course at Conestoga College to become a Certified Engineering Technologist. When he left Magna and returned to Linamar, Frank called him to his office and asked, "Did you learn anything?"

"Yes," replied Wade.

"Are you going to leave again?"

"No."

"Good," said Frank, and that was the end of the welcome-back conversation.

Wade became plant manager at Cemtol with 250 employees and $60 million in annual sales. "That's when I really changed. I had a smaller plant but I had more technical people than five plants put together. Whenever anyone asked for help, I always agreed and never put through an inter-company charge. I just let them go for a week here or a week there."

At the time, most plant managers didn't act the same way. "Everybody defended their four walls. But now we're so big and global that you have to be more insightful of what the other guy's doing. If I have a quality problem it affects other plants that are selling to the same customer but don't have a problem," said Wade. His helpful attitude was noted and is now being repaid by others. "I can call pretty well anybody."

In 2003, Wade was named vice president of operations in Germany when Linamar acquired Salzgitter Antriebstechnik, renamed Linamar Antriebstechnik, to make hydro-formed camshafts for major European manufacturers. In 2005, he was appointed group president of Asia. "I never felt I stepped into something I wasn't ready for. My biggest weakness was on the commercial side — the right pricing and the right quality. Jim [Jarrell] mentored me on that."

Among Wade's many successes was a turnaround at a plant that Linamar bought in Wales in 2008. "The first day I walked in, radios were playing and newspapers were open everywhere. It was just a non-professional facility." When he arrived there were 520 employees making 2,000 power takeoff units a week. A year later, there were 202 employees making 3,000 units a week. During the same period scrap was reduced from 20 to 30 percent to less than 4 percent. Casual absenteeism, which had been running as high as 40 percent, became non-existent. "I was in their face every day. I kept saying, 'Guys, you're going to have to change.' And they did." In 2010, Wade was named vice president of operations and quality manufacturing, which meant he was in charge of standardizing quality levels in all plants. In 2011, he was promoted to vice president of the driveline group.

~

Frank played a similar mentoring role when Leigh Copp was a grade twelve student at Centennial Collegiate and Vocational Institute in Guelph. Copp was not enjoying school but liked science and technology so focused on courses such as machine shop and electrical shop. Copp's father, David, arranged a meeting with Frank through a mutual friend.

When they met on a Saturday morning in January 1986, the seventeen-year-old Copp told Frank he was tired of school and wanted to start an apprenticeship program. "A job's a lot like a girlfriend," said Frank. "It's okay for a little while but then you get bored and you want to move on. I'm not going to waste my time on an apprenticeship for you because you're going to get bored and move on and then we've both wasted our time and I've wasted my money."

Copp assured him he was interested.

"Will you work hard?" asked Frank.

"Better than anybody," Copp replied. "Just give me a chance."

"I'll give you a summer job, but you've got to finish grade twelve first."

Copp passed grade twelve and that summer worked in the maintenance department. Every year after that, he would have another conversation with

Frank who would urge him to complete just one more year in school. Because of Frank's carrot-and-stick approach, Copp spent three years at McMaster in Hamilton in engineering physics and then took the four-year electrical engineering course as well as a master's degree at Ryerson in Toronto. All that time, he worked summers at Linamar, doing "doubles," which meant eighty hours a week, to help pay for his education.

After Copp graduated in 1995 and joined Linamar full time, Frank held a small celebration party for Copp, who finally revealed the truth about all those conversations when Frank promised more work if he would just continue his education for one more year. "I didn't tell you, but when I finished grade thirteen, I would have never quit school. I put you on, you didn't put me on," Copp told the gathering.

Their close relationship has continued. "Over the years we've had many one-on-ones. Frank has been a phenomenal influence on me." Frank continued to spur Copp on by changing the incentives from summer jobs to possible promotions. On one occasion, Copp was up to his elbows in gunk trying to fix a coolant pump in a broach pit. "It's one of the most disgusting machines that we have. It's like a sewage system," said Copp. It was a Saturday afternoon in 1989 and Frank, still wearing his whites after playing tennis, showed up at the plant unannounced.

"How are you doing?" Frank asked Copp.

"Well," he said, gesturing to the goo that had splattered on his uniform.

Said Frank, "You've got to learn to do this too, or how are you ever going to understand what's going on beneath you when you become a manager?"

Commented Copp, "I had a number of instances like that with Frank. The fundamental philosophy of Linamar was that all the managers and engineers spent time on the shop floor before they got a desk."

Copp is now engineering manager at the Centre of Excellence where he runs Linamar Advanced Systems, a twelve-member team that designs and builds control systems and automation for the various plants. He is also Linamar's expert in induction hardening, a process that heat-treats transmission parts so they are hard on the outside but soft on the inside, which is the best for longevity. Traditional heat-treating hardens parts all the way through and does not create a ductile, resilient component.

Copp has an equally close relationship with Linda that dates to her first few months at Linamar in 1990. When she was working the jig-boring mill at Hastech, the machine crashed. Linda had arrived for her shift and cycled the machine without checking first to see if anything had changed. In fact, the previous operator had changed some of the settings. "It was a good lesson," recalled Linda. "Never assume what was true yesterday is true today." Copp was summoned to get the machine up and running again.

A year later, when Linda was a materials manager, an outside supplier had a machine problem that was affecting production at Linamar. Linda drove Copp to the nearby plant where he fixed the supplier's machine so production at Linamar would be maintained. "She's always got a 'hello' and a 'how are you?' She remembers my roots," said Copp. "I know that when something really, really dire is on the horizon, I can walk into Frank's or Linda's office and say, 'You need to know about this.'"

～

The days are long gone at Linamar when managers were people like Ernest Severa who were trained in Britain or Europe before coming to Canada. Nor are there enough people like Brian Wade or Leigh Copp to fill all the openings for skilled workers as Linamar grows globally. Increasingly, the company has to hire workers with little or no experience while creating more and more training programs to teach them the necessary skills.

Much of Linamar's training, from driving a forklift to leadership programs, is carried out at the Centre of Excellence. Among the 320 employees who work at the centre are a dozen individuals taking the three-year apprenticeship program. The rest of the apprentices, 250 in all, work at different plants in Guelph. "If I could get all those apprentices fast forwarded now, I've got jobs for all of them. Future leaders, future succession, I feel comfortable, but the technical people is where we have a gap," said Jarrell.

The centre also houses a separate design-build business, McLaren Performance Technologies, which focuses on transmission gears and cases. McLaren's test facility in Livonia, Michigan, conducts research and development on engines. "I see the design-build team growing as we continue to take on increasingly complex modules and ultimately systems. Ultimately, it will become the majority of our business. The next ten years are going to be about our customers outsourcing more than they are now," said Linda. "About 70 percent of the engine and transmission content is still being done in-house by our customers. The first wave will be to get that all outsourced. The next wave will be design involvement in terms of modules for engines and transmissions that would be designed by the suppliers. It's already happening in driveline systems. At the moment, the axle and the all-wheel drive or rear-wheel drive systems are being purchased in their entirety from the suppliers who have the design responsibility."

Linamar acquired McLaren, a storied name in automotive engineering, in 2003. Originally established in 1969 to develop engines for Bruce McLaren Motor Racing, McLaren now specializes in product design, development, testing, and analysis; product engineering; and prototype building services for the automotive industry. One of the innovations produced by McLaren since the acquisition by Linamar was Opti-Power, which uses custom cylinder heads to optimize the fuel-air flow prior to the combustion cycle. While the process had previously been used in racing, it had never before been used in production vehicles. "These custom cylinder heads for racing typically cost thousands of dollars so they're unsuitable for mass production," said Linda. "Our real achievement is that we have found a way to machine these optimized cylinder heads at a normal production cost." Opti-Power was used in the Corvette Z06 and the 2008 Dodge SRT's V10 engine that produced 600 horsepower. Linamar also machined the intake and exhaust ports of the V8 engine in the 2012 Mustang Boss 302. "This technology is definitely not confined to high-powered vehicles," she said. "The same method can help produce a fuel-efficient family car." Just what you'd expect from a family business.

20

STEERING THE CANOE

LINDA HASENFRATZ RESUMED HER seat at the same boardroom table
where she had just spent the last six hours working with the Linamar board
of directors. Despite the demanding nature of the lengthy board meeting
that reviewed strategy for the coming year, she still looked chic in a stylish
two-piece suit, her long blond hair falling exactly where it should, lipstick
and makeup refreshed during the brief break. It was 5:00 p.m. on August
10, 2011, the scheduled time for the regular conference call held every three
months to talk about Linamar's earnings with analysts from brokerage firms
across Canada.

This day's topic was the second quarter financial results just made public
after the markets closed an hour earlier. Linda glanced around the twenty-
foot long table at the members of her executive team who were on hand to
provide detailed information. Present were President and COO Jim Jarrell,
General Counsel Roger Fulton, Chief Technology Officer and Executive
Vice President of Marketing Mark Stoddart, and Chief Financial Officer
Dale Schneider.

After the conference call operator had launched the proceedings, Linda
opened her thick black binder, leaned toward the speakerphone parked in
the centre of the table, and then rattled off some numbers that included
record sales in the second quarter of $743 million, up 30.7 percent from

the same quarter a year earlier. Profits were $28 million, up 11.6 percent year-over-year. Skyjack sales had doubled year-over-year with prospects for continued recovery in the industrial segment.

Looking ahead, Linda cited industry expectations for moderate growth of vehicle production in 2011 of 12.7 million units in North America, 20.3 million in Europe, and 36.3 million in Asia, increases of 6.3 percent, 5.9 percent, and 3.9 percent, respectively over the previous year.

Content per vehicle, a way of measuring Linamar's market penetration, had also continued to improve. In North America, content per vehicle was $142.83 up from $92.84 in 2005, $11.33 in Europe from $7.66, and $3.44 in Asia from $0.07. "Growing market share is particularly critical in softer markets as is evidenced by our great sales growth at the moment, despite auto production levels being less robust on a global basis," she said.

Linda told the analysts that Linamar was planning four new plants, one in North Carolina, one in Guelph, and two in China — one of which will be in Wuxi, where Linamar already has a factory, the other in the Tianjin area. "We are also continuing to explore India as well as Brazil as potential expansion sites over the next few years," she concluded, and then turned the meeting over to Dale Schneider for a more detailed financial review.

Following Schneider's presentation, the analysts asked questions on such topics as profit margins, raw material prices, interest expense, and electric vehicles. Linda closed the session with a summary of her main messages. "First, we're thrilled to see both sales and profits growing in double digits over last year and notably another record high for quarterly sales. Our back-log of new business, now $2.5 billion strong, is the driving force that will continue this trend of both sales and earnings growth over the next several years. Secondly, it's great to see the industrial segment break into a profitable position after nine quarters of losses. Lastly, we are very pleased with the finalization of another tranche of well-priced long-term debt that secures the company's access to capital to grow."

The conference call, which lasted a little less than an hour, is one of the many ways that Linda, as CEO, regularly reaches out to Linamar's various stakeholders. "One of Linda's strengths is her connection to the outside world, her ability to deal with the analysts, shareholders, agencies, and governments," said Jarrell. "She has a very good presence and good optics for the company. She plays that role well. Linda's the visible presence, Frank's the money, cost,

lean, lean, lean, and I keep everything flowing." For his part, Frank believes
Linda has many talents that he does not possess. "I'm too direct. I go too
quickly to the point instead of playing it up and convincing the other party,"
he said. "She's more willing to take time with people. There have been occasions when I lost my temper. You should never do that in business."

~

Among all of the auto parts companies in the world, Linamar is the largest
devoted solely to making precision-machined components, focusing on highly
engineered systems including transmissions, engines, brakes, steering systems,
and suspension systems. According to the July/August 2012 issue of *Report
on Business*: "The Top 1000," Linamar ranks 157th among all businesses in
Canada based on an annual profit of $101 million. Measured by annual rev-
enue, Linamar's $2.9 billion in revenue is topped in the automotive sector only
by Magna, Ford, and Honda. In January 2012, Linamar had almost 16,000
employees in 39 plants with 8,016 employees in Guelph, 3,347 in Europe,
3,237 in Mexico, 702 in Asia, and 477 in the United States. Linamar's target is
to have 25 percent of employees technically focused, a description that covers
such roles as engineers, skilled trades, and quality control.

In many specific products, Linamar is the clear leader. More than 80
percent of its business is in powertrain assemblies and parts. The company
is one of the largest independent producers of automotive gears in North
America and the largest producer of machined cylinder heads in the world.
In addition, Linamar has 37 percent of the North American market share
in differential cases, 34 percent of the market share in camshafts, and 22
percent of the market share in cylinder heads. Skyjack is the largest scissor-
lift platform maker in the world.

Beyond such numbers, being productive and competitive are the other
main gauges of success. "Competitiveness is really all about innovation and
efficiency in terms of the products and processes you develop, and the ability
to be continuously improving both of them. In turn that involves planning,
purchasing, managing your people, your costs, as well as the taxation and
regulatory regime," said Linda.

While some companies use sales per employee, Linamar measures productivity using value-added sales, a figure that does not include the cost

of materials that go into making the products. For Linda, productivity is best measured by value added sales per employee. "Politically there's lots of talk about poor productivity for Canadian companies. They use sales per employee as a measure but that's not a good measure because all we'd have to do to improve our productivity is outsource 90 percent of what we do to China. Does that make us more productive? We'd still have our sales, but we'd hardly have any employees. That, apparently, would make politicians happy. I honestly don't think they really think these things through. I have yet to see anything that accurately measures productivity compared to competitors, which would be a value-added calculation. That's the one that really matters. At Linamar our competitiveness and efficiency goes up every year."

Identifying and taking advantage of opportunity requires passion, edge, and acumen, according to Linda. "Successful businesses inevitably have that entrepreneurial spirit of passion and motivation and focus on performance firmly rooted in their leadership. That is certainly true at Linamar where our founder, my father, is the consummate entrepreneur. His spirit continues to inspire many more entrepreneurs within our company."

In an entrepreneurial culture like Linamar, Linda believes extolling success is important. "We need to take the time to celebrate when we win, to acknowledge the great achievements of our people, and do so regularly. Positive words of praise go much further and are remembered longer by more people than negative words of criticism. But don't get too carried away. Success isn't forever, just like failure isn't fatal. If you win, celebrate, then get back to work. If you lose, mourn the loss, then get back to work."

⁓

A successful strategy is the best way to have more wins than losses. The all-important annual strategic planning process begins in late July when Linda meets with her senior executives to review the different areas of the company, analyze strengths and weaknesses, and then study the opportunities and threats in the marketplace. Once they've identified goals for the next year and the next five years, Jarrell discusses those goals with the fourteen people who report to him. The executive group then revisits the topic and the result is presented to the August meeting of the board of directors for approval.

In September, the strategy is shared with the top cadre of the Linamar leadership at the Annual Strategic Business Review Meeting (ASBRM). Four hundred supervisors and managers gather at the Centre of Excellence — with 300 more watching and listening via WebEx in other countries. In November, directors receive an in-depth presentation about products, customers, and growth followed in December by an update on the financial plan. At the other board meetings during the year, in March and May, each of the major groups makes a presentation so directors continually hear about progress in all areas.

During the strategic review, Linda seeks the right balance between risk and reward, performance and innovation, systems and freedom. "Our customers and our shareholders want consistent, sustainable earnings growth and our customers want consistent, cookie-cutter performance. I can go to this plant, I can go to that plant, and I know I'm going to have the same system, the same quality, and the same high performance. But we also want the innovation, ingenuity, and speed that comes from the entrepreneurial approach of letting people run their own businesses," she said.

At the ASBRM in September 2011, held in the tech hall at the Centre of Excellence, the mood was upbeat with tentative overtones bearing in mind the volatility of stock markets, the fragility of Europe, and the political bickering over debt and deficits in the United States. In her opening remarks, Linda cited Avery Shenfeld, chief economist at CIBC World Markets, who has said that any recession that might occur would be shallow. "No economist is sticking their neck out and saying we're definitely headed into another recession. On the other hand, there are lots of other folks out there who are making those kinds of comments. That kind of conflicting messaging is really having a detrimental impact on consumer confidence. The sooner we can see some clarity on where things are going, the better. It's the uncertainty that creates the issue," Linda told the gathering.

Despite worries about a double dip, automotive sales have held up well. "There is some pent-up demand. We're barely covering scrappage rates at current levels of production," she said. In North America, year-to-date sales in 2011 were 11 percent higher than in 2010. Sales in Europe were flat but production was up 10 percent because one-third of all vehicles made in Europe are exported. North American vehicle production is expected to go from about 13 million in 2011 to 15 million in 2013, with Europe up from

20 million to 22 million and Asia rising from 36 million to 42 million in the same period.

Other numbers flashing on the giant screen behind the podium demonstrate that Linamar has bounced back from the recent recession. Employment more than doubled from 7,000 in June 2009 to 14,900 in June 2011. In 2009, there were only seventy-five new program launches; in 2011, there were 214. "We are keeping a close eye on the situation and we know how to react if we start to see things start to turn down," Linda said. "If there's an issue with the launch of a new program, we want to know about it. Raise your hand so we can send in some resources and get things back on track because one leak can bring down the ship. We're in it together. We're a team."

In addition to presentations by other Linamar executives, the ASBRM also included video clips intended to leaven the proceedings and deliver key messages. One video from the movie *The Matrix* showed Keanu Reeves sparring with Laurence Fishburne using kung fu choreography enhanced by special effects. "We don't expect to see you do somersaults over the Ford purchasing guy but in the video he's courageous, results oriented, and sets himself a vision and a strategy. He manages risks, has balance and respect for his opponent, he's ingenious, has a strong work ethic, and shows perseverance and responsiveness just like we need to in a marketplace that is always changing."

Another video clip, this one meant to illustrate leadership, featured Mel Gibson as Scots hero William Wallace in *Braveheart* facing a vastly superior English army. In the initial banter before his famous "Sons of Scotland" speech, the shouted answer from his ragtag troops to Wallace's question "Will you fight?" is "No, we will run — and live!" Replied Wallace, "Aye, fight and you may die. Run and you will live at least awhile. And dying in your beds many years from now, would you be willing to trade all the days, from this day to that, for one chance, just one chance, to come back here as young men and tell our enemies that they may take our lives but they'll never take our freedom." Of course, in the movie, Wallace's words carry the day and the fired-up Scots are victorious in battle. "I know we're not fighting battles for our country or our freedom," said Linda after the video had played. "But that enthusiasm, good decision-making, good planning, good execution, and good communications, that's what will make all of us great leaders."

Linda with Linamar officers. Front row from left: Jim Jarrell and Mark Stoddart. Second row from left: Dale Schneider, Ken McDougall, Brian Ahlborn, Brad Boehler. Back row from left: Kai-Uwe Wollenhaupt, Roger Fulton, Henry Huang. (Absent Nick Adams.)

Next came a live question-and-answer session with Frank, who did fight for his freedom, that highlighted his leadership style and how he wants to be remembered. "Not everybody is capable of being a leader. All of us have a limit. Don't push people over that limit because it could be very bad for that person and for the corporation. Technical knowledge you can teach. Personality you cannot. Once you're twenty-five you aren't going to change. I once walked through a plant with I guy I had interviewed. He lagged behind me all the time instead of being interested in what we were doing. He'd never make a leader. He's a follower," said Frank.

Some people who appear tentative can be trained to be leaders but only if they know deep within themselves that they are truly capable. "Believe in yourself. That's the first thing. Take advice from others and sort out what's good advice and what isn't. If you don't believe in yourself, if you can't project that you truly believe, it's not going to happen."

Frank also told the group that he wanted to be remembered as a founder who created a corporate culture that will continue long after he's gone. "We developed a few numbers and rules years ago that came from my family. Never spend more than what you have. Or never spend more than you know you're able to pay for. Never borrow more money than one year's cash you're generating. When you spend $1 you need to generate $2 in revenue and you should make about 7 percent profit. Run a tight shop. Learn from the past, but look ahead."

After Frank left the stage to applause, Roger Fulton reported the results of an employee engagement survey carried out in the spring. Almost 12,000 employees participated, or 84 percent of the total work force. The usual response level for such questionnaires is closer to 60 percent. Each respondent took an average of twenty minutes to answer sixty-four questions about themselves and their attitudes toward Linamar. The profile that emerged showed a young workforce: 70 percent are under forty-four and 43 percent under thirty-five. About half have been at Linamar less than three years. English was not the first language for 65 percent of respondents.

In terms of their relationship with their bosses, 91 percent said that during the last year they'd had a conversation about their performance;

77 percent said it was a fair conversation. More than 25 percent had held three or more positions during their time with the company. Seventy percent said they felt safe in their jobs, both emotionally and physically.

After presentations by various group leaders about their specific strategies, Jim Jarrell returned to the podium. "That's our current battle plan. We know it will change and it will evolve. All organizations need to make three groups of people happy: customers, employees, and shareholders. All of us struggle, juggling the balance that happens when things get tough and there are tough decisions to be made," said Jarrell. "Consider the three — customers, employees, and shareholders — as balls you have to juggle. How do you do that? Now, let's see these balls as being made of glass. You drop one of them. It might get marked or nicked; it actually might get fractured. If that happens, how do you recover? A lot of companies will rank these three. Southwest Airlines, for example, has a pyramid with employees on the top. At General Motors, the shareholder is first. At Linamar we think of all three."

Jarrell asked how many people recently had to work seven days a week to satisfy a customer. Hands went up throughout the audience. "The question on its own is a little absurd. Why? I guarantee you if we worked seven days a week, 100 percent of your quality people will leave. What happens then? We can't produce a quality product, which means I can't ship to my customer, a situation that will eventually impact the shareholder. Instead, we need to add more people, add more machines, because we need to make sure that quality people are satisfied in this organization. It always comes back to balance, and keeping these three glass balls in the air," he said.

Is Linamar in balance or off balance? "That's a question you should think about when it comes to planning. We have a Stepping Stool metric system. We can see we're yellow on our customer leg. We're green on our employee leg and we are red on our financial leg. On the metric system, we would show ourselves to be off balance. However, when I think where we've come during the last couple of years, on the management philosophy of balancing our Stepping Stool, I think we're moving to a more balanced approach. That's critical for all of us to know in our day-to-day thinking," he said.

Jarrell's remarks were followed by a video that's used in the LLDP leadership program to underline the importance of communications. The video showed a beggar sitting in a city street with a hand-lettered sign that said, "I'm blind. Please help." Passers-by paid scant attention. A woman stopped, rewrote his sign, and coins began clattering into his cup. The video ended by revealing the new words: "It's a beautiful day and I can't see it." Said Jarrell, "The video talks about changing the way of communicating. In my view, the more we are interconnected as a team, utilizing the talents of all of the individuals in this room and around the world, the more we will be fast-paced, we will grow, and we will set this company on fire."

After a presentation of cash awards to half a dozen employees who had come up with the best new product ideas or suggestions to save costs, Linda brought the meeting to a close. "We've talked a lot about being one team. If we're one team, we all need to know what's going on in the organization. Our ability to change is directly linked to our ability to be successful. We need to lead, not push, our people. Leaders need to lead by example. Balance is the key."

Linamar's corporate culture is more than a few finely crafted sentences framed and hanging on a wall. "This is who we are, how we need to work, and work better as an organization in order to be successful. We've got a great opportunity ahead of us at Linamar. There's a huge market we're focused on. We've got great technology and fantastic people to make our road map a reality."

The final video, a collage of scenes from various sports movies featuring a bevy of actors from Gene Hackman in *Hoosiers* to Sylvester Stallone in *Rocky*, celebrated teamwork, leadership, performance, and victory. With the major league baseball playoffs approaching, Linda ended the four-hour meeting by saying, "Let's get out there, team, and hit it out of the park!"

⁓

Increasingly, the game is both changing and more challenging. Twenty-five years ago, the auto manufacturers started looking for ways to streamline their costs and make their operations more flexible. The answer was in outsourcing. They began by outsourcing low-value parts then moved on to seating, instrument panels, and bumpers. Eventually the OEMs began offering a few contracts for engines, transmissions, and the driveline, the three areas that make up the powertrain. "The powertrain is the last area of the vehicle to be outsourced precisely because it is so important to the consumer. The powertrain represents around $3,000 content per vehicle, a significant percentage of the overall cost," said Linda. "Coupled with a market of more than 50 million vehicles per year this represents a market potential of $150 billion which will grow to $250 billion in the next ten years."

At the moment, Linamar has only $1.5 billion in sales to this sector, a 1 percent market share, because powertrain outsourcing is still in its infancy. "But with every new platform launched they are outsourcing more and I have no doubt will eventually outsource it all. This is hugely exciting to us as it means we can grow this part of our business to $6 to $8 billion annually just by doing what we are doing now for more vehicles in more parts of the world," said Linda.

Another sector with potential for growth is alternative energy. Wind and solar comprise only about 2 percent of Linamar's total sales but the company is aiming for that to become as much as 10 percent. Wind turbines are growing more quickly than solar possibilities with Linamar making machined components inside the gearbox for wind turbine manufacturers. Linda noted that years ago Linamar started talking about diversification. "To us diversity meant taking the same things that we're making today or processes we're expert at and selling them to new customers or to new geographic markets. Wind is a great example because we're manufacturing shafts, gears, covers, and housings, the same kind of things that we make for our automotive customers, but on a much larger scale. We're taking a process expertise that we already have — precision machining to very high tolerance — scaling it, and taking it to a brand new market that has a huge amount of opportunity."

The market, which is well advanced in Europe, is just opening up in North America so there isn't a well-established supply base. The parts are so large it makes no sense to ship them from European makers. As a result, in 2010 Linamar formed a strategic alliance with German-based NCB Lohmann GmbH to develop and build wind turbine components for customers in North America where the market is an estimated $4.5 billion a year. "It's a great opportunity for us to get in on the ground floor as a pre-eminent supplier of machined components for a market that is really just starting to emerge in North America. We've just won our first contract, maybe $50 million when it's all ramped up, but we see the potential to grow quite a bit from here," she said.

In solar power, Linamar worked for three years with Stirling Energy Systems Inc., of Scottsdale, Arizona. Stirling's solar dish converted the sun's rays to energy for electricity grids using a closed system of hydrogen gas that drives the pistons of a combustion engine designed and made by Linamar. Stirling had contracts with two California utility companies but was unable to raise the necessary investment funds and filed for bankruptcy in 2011. "For Linamar, making the solar engine is a another great way for us to take a process and a product that we know and take it to a whole new industry where there's significant growth potential in terms of revenue," said Linda. "We were expecting $200 million a year minimum out of this project. So it's a little frustrating that our customer was not able to get funding because the technology's there and the desire seems to be there on the part of consumers and the U.S. government. In his 2011 State of the Union address President Obama said 80 percent of energy should be supplied from renewable or efficient sources within the next twenty to thirty years."

Despite such setbacks, Linamar remains on track to reach its target of $10 billion in revenue and $1 billion in operating earnings by 2020, a level of growth that requires a 15 to 20 percent annual increase in revenue and will result in a healthy 20 percent return on equity for shareholders. For a time, growth was running at 30 percent but debt levels were rising too quickly. Growth of a more reasonable 15 to 20 percent can be financed by cash flow, which means the company won't have to take on burdensome debt to pay for new plants, new equipment, and expansion into new markets. At the end of 2011, as the company looked ahead to the interim goal of $5 billion in sales by 2015, there was already $4.1 billion in business booked.

As part of the strategy to increase European sales and market share, in 2011 Linamar bought the three commercial and industrial divisions of the Famer Group of France. Famer's main business is making parts for commercial vehicle manufacturers as well as Peugeot and Renault. "It's critical to have actual business on the ground in France in order to be able to really make headway with these customers. It's more of a nationalistic thing than a regulatory requirement. Once you're in then you can supply from other locations as well," said Linda.

The Famer facilities in St. Romain en Gier, St. Etienne, and Montfaucon employ 300 workers making cylinder heads and gears, as well as other

engine and transmissions parts, with an annual revenue of €50 million
(C$70 million). By building new plants in China, Linamar is following a
different method in the same strategy: making auto parts for client firms
in the geographic regions where those clients are situated. Asia and Europe
combined represent a vehicle market more than four times larger than
North America.

By 2015, Linamar will have doubled in size to eighty plants and 30,000
employees. "That means we need thousands of new supervisors, managers,
and skilled people so that has become our top priority," said Linda. "In particular we have to make sure that we're identifying our top talent, and getting
them into succession programs and development programs to take on the
next role. Attracting the people that we need and motivating the whole group
have become key priorities for us." Those thousands of newcomers will stand
on the shoulders of those who have gone before.

21

Doing Well and Doing Good

AFTER THEY WERE MARRIED in 1960, Frank and Margaret never moved very far. Margaret's dowry was her grandmother's 1950s bungalow and 150 acres on Silvercreek Parkway north of Guelph near where Frank had lived briefly with his Uncle Jake. In 1967, Frank and Margaret replaced the bungalow with a two-storey, five-bedroom family home that had black shutters and six white columns across the front in the Southern Colonial style.

In 2000, Margaret had a regular mammogram that found breast cancer. A double mastectomy followed by chemotherapy and radiation gave her four years of freedom from the disease. In 2004, the couple began building a new residence immediately behind the dwelling where they'd raised their children. Frank set aside his usual parsimony; no expense was spared. Over the next two years Margaret created her dream house — a 13,000-square-foot mansion with a porte-cochere and three-car garage.

The foyer is a two-storey open atrium with a glittering chandelier, interior balcony, and stunning views through the house to the garden. Hanging on the atrium's upper walls are several museum-quality paintings including a nineteenth-century scene of a Hungarian field market. There are also individual portraits of Margaret and Frank created by renowned Canadian artist Ken Danby. Margaret is shown seated on a piano stool, with the piano behind her, wearing a lace top that was so detailed even Danby complained about the inordinate amount of time it took him to paint it properly in his photorealistic style. Frank is shown leaning in a light-hearted manner against the front of his office desk. On the desk is a small holder prominently displaying his business cards, ever the effervescent salesman.

The main floor boasts twelve-foot ceilings and abundant light streaming through floor-to-ceiling windows. Furnishings are an eclectic mix of modern and antique pieces set off by puddled drapes, Japanese screens, and silk carpets. There's a dining room with an eighteenth-century Sheraton table that can easily seat thirty; a formal living room with a grand piano; a book-lined library where Frank works; a guest bedroom; an eat-in kitchen with a cooking island; a family room featuring a large, framed colour photo of Margaret, Nancy, and Linda on Linda's wedding day; and a sunroom that's Frank's favourite spot to sit because he feels like he's right in the midst of the garden with its patio, plantings, waterfalls, and gazebo.

Upstairs are his and hers bedrooms with en suite bathrooms, two more bedrooms each with twin beds for sleepovers by the four grandchildren, and an exercise room where Frank works out daily on a treadmill and with free weights. An elevator links the floors and there's a wine cellar in the basement. During construction, Margaret's cancer returned. They moved into their dream house in December 2006 and were only able to celebrate two Christmases there before Margaret died in April 2008. She was sixty-seven.

The funeral service was held in Knox Presbyterian Church where Margaret had sung in the choir. According to John Rennie, who owned the shirt factory where she'd worked as a teenager, "She was the most charming, outgoing person" who greatly contributed to her husband's success. "I don't think there's any question of that. It was a husband-and-wife team," Rennie told the *Guelph Mercury*. "She was a spark," added William Thorsell, CEO of the Royal Ontario Museum, which received a $500,000 bequest from Linamar. "She was a very warm, smart woman."[16] In their social circle, Frank and Margaret were the perfect pair. "They were an interesting couple, a great couple, a solid couple. Margaret totally stood by Frank yet Margaret had a line where she would look up and say, 'Hasenfratz.' And he was supposed to listen," said Sandra Chiarandini. "She had wonderful things and Frank let her have them. She was a beautiful woman."

Frank now lives alone in the house, aided by two housekeepers: Caroline and Katalin. There's also a resident Brittany that Frank calls a watchdog because she watches and watches but then does nothing.

~

Frank's lifetime accomplishments have brought numerous awards. In June 2011, the University of Guelph gave him an honorary doctorate. "After half a century in Canada, Frank Hasenfratz has risen from a poor political refugee to a respected business leader on the international stage," declared the citation read by University of Guelph President and Vice-Chancellor Alastair Summerlee. "His ingenuity and business acumen have created not only the largest employer in the city, but have positioned Guelph as a major producer of automotive parts and industrial equipment. His contributions as a local and international business leader; employer; and supporter of sport, the arts, and healthcare have been immeasurable and his story serves as an inspiration to future generations. He reminds us of why Canada is a beacon to the world."

In his speech to graduates, Frank revealed some of the secrets of his success. "If you move into a management position, hiring the best and brightest people you can find will always work in your favour. Don't ever be

Frank and University of Guelph President Alastair Summerlee on the occasion of Frank receiving his honorary doctorate in 2011. (**Guelph Mercury**)

threatened by an employee of yours who you perceive to be better than you. They will only make you look good! Don't forget for you to be promoted yourself, you should be grooming someone to take your place successfully. And make sure that person is teaching and grooming someone to replace him or herself," he said.

As for learning, something his audience had spent most of their young lives doing, their education had only just begun. "Never believe that you know it all. You can't. I keep finding myself thinking, okay, I've really got a handle on this now — the job, the company, management, the industry, whatever — and then looking back a year later and realizing how much I didn't know at the time. For those of you who thought you could pack away the notepads, sorry! Better pull them back out! We must all learn to embrace new knowledge and figure out how to convert it into practice. Be inquisitive. If you don't understand something, ask. Believe me, you will look much more foolish when you've made the wrong decision because you didn't really understand the situation at hand rather than asking a question at the time," he said.

He encouraged the new graduates to seek challenges rather than work merely for the money. "I have moved through many different disciplines, each time starting at square one with no knowledge of that discipline, but I never took jobs for the money. If there was no chance of learning, I moved on. With each success, you grow a little stronger and more confident. With each team whose respect you have won, you create a bigger network to draw on in the future. Whatever you do, measure it. Score keeping is most important. The thing you don't measure doesn't get done."

Frank urged his audience to learn from their own mistakes and the mistakes of others, promote change and improvement, and always use common sense. "Ingenuity is a lost skill in today's multinational conglomerates. Ingenuity and innovation in product and processes is what sets you apart from your competitors to let you deliver better products more consistently, and make more money doing it. We all need to approach business from a small company perspective — what makes sense to do? If you behave in your job like an entrepreneur running his own business, believe me, you will catch the attention of management. They will pay attention to you because you will be getting results cost effectively — something every company needs."

While that was Frank's first honorary degree, it was far from his first award. In 1995, he received the Award of Excellence as Person of the Year from the Yves Landry Foundation, established in honour of the former CEO of Chrysler Canada. In 2006, the Republic of Hungary made him a member of the Knight's Cross of the Order of Merit. The presentation by the Hungarian Ambassador to Canada, Dénes Tomaj, took place at Linda's house with family in attendance on the fiftieth anniversary of the Hungarian Revolution. In 2007, Frank was named to the Canadian Manufacturing Hall of Fame for his significant contributions to Canadian manufacturing. Among his fellow nominees that year were two other automotive pioneers, Colonel Sam McLaughlin and Gordon McGregor, who launched businesses early in the twentieth century that became the Canadian subsidiaries of General Motors and Ford, respectively.

Many other Hungarian immigrants have also become leaders in Canadian business. They include Leslie Dan who launched Novopharm, a pharmaceutical firm; Robert Lantos, a film and television producer; Peter Munk, chairman of Barrick Gold; Anna Porter, founder of Key Porter Books; and Andy Sarlos, a Bay Street financier.

For all the honours paid to him, Frank never boasts. "He'll tell you about these things but he'll tell you in an off-handed way. It's not like he's bragging," said Rudy Chiarandini. When Frank showed Chiarandini his Knight's Cross, which hangs on a sash for ceremonial occasions, and the small, green lapel badge for everyday use, Chiarandini asked, "Why isn't it on? Frank, you should be proud you have it and wear this on your lapel all the time." Frank reluctantly took the smaller version out of the package and pinned it on his suit lapel for that occasion. "He just doesn't want to push himself in that way on people," said Chiarandini. "The less work I do, the more recognition I get," said Frank. "When I worked day and night, nobody recognized it."

Linda's achievements in her first ten years as CEO have also been widely honoured. In 2003, Ryerson University awarded her an honorary doctorate in Engineering and she has been among the *Automotive News'* "Leading Women" for several years; was one of the "Top 40 Under 40," in 2002;

and was named "Outstanding Business Leader of the Year" by Wilfrid Laurier University. Her role as a director of the Canadian Imperial Bank of Commerce since 2004 has been particularly rewarding. "I've really enjoyed being on the CIBC board. It gives me great insight into general economic conditions on a global basis. There are a variety of directors who run a lot of different businesses giving their thoughts. I find that really useful in terms of understanding and making my own judgment call on where I think things are going economically. A bank board obviously keeps you in touch with what's happening in terms of credit markets, debt availability, the cost of debt, and different types of insurance. I've learned a lot that has helped me in my role as CEO," said Linda.

Linda is also on the board of Faurecia, an automotive supplier based in Nanterre, France, with annual sales of €14 billion, as well as the Canadian Council of Chief Executives, and the Original Equipment Suppliers Association (OESA), of Troy, Michigan, where she served as chair during 2008–09. "It was the most difficult year in the history of our association, that year when Chrysler and GM went bankrupt," said Neil De Koker, president and CEO of OESA. "We prepared a fifty-six-page document appealing to the U.S. government for assistance and why it made sense because the banking community was not providing financing for suppliers just like financing wasn't provided for GM or Chrysler. Linda was very successful in dealing with the minister of industry in Canada to get support for the supplier community in Canada."

Linda's role at the OESA was all the more unique because the automotive industry is dominated by men. Of the twenty-nine OESA board members, only three are women. The other two are Kim Korth, CEO of Supreme Industries Inc., and Jacqui Dedo, chief strategy officer at Dana Holding Corp. When Linda stepped down as chair, De Koker presented her with a gift at the annual meeting. She gave him a hug and a kiss, saying, "This is one chair you can kiss."

According to De Koker, a daughter taking over from a father is very unusual in the automotive sector. "Especially in a high tech area such as Linamar is involved with — engines, transmissions, and machining centres. Anybody who joined, Frank put them on the floor for a few years and made them learn hands on what the company is all about. Linda uses that knowledge every day, how decisions are made, and what kinds of decisions are important to the success of the manufacturing operations. I don't think it made a difference to Frank that she was male or female. She was his child, she showed an interest, and she was going to run the company," said De Koker. "Linda has a good sense of humour, a very focused manufacturing viewpoint, a can-do attitude, and is a great analytical thinker on just about any subject."

Over the years, governments have been eager to seek Linda's counsel. In 2006, Canada, the United States, and Mexico created the North American Competitiveness Council (NACC), a trilateral advisory body of business leaders charged with improving competitiveness. The mandate of the group was to provide governments with recommendations on issues such as border facilitation and regulation, as well as offer views on competitiveness in key sectors including automotive, transportation, manufacturing, and services. The group met annually with ministers and on an ongoing basis with government officials.

Each country was represented by ten members. Linda chaired the Canadian group that included Richard George of Suncor, Rick Waugh of Scotiabank, and Paul Desmarais Jr. of Power Corp. The U.S. was represented by executives from Merck, Lockheed Martin, General Motors, Whirlpool, and Chevron. Mexico's members came from Finca Montegrande, TAMSA, and Avicar de Occidente, among others.

The first report by the NACC was presented to President George W. Bush, President Felipe Calderón, and Prime Minister Stephen Harper in August 2007. Further reports were submitted in 2008 and 2009. Among the main recommendations were more energy sharing as well as regulatory harmonization and reduced paperwork to ease border congestion. Linda was pleasantly surprised to find that despite the fact that the CEOs were from three different countries, there was consensus around the key issues that needed to be addressed. Specifically, Linda supported efforts to create a Canada-U.S. perimeter security pact or, even better, eliminate the border. "I know there are lots of concerns about sovereignty and privacy issues but those issues can be addressed. Look at the European Union, they've very successfully dealt with those issues. We need to learn from their mistakes in a number of areas but the EU includes countries that for centuries hated each other but somehow managed to feel comfortable with their sovereignty, identity, and privacy issues for the greater good of having an economic unit that can work together and have goods and people flow seamlessly across those borders. It's just foolish of us as North Americans to not follow suit on something that can help us be more competitive on a global stage."

Linda would reduce the number of customs forms required between Canada and the U.S. and extend the trusted traveller programs beyond Nexus to pre-approve commercial importers and exporters at a dedicated crossing where they wouldn't have to stop at all. "The perimeter security deal approved by Stephen Harper and Barack Obama in December 2011 was a step in the right direction. The ultimate answer is to create a strong perimeter and eliminate the border altogether. From France to Germany there's no border. You don't have to stop; you just keep going. If Canada and the U.S. have a common goal that we both feel is important and critical to our ability to compete on the global stage, then we will work through those issues. If France and Germany can do it, surely Canada and the U.S. could do it."

After the trilateral NACC concluded, Linda then chaired a panel created by federal Environment Minister Jim Prentice on energy efficiency and research and development. Linda was also asked by Glen Murray, then Ontario minister of research and innovation, to be part of a small group of business people and academics looking at what government needs to do in order to spark more innovation.

Linda regards fulfilling such requests as an important contribution to society. "For me it's a good opportunity to interact with other business leaders and build relationships with politicians. It's a national sport to complain about what a poor job our politicians are doing for us. That's not helpful. If you think something should be done differently then you have to speak up and make those recommendations. If they're not acted on, then you can complain. But you can't really complain if you're not doing anything about it."

Her work with policy and advisory committees also has a commercial value for Linamar. "At the clean energy dialogue group I met lots of people doing interesting things in energy and battery development. As a result, I made some business connections that are potentially leading to commercial opportunities for us in terms of hybrid vehicles. So, there's absolutely a direct link between some of those events, people that I've been able to meet, and business that we've been able to subsequently transact."

∽

As pillars of the community, Frank and Linda are generous philanthropists. Recent donations from the family and Linamar include $1 million for a magnetic resonance machine, emergency health services, and vascular surgery at the Guelph General Hospital, $1 million to the University of Guelph to provide ten $2,500 engineering scholarships annually, $450,000 to St. Joseph's Health Centre, and more than $200,000 each year to the United Way. Frank also donated $500,000 anonymously to the Guelph General. He has also quietly helped countless people. An employee suffered a nervous breakdown; his pay was continued for two years until he recovered and returned to work. A plant manager died; Frank paid off his mortgage so his wife could stay in the house, debt free.

A Linamar-sponsored program at the 800-seat River Run Centre was inspired by a conversation Frank had with Peter Gifford, a Guelph lawyer and past chair of River Run, about how young people in Hungary grow up with an appreciation for the arts that lasts all their lives. Gifford passed the comment on to Rob Mackay, then manager of the performing arts centre in Guelph. Mackay had been looking for a way to get Linamar engaged. Local business leaders Ken Hammill and Doug Bridge called on Frank and told him that Mackay had developed a program for local students based on Frank's comments to Gifford. When Frank heard the idea, he smiled, and said, "You got me." Since 2000, Linamar for the Performing Arts has been providing all 14,000 Guelph elementary school students free admission twice a year to see music, dance, and drama at River Run.

As vice-chair of the Royal Ontario Museum Foundation, Linda held five garden parties that raised a total of $750,000, an amount that included a donation from Linamar, for the museum's capital campaign. Linamar also established the Guelph School Visits Bursary Fund that provides free admission to Guelph-area students visiting the museum. Over the past ten years, Linamar has donated more than $1 million to support local sports teams, community events, and venues such as Taste of Guelph and the Guelph Civic Museum. "Philanthropy is an important role that we as leaders in a community need to play. We need to support the communities that we live in," said Linda. "For example, if you want your hospital to thrive and have the best doctors and equipment, it's not going to get that unless you help it. Having such a strong employee base in Guelph, if we can support our hospital then we're making Guelph a better place for our employees to live."

~

During the last thirty years, Linamar has undergone dramatic growth and change. In 1980, there was just one plant, today there are thirty-nine. In 1980, the lion's share of the business was in defence contracts. A part manufactured for the military might take a week to produce with government inspectors keeping a close eye on each step. Today, one plant can produce tens of thousands of parts a day. Customers are so trusting of Linamar's production systems and quality control that the company's output goes directly to the assembly line at Ford, GM, or Chrysler without any further scrutiny by the customer.

Through it all, Frank has worked hard to create a way of doing business that will continue long after he's gone. "I love working. I love coming in here. Somebody tells me they've got a problem. Great, what is it? I enjoy what I do. My biggest strength is my technical knowledge. Why do you think CAT is so successful? I look at things, analyze them, and people love to do the CAT with me."

There also continue to be those occasions when Frank reminds others of steps that somehow everyone else forgot. For example, in 2011 when Linamar was planning to buy $40 million in new equipment, double the workforce, and create 138 new jobs at its plant in Florence, Kentucky, Frank asked those involved from Linamar what help the state was offering. None, came the reply. No one had asked. "Don't place any order, get to the government right now. Kentucky will pay a portion of your training, your labour, new people you hire, or some of the capital," he admonished them, pointing out that Linamar had just received about $12 million from various levels of government after taking over a former Volvo plant in Asheville, North Carolina, and creating 400 jobs. In the end, Kentucky provided $4.5 million in tax incentives through a business investment program.

Frank argues that government grants, loans, and other helpful offers should always be available because Linamar and its employees pay plenty of taxes in return. In 2011, Linamar and its employees paid $180 million in property and income taxes in Canada. If Frank had his way, manufacturers would pay no tax at all because of the many spinoffs industry brings to the rest of the economy. "The average employee makes $50,000 so three times that goes from Linamar to outside companies, suppliers, contractors, accountants, and lawyers. Manufacturing is the engine of well-being. Manufacturers and farmers are the only ones who produce tangible goods."

~~~

Even though he is no longer involved in the strategic direction of the company, Frank continues to offer his opinion on a wide range of topics. "The Frank I know will give you his blunt, everyday, upfront, transparent view," said Jim Jarrell. "Linda and I will be meeting and he'll come in and say, 'I don't think this is right. I would never, ever, ever, in my life do something that stupid. But you guys go off and make your own decision.' We laugh and we just sit there and look at each other and think, 'How do you respond to that?' But if we think through the issue and we think this is the way we should go, then that's what we do. He doesn't drive me crazy. I guess I'm just immune. I want him to tell me what he sees, because I can't improve things if I don't know."

For some time to come, Frank will be very much present, both in his role as board chair and while travelling abroad to conduct CATs. "This is his passion day in, day out. He likes to contribute and he does contribute but long-term we've got to have somebody who can also be the next set of eyes and ears like Frank to continue that passion," said Jarrell. "There are a couple of guys in the background who probably have a bit of that personality. It will never be Frank, because there is only one Frank, but the key is to try and keep that passion for lean reduction and the passion to get it done right now. We all believe that we've got that as part of our heritage," said Jarrell.

Frank's friends have tried many times to figure out what makes him tick. "He's very much interested in the *Monopoly* game of life. In *Monopoly*, you try to amass funds and that was part of the deal of what he was doing. But he liked what he was doing so therefore it's not work," said Bob Young. "He was in the right place at the right time and he was ingenious. If we had more Frank Hasenfratzes in this country, we'd be in better shape than we are. The country did a lot for Frank and Frank did a lot for the country."

According to David Allan, the Walwyn senior vice president who took Linamar public in 1986, Frank is a rarity among industrialists. "He's a most extraordinary person, he's a force of nature. There are few others like him and he hasn't lost his touch over the years. Anybody who can run a business where the price of the products they sell to the Big Three is mandated to decline every year through the life of the contract, that separates you from the great majority of other businesses," said Allan. "As the Big Three outsourced more and more of their production, that's what made Linamar. The error that Frank identified at Chrysler, GM, Ford, Jaguar, you name it, was you can't have a business with large factories that have three or four thousand employees. You don't have a culture, you don't have anything, you just have robots coming in and leaving at the end of the day."

The entrepreneurial approach to business instilled by Frank will always be the beating heart of Linamar. "He's in every day and he's detailed in the same way as he's always been. Because he goes around the world regularly to every plant he can bring ideas to the other plants," said Brian Wade. "We have people in the organization like myself, Rick Nelson, and many, many others who have taken the tool Frank created and the ideas and just keep working with them. It has become part of our culture."

The fact those "others" exist is proof of the importance of being surrounded by strong people. "The last thing my father would want is to have created something that's going to collapse when he steps out. That's not the kind of person he is. There are some people out there who are that way. They like the idea that they're the cog in the wheel," said Linda. "To me, your greatest success is the success of your company after you leave it because that says what you've done in terms of leadership, development, systems, and creating something that has longevity."

When her own time as CEO is concluded, Linda would like to see one of her four children have the opportunity to take over the role. "They're all potential candidates. They're smart and they all have great leadership tendencies that I've seen already. So the question is, 'Who's going to be interested and have the technical and business aptitude to step in?' I'd love to see one of them want to do that." When Linda does step down, Jim Jarrell is in line to become CEO. Among his many duties, he would put in place the next succession plan that could lead to another Hasenfratz — or someone else — at the helm.

In Frank's mind, one of the most important reasons for Linamar's success has been choosing the right people all along the way. "I love it when people say, 'Where would you be if you didn't have Jim Jarrell, if you didn't have Linda, if you didn't have Frank Carpino?' Well, I was the one who picked them. If you want to be successful, no one man builds a kingdom." And yet, all it took was this one man to launch a business in a basement that spread to a garage and then grew right around the globe.

Epilogue

In the spring of 2011, Frank Hasenfratz visited Hungary during a tour of one of his many companies worldwide. While there, he made a side trip to the village of Szár, where he was born. The residents of this village rise early, as their ancestors did for generations. This time of year, the farmers are carefully preparing the earth for the planting of the new crop, and tending to the many tasks that need to be completed for the spring planting.

Frank Hasenfratz is the famous son of this community, the celebrated, well-known Canadian entrepreneur. He takes a brisk walk toward the village green, greeting neighbours, stopping to visit childhood friends and family acquaintances. One of those friends is János Laub whose family was also evicted from this village to the hamlet of Vérteskozma, along with the Hasenfratz family in 1948. Laub is the local historian, meticulously gathering stories from that era, documenting, publishing, and writing about the sad events of the past.

In hindsight, Frank is philosophical about the many hardships he and his family had to face as he was growing up. He views every obstacle endured by his family as something that simply had to be surmounted. In the long term, he believes, what seemed like devastating tragedies eventually led to improvements in his life. The cruel confiscation of the family's home and land, the tragic eviction to Vérteskozma, led to a much better education for Frank and his brother, Marton. Taking part in the Hungarian Uprising in 1956, as a soldier whose entire unit defected to the insurgents, forced him to flee his homeland. This, in turn, through much hard work and persistence, resulted in a much more rewarding and successful life in Canada than otherwise would have been his lot.

~

During this particular trip, Frank was reunited with one of his co-combatants, László Huszár. The two last said goodbye to each other more than fifty years ago. Frank remembered him as a muscular, handsome, determined young corporal, and an excellent water polo player. "László was such a dedicated fighter, he always wanted to be on top of the vehicle we were riding in, always wanted to lead the charge in the front line of battle."

The two sat together and reminisced about their life in the military, sharing stories about boot camp, and all the practical jokes they played on the others. The contrast between the two men, of similar ages and backgrounds, is striking. The one who left, Frank, is energetic, fit, quick to laugh, and looks much younger than his seventy-six years. The one who stayed, László Huszár, is thin, frail, and weak, his voice at times barely audible. Deep lines are etched into his formerly handsome face.

As the two army buddies talked about the fighting at Soroksár and Jutadomb, however, Huszár turned strangely quiet and became choked with emotion and tears. He frequently stopped, often in mid-sentence, turned away, buried his face in a handkerchief as he wiped the tears from his eyes and blew his nose. Each time it took him longer to collect himself and face his old friend. At one point, he looked at Frank and said, "Forgive me, I can't help myself, the time following the Revolution was unbearable. The secret police visited me, harassing me regularly at my place of work — for over ten years. My nerves aren't what they used to be." Finally, Huszár realized he couldn't continue. Without saying another word, Huszár quietly wiped his eyes one last time, stood up, shook hands with Frank, put his hand on his friend's shoulder, and shuffled off.

Appendix:

<u>Words to Live By</u>

- There's only one job you start at the top, and that's when you're digging a hole. And guess where you end up? At the bottom of the hole.

- Whenever you go into a plant, you learn something or you teach something. If you don't do either, it was a waste of time.

- Any entrepreneur needs help to succeed.

- If you have good supervisors who stay a little bit under-employed, they will do great things because they not only will do their job inside out but also will bring about change.

- Whatever you do, measure it. Score keeping is very important. The thing you don't measure doesn't get done.

- Tell me how you're going to do something, don't tell me how you can't.

- Ingenuity and innovation in product and processes is what sets you apart from your competitors.

- If you move into a management position, hiring the best and brightest people you can find will always work in your favour

- In negotiations, don't want something too badly; if you do, then you're going to compromise somewhere on the price or the terms.

- Be with your people every day. Don't push them; lead them.

- Never believe that you know it all.

Notes

1. *The Financial Post*, May 10, 1986, 21.

2. *Ibid.*, May 18, 1987, 8.

3. *Ibid.*, May 10, 1987.

4. *Globe and Mail*, April 28, 1986, B1.

5. *The Financial Post*, May 18, 1987, 8.

6. *Globe and Mail*, March 10, 1988, B7.

7. *Ibid.*, March 30, 1992, B1.

8. *Guelph Mercury*, October 27, 1990.

9. *The Financial Times of Canada*, March 18, 1991, 10.

10. *Globe and Mail*, September 25, 1991, B6.

11. *The Financial Post*, October 26, 1993, 18.

12. *Ibid.*, December 18, 1996, B18.

13. *Elora Sentinel and Fergus Thistle*, March 9, 1993, 20.

14. *Guelph Mercury*, April 2, 2005, Q1.

15. *Windsor Star*, January 22, 2009, C1.

16. *Guelph Mercury*, April 19, 2008, A1.

INDEX

Numbers in italics refer to illustrations and their captions.